AN LEABHARLANN

COLÁISTE NA hOLLSCOILE, CORCAIGH

Níl sé ceaduithe an leabhar seo a choimead thar an dáta is déanaí atá luaite thíos.

This book must be returned not later than the last date stamped below.

The Library, University College, Cork

M.O.5637

THE CHURCH AND UNITY

The Church and Unity

An essay by B. C. Butler

Geoffrey Chapman
London

A Geoffrey Chapman book published by
Cassell Ltd.
35 Red Lion Square, London WC1R 4SG
and at Sydney, Auckland, Toronto, Johannesburg
an affiliate of
Macmillan Publishing Co. Inc.
New York

First printing 1979
ISBN 0 225 66245 0

British Library Cataloguing in Publication Data

Butler, Basil Christopher
    The Church and unity.
    1. Christian union
    I. Title
    262'.72   BX8.2

Nihil obstat: R. J. Cuming, D.D., Censor
Westminster, 7 April 1978

The Nihil obstat is a declaration that a book or
pamphlet is considered to be free from doctrinal
or moral error. It is not implied that those
who have granted the Nihil obstat agree with the
contents, opinions or statements expressed.

Printed in Great Britain by
Billing & Sons Limited,
Guildford, London and Worcester

Contents

Introductory

Experts – and in these pages I trespass on the ground of several different kinds of experts – will easily understand why this book is called an essay, not a treatise. A treatise, Bernard Lonergan tells us, 'undertakes to define all its terms implicitly or explicitly, to prove all its conclusions, and to accept every conclusion that follows logically from its premises. ... its function primarily is to present clearly, exactly, and fully the content and the implications of a determinate and coherent set of insights.' The reader will rapidly see that, if such had been the undertaking of this book, it has woefully failed of its aim. But Lonergan also points out that we are never in a position to write a good treatise on the subject of human experience; and it is human experience, as raised to a supernatural level by a divine Act, that is the concern of this book.[1]

My concern is with Christianity as a real factor in human history. I have not set myself the task of proving that Christianity, as lived by men, is a reflection, indeed an embodiment, of a divine Act. I have assumed this truth, and therefore my immediate audience is conceived as being such as are themselves Christian believers. Others can understand the book if, 'for the sake of argument', they can temporarily suspend their unbelief.

A first chapter looks back to Christianity as it was understood in the first century of our era. I have not, indeed, embarked on a scientific historical reconstruction of 'the historical Jesus' – the task would have been enormous, and I am conscious of my limitations. Christians, in any case, know by faith that Jesus, the son of Mary of Nazareth, is the Word of God incarnate, that he was 'crucified under Pontius Pilate' and 'rose again the third day'; similarly, they know that 'he is seated at the right hand of the Father' and has poured out his Holy Spirit on the Church and its members. In the first chapter, then, I address myself to the reflection and perceived implications of these truths in the consciousness of the primitive believers, particularly as that consciousness is revealed to us in the Pauline corpus.

In the second chapter I argue that, rather than seeking a definition of the Church, we should try to find and explore 'models' of it, without maintaining that any single model can exhaust the significance of the object which we are seeking to understand. I state my intention to use the model of 'communion' and proceed to explain what I mean by this term.

In the third and fourth chapters I consider the Christian revelation as the incarnate Word of God. I seek to penetrate some of the implications of the notion of an incarnation of God, and I argue that, 'word' meaning 'communication', God the Father communicated himself to Jesus in the latter's humanity by the way of revelation, and that this communication was for further communication to the rest of us human beings.

Having explained what I mean by 'communion', I substitute for that word the transliterated Greek word *koinonia* when referring more particularly to the Church as the Christian communion. And in the fifth chapter I suggest that the farewell discourse(s) in the Fourth Gospel may throw some light on the Church as koinonia.

Chapter VI reverts to the external history of Christianity in the apostolic age, and suggests that the koinonia was realized not just as a number of separate local churches, but also as a universal fellowship of all believers. This fellowship was not destitute of organizing elements. From the start there were the 'apostles', and as the apostolic age draws towards its end I direct attention again to a somewhat neglected piece of evidence from Clement of Rome for a succession to the authority of these original leaders.

The seventh chapter offers a very sketchy survey of post-apostolic Christianity, so far as such a survey can throw further light on the notion of the koinonia. I emphasize here, and throughout the rest of the book, that traditionally the koinonia has been perceived as an indivisible visible fellowship, such that – in principle – 'schism' is always *from*, not *within*, the Church.

In Chapter VIII I turn to the objection that has been raised in modern times against this notion of the Church, an objection based on the fact that Christianity exists (and, it is implied, bears fruit) in a number of different Christian bodies in separation from one another. It may be noted that the objection seems rarely to appeal to the existence of non-Catholic Christian Churches in the patristic age in its own support, but to confine its attention, in the main, to the Churches whose separate existence dates from the sixteenth-century Reformation or from subsequent 'schisms', and more especially to the apparent schism between the Roman Catholic Church and the Eastern Orthodox Communion, a separation that is usually dated from the year 1054, and of course, most regrettably, still persists today. The objectors ask: Is it not totally unreasonable to pretend that the Church is undivided, when most manifestly it is not? I have paid particular attention to this objection as stated by the late Dr Greenslade. He and I agree that one cannot rest in the ecclesiology of St Cyprian – on this point we are in agreement also with St Augustine. There are two components in Cyprian's ecclesiology: his insistence on the indivisible visible unity of the Church, and his strong contention that outside the Church there are no real sacraments. Augustine retained the former component and abandoned the latter. Greenslade did the opposite: he retained the second component of Cyprian's position – the impossibility of sacraments outside the Church – but aban-doned the former. I have followed here not Greenslade but Augustine; but I have acknowledged that Augustine's own statement of his position needs further development, and have sought authority for such further development in the teaching of the Second Vatican Council.

In the ninth chapter I have tried to 'place' Christianity within a world view, a view that sees the created order not as static but as dynamic, developing, and permeated by a single divine purpose to be realized in the kingdom of Christ consummated and 'handed over' to his heavenly Father.

The tenth chapter includes an effort to work out what I think would be the consequences, ultimately fatal to Christianity, of abandoning the traditional view of the Church as an indivisible visible unity. I here argue that the choice is between revolution and development, and I give my support to development as the preferable alternative.

I have thought it worth while to devote a separate chapter, the eleventh, to the special problem of the 'estrangement', now of a thousand years more or less, between the Roman Catholic Church and the Eastern Orthodox Communion. Here I have argued that our Orthodox friends, so devoted to tradition, have given less than due attention to a strand in their own ancient tradition which recognized, with whatever qualifications, a 'primacy' of the See of Rome which cannot be fairly described as merely honorary. Indeed, what place has the notion of 'honour' in a religion that looks back to a crucified Redeemer?

The final chapter includes a sort of apology to my ecumenical friends for a book which will seem to many of them to question the very principle underlying their efforts. But it also contains a reminder to Roman Catholics that not everything in the contemporary stance and practices of their Church can claim the status of *articuli stantis aut cadentis ecclesiae*. I have here singled out the extreme centralization which, in modern times, has been both a bulwark of the Church in a world of polemics, controversy and secularization, and also a dead hand upon the spontaneity, and a grievous limitation of the legitimate autonomy, of the local dioceses and regions, not to speak of the due liberty of the individual Christian conscience; and which is still a serious obstacle to the union of Christians for which we all pray.

That 'schism' is a condition of things which is regrettable and should be altered is a conviction common enough at the present day; it is one of the strongest motives behind the ecumenical movement. That schism is objectively illegitimate is also widely, though not so widely, held; there are still those who would say that, in the circumstances in which one section of Christians moved – or were driven – out of communion with another and thereafter continued to operate in or as a separate 'church', the founders of the schism could, in conscience, 'do no other'. Whatever position is adopted in this debate, it is surely true that, apart from schism as an objective state of affairs, there is such a thing as a sin of schism. In the eyes of God this is the heart of the matter. Cajetan argued that schism is a sin, not precisely against obedience but against charity. He sees the Church as an embodiment of the virtue of charity in a community of mutual forbearance and esteem. Schism is the ecclesial expression of egoism, whether individual or collective. As such – and I here speak, be it noted, not of schism as a sociologically observable fact but of the sinfulness of an interior determination of the will – it is clean contrary to the gospel. But it is also, thank God, much rarer than sociological schism. A man can be born into, and grow up in, a sociological schism in the utmost good faith and, in the communion of a 'schismatic' Church, attain to the heights of sanctity. What is true of an individual can also be true of a group. When a Church has come to realize that division between Christians is an evil that needs to be overcome, and when in consequence it has deliberately committed itself to the ecumenical enterprise, then it has exorcized the 'sin' of schism. When our hearts are all dedicated to Christian unity the real evil of schism has already been overcome. It may still remain to work out the consequences of such dedication.

This sharp distinction between sociological schism and the sin of schism involves a development beyond the position adopted by St Augustine in his long controversy with the Donatists. It may be helpful here to enlarge somewhat on the point at which I hold that Augustine has to be invited to move further along a road which, it seems to me, would not be unattractive to a man who wrote, in his *Confessions,* that one would not be seeking God unless one had already found him or been found by him.

Augustine held that true sacraments – what theologians call 'valid' sacraments, that is to say sacraments which conform to the conditions laid down for their genuineness by God – can be found and administered outside that communion which is called the Catholic Church, which itself is an indivisible visible unity. Valid sacraments can be found, then, in 'schismatical' Christian communions. He does not, however, seem willing to admit that sacraments thus received can be of any benefit to the recipients of them so long as these recipients are and remain in a state of schism. For instance, their baptism does them no good unless, and until, they seek and are granted admission into the visible Catholic unity; at that point their baptism begins to take effect (and they are not, of course, 'rebaptized'). Yet he maintains that a man, if he is in proximate danger of death and wishes to become a Catholic Christian by baptism but is unable to secure the ministrations of a Catholic minister of baptism, may and presumably should seek baptism from a schismatical minister (if the danger of death passes he would of course be bound to enter into the visible communion of the Catholic Church).

Augustine's treatment of the case of the man who wishes to become a Catholic Christian but cannot find a Catholic minister of baptism is clear evidence that he is genuine in maintaining the validity of sacraments duly administered by persons whose only defect is their schismatical allegiance. His reluctance to admit that *schismatical* recipients of schismatical sacraments get any fruit out of these sacraments may be presumed to illustrate both his conviction that schism is itself a grave sin and also his failure to advert to the fact that a man may *de facto* be 'in schism' without any fault on his part.

This failure to advert to the distinction between objective and subjective moral evil was perhaps an effect upon Augustine of the general culture of his time.[2] There can be no doubt that the distinction is a valid distinction and of the greatest importance. It means that there may be a complete absence of guilt in the fact of schism – and this is entirely consistent with the view that schism in itself is, objectively, a sin against the gospel.

I therefore hold, with the Second Vatican Council, that Augustine's position should be 'developed' to take account of the distinction between objective and subjective moral evil. The development preserves everything that is essential to Augustine's ecclesiology. And it makes that ecclesiology credible in an age like our own when we are acutely aware that people can be at odds about matters of supreme importance (e.g. the existence of God) and yet be in perfectly good faith.

This development of the Augustinian position invites us to a further step. Not only are individual 'schismatics' to be presumed – pending convincing evidence to the contrary – to be in good faith, and in consequence able to benefit from the sacramental and other ministrations of their own communions, but the 'schismatical' communions themselves can and should be presumed to be, collectively, in good faith. They are therefore Christian communions composed of genuinely Christian members; both they and their members are 'in favour with God', to borrow a phrase from St Luke. In the following pages I have frequently abstained from calling them 'churches'; and I have reserved the technical term *koinonia* as a designation of the Catholic Church. To some extent, these are matters of linguistic convenience; and in fact Catholic usage refers to the Eastern Orthodox separated bodies as 'Churches'. But I have wanted to preserve in its purity the traditional truth that, objectively speaking, the Church has a guaranteed indivisible visible unity of communion. It may seem somewhat arrogant to maintain that, while other Christian bodies are subjectively above reproach, only the Catholic Church is both subjectively and objectively in the right way. But that was the truth that brought me into the full communion of the Catholic Church, and I hope it may not be considered offensive if I proclaim it as truth.

Nevertheless, the distinction between objective and subjective correctness enables the Catholic Church to give full recognition to the other Christian bodies as genuine Christian communions. Their members are accepted by us 'with affection and respect' as brothers. In particular, if they have been validly baptized (and mutual recognition of baptism has been a feature of the ecumenical movement), they 'are brought into a certain, though imperfect, communion with the Catholic Church' and are 'properly regarded as brothers in the Lord by the sons of the Catholic Church'. The ecclesial bodies to which they belong receive and bestow the grace of God, and the sacred actions of the Christian religion, performed by them, 'truly engender a life of grace and can be rightly described as capable of providing access to the community of salvation'. These Christian bodies, then, have genuine 'significance and importance in the mystery of salvation'.[3]

The notion of 'imperfect' (yet genuine) communion expressed in the Decree on Ecumenism is an important one. In the above quotation it is applied to individual Christians in the 'other' Christian bodies. But a later passage speaks of the 'work of restoring the full communion that is desired between the Eastern Churches and the Catholic Church',[4] implying that there is real but incomplete communion between (not only individual Eastern Orthodox believers but) the Eastern Churches as such and the Catholic Church. More recently the Pope has spoken of the 'almost complete communion' already existing between those Churches and the Catholic Church.

Such language is a healthy reminder that the notion of 'communion' is extremely rich and capable of many different kinds and dimensions of realization. The ensuing pages of this essay explain communion as a relatedness founded in common 'possessions' (such possessions being either material or spiritual). Whatever Christian truths and gifts, therefore, are held in common by individuals or by Christian groups (two or more) are in themselves bonds of union between them. Supreme among such gifts is the gift of the grace of Christ through the Holy Spirit by which men and their societies are related to God the Father. Through such gifts there is genuine communion between us

Christians as individuals and between our several ecclesial bodies. But complete communion involves a shared acceptance of the whole mystery of the redemptive 'economy', and included in this mystery is the guaranteed visible unity of believers in a single grouping. This gift of unity, it is maintained by the Second Vatican Council, exists in the Catholic Church. It is, we may say, the supreme contribution of the Catholic Church to the ecumenical movement. But neither the Council nor the present author denies that there are very serious imperfections in the Catholic Church as it historically exists at the present (or at any other) time; and it is obvious that we have much to learn from the Christian bodies at present united to us by a communion that remains 'incomplete'.

A further observation seems to be called for. Once we have acknowledged the twin truths *(a)* that the whole of humanity has been redeemed in and by Jesus Christ and the outpouring of his Holy Spirit, and *(b)* that subjective error can be absent when objective error is present, then the principles, aims and processes of Christian ecumenism can provide an analogy for our relations with other religions, other philosophies, and ultimately the whole of mankind in its pilgrimage towards the hidden goal of all God's purposes for us. In these other incorporations of belief, and even in honest agnosticism and the quest of true values that can accompany professed atheism, we can recognize not only human good will but that without which such good will is, according to our own faith, by and large impossible, namely the grace of God in Christ. That grace is a bond of communion between all of us in our earthly pilgrimage.

The notion of communion thus begins to disclose its power and scope. Realized most fully, here on earth, in the koinonia in which its completeness is guaranteed and its reality comes to full expression, to the extent that this is possible in a state of affairs which is for ever moving from imperfection to greater perfection, it is at the same time very truly realized in the communion, in various degrees incomplete, that binds us all together in our grace-given subjective good will and our adherence to the truth to the extent that we have arrived at truth. The philosophic notion of the *societas humani generis*, the fellowship of man, becomes concrete in the Christian vision of a unity given by Christ, and preserved and promoted towards an ever-growing realization by his Holy Spirit.

Communion easily develops into community, and this development of the koinonia is presented in these pages – perhaps with
insufficient argument but at least with the power of a strong
Christian tradition behind it – as essential to the Church. But
community leads inevitably to institution; even in the community
of the human family there are rules and indeed an indispensable
hierarchy: when opinions differ on a decision to be taken,
someone's word has to settle the issue. I am very conscious that to
some it may seem that I have in this essay attached too much
importance, and devoted too much attention, to the 'institutional
element' of religion. When one is enjoying good health one need
not reflect too much on the harmonization of bodily functions. It is
when one is ill that these things demand attention. A divided
Christianity is very ill indeed. It is necessary not to acknowledge
the symptoms of the illness, but to diagnose it. There is little to be
gained by pretending that the illness does not exist, or by inviting
believers to act as though everything could be put right by a
mindless coming together in an external unity that would have no
theological rationale. If my diagnosis is correct, the key to our
problem is found in a very simple fact: that – to extend the scope
of a saying of Augustine that was primarily uttered with reference
to the particular circumstances of the Donatist schism in northern
Africa – 'there is no justifying reason for schism'. If I am correct,
it is not the case that serious defects cannot show themselves in the
one universal communion whose unity is guaranteed by the Holy
Spirit himself; even if Christians were all sinless, the mere fact
that we are human, and that human beings attain maturity only
by slow process, would mean that the Church militant can never
live at the level of its divine calling. But the remedy for defects in
the Church is not to separate oneself from the community –
whether by an individual secession or by a group movement into
schism, but to stay within and pray and work for improvements
here and there.

Meanwhile, it is important to realize that communion, in its
Christian form as koinonia, is not simply an association of
believers here on earth. The risen, reigning, and active Christ is a
member of the koinonia; and so is his heavenly Father: 'Our
fellowship is with the Father and with his Son Jesus Christ'. It is
indeed of the essence of Christianity that our fellowship should be
with one another. But where, in all good faith, this fellowship is
not actualized but nevertheless communion is not lost with God

and Christ, then, though direct communion is absent, there is an indirect communion between separated Christians which is of immense importance. The Second Vatican Council spoke, in this context, of an 'imperfect' communion of baptized but not Catholic Christians with the Catholic Church. Imperfect it undoubtedly is, since it does not incorporate them into the full visible unity of the koinonia. But communion mediated through Christ and embracing all who genuinely try to serve him is not, for that reason, unimportant or insignificant.

What separates from God and Christ is not sociological schism but the sin of schism. The sociological fact leaps to the eye in the tragic situation of the Christian Churches today, the divisions between East and West and the divisions also within the East and the West. But who can suppose that the multitudes who, in the heart of Russia, in the Near East, in North-Western Europe and in North America and the third world, are following Christ as they have come to know him in the only Christian communion that has really brought its message home to them, are committing the sin of schism? And where sin is not present to establish a barrier between the individual person and the grace of the Holy Spirit, there communion with Christ is deepened with every unselfish act. As love laughs at iron bars, so holiness laughs at sociological conditions when these are accepted or rejected in all good faith. Christ is alive in every humble believer, indeed in every man and woman of good will even if such persons do not acknowledge, perhaps have not even heard, his name. And where he is alive, there, through human behaviour that is instinct with his Spirit though not labelled outwardly as his, he is proclaiming his presence and his redeeming work. And it may well be that, across the barriers that still divide our Churches, we can recognize something of this holiness and can respond to our brothers in Christ.

None of this means that we may resign ourselves to sociological schism. None of this means that there is not, discoverable by everyone if its presence is made manifest to him, that indivisible koinonia which is the God-given home of us all. None of this means that we must give up trying to discern God's will for his faithful. This book is written because its author is profoundly convinced that subjective good will is called upon to find what is the will of God in the objective order; and because he believes that

that objective order of God's will is shown to us in the Christian tradition properly interpreted.

All the time, moreover, the world waits for the message of the gospel. That message supervenes upon human subjective good will to assure us that man's goodness is not just an eccentric by-product of evolution in a mindless, valueless world, but is the reflection in history, amid all the ambiguities, the frailties, the ironies of our human condition, of the omnipotent and absolute love that is God. We Christians have something to contribute to the world's drama over and above our good will – there is plenty of that about elsewhere, though never enough. We have the divine message, the Word incarnate, and the assistance of the Holy Spirit to guarantee the integrity of that message. What the world, however, is tempted to see, when it observes our Christian divisions, is a set of groups of searchers for a highly uncertain and in any event wordless Absolute. For the sake of the world we are engaged in our own ecumenical movement. And for God's sake we have to bring to that movement not merely good will, still less national or cultural prejudices and provincially vested interests, but the clear intelligence of mature persons who know by faith that Christ is not only the way and the life but the truth.

My debts to others for anything that is of value in the following pages are so many, so various, and in many instances so unspecifiable, that I resign myself to mentioning only two. First, I owe to Bernard Lonergan more than I can easily say. The first work of his that came to my knowledge was *Insight,* which I read shortly before the Second Vatican Council. I have expressed elsewhere something of what I owe to that book; and subsequent books or collections of papers from his pen have helped me to grapple with the abundance of new problems which the last two decades have forced upon our attention. Secondly, I thank Mrs Audrey Andrews for her marvellous help in the preparation of the manuscript, her typing skill, and her quiet encouragement.

Quotations from Scripture usually follow the Common Bible. Other versions are occasionally followed.

Note: I have assumed in these pages that, like the Anglican Communion, the great world Churches of continental Protestantism refrain from claiming, each for itself, the exclusive title to be the Church of Christ. These bodies should of course be allowed to speak for themselves. I note, however, that Karl Rahner says that such 'ecclesial relativism', as he calls it, was 'completely foreign to the early churches of the Reformation period'.[5] If Rahner is right, then since the Protestant reformers were severally responsible for the formation of a number of contending Protestant churches, logic would demand that each of these churches must claim for itself to be exclusively the Church of the Apostles' Creed. Whatever may have been the case in the sixteenth century, I doubt whether this is effectively claimed by these several bodies today. If I am wrong about this, the wording of numerous passages in the ensuing essay requires modification. I do not think that the essential argument is seriously affected. In practice, it would mean that the inquirer from outside, convinced that the Church is an indivisible visible communion, would have to consider not only the Catholic Church and the Eastern Orthodox Communion, but a number of Protestant bodies also. I venture to think that such knowledge of pre-Reformation Church history as is possible to a non-professional would suffice to persuade him that the Reformation was of such a revolutionary character as to constitute a break in continuity which is impossible if, ever since the first Christian Pentecost, there has been, and will continue to be, one Church in the terms of the argument of this essay. Ordinary common sense can see the humour of the note in *1066 and All That* against the year 1570 (excommunication of Elizabeth I): '(In this year) The Pope seceded with all his followers from the Church of England'. Common sense would react similarly to the proposal that the Lutheran Church of the sixteenth century is identical with the Catholic Church of the fifteenth.

Chapter I

Origins

There are great historical realities – in our own country, for example, the major political parties – which can be sufficiently understood for practical purposes without delving into their origins in the distant past. If the rungs by which they ascended were base, they can afford to despise them. They stand by what they are today and they stand for what they propose for the future. Napoleon's parentage does not matter; what matters is what he offers and threatens today.

With Christianity, things are different. What differentiates Christianity from other world views and, more particularly, from other religions, including those to which it is most akin, is Jesus Christ. Jesus Christ 'suffered under Pontius Pilate', at a date roughly ascertainable during the principate of Tiberius Caesar. It is true that he is the Word who was in the beginning with God and was God; that he is the eternal creator. But this we know, only because 'he was made man', made that particular man, Jesus son of Mary of Nazareth. That man is not only the final hope of the believing Christian. He is the historical origin of the Christian religion but also its abiding meaning. Christians cannot leave Jesus as an interesting but practically unimportant object for study by academic historians.

Jesus Christ is not only the Founder of Christianity, as he is described in the title of the late C. H. Dodd's splendid book. He is the living and abiding link between man and his environment on the one hand, and the Absolute Mystery which we call God on the other. And it was in his historical life, his resurrection, and the consequent outpouring of his Holy Spirit, that he showed us what that link is, and showed us what God is: 'He that hath seen me hath seen the Father.' The historical and risen Jesus is not only the messenger of God; he is the message.

Being historical, he is the object of historical investigation. He lived nearly two thousand years ago in Galilee and Judaea. We know him, as historical, through the medium of records and traditions. The records are almost exclusively those gathered together in the pages of the New Testament. Traditions are those that lived on in the Church. Neither source is as abundant and unproblematic as we might wish. Both, as being data for historical reconstruction, are subject to the methods of historical research and evaluation that are recognized as valid by academics. And academics are quick to point out that virtually all the evidence comes from within the Christian movement itself. It is as though we knew nothing of Lenin except what Communists have been prepared to tell us.

This essay is written by a Christian and, in the first instance, for Christian readers. It therefore assumes the truth of the Christian doctrines of the incarnation and the triunity of God. It cannot, however, assume that all historical questions about Jesus have yet received definitive answers; though it does assume that the New Testament books are 'inspired by the Holy Spirit'. And since it is from Christians that we know about Christ, I propose to turn without more ado to some New Testament evidence as to what the primitive Church believed about him and about the world as that world was, in their view, changed by his life and work, his death and resurrection. The question, for the moment, ceases to be: What was Jesus?, and becomes: What is Christianity? And in particular: What is the Church, to which Christians profess their allegiance when they recite the Creed?

Christianity dates not from the birth of Jesus but from his resurrection. That God had raised him from the dead is the root conviction and the root proclamation of the Christianity of the New Testament. If we can here rely on the Acts of the Apostles, it was this that Peter preached in Jerusalem after the 'charismatic' occurrences of the feast day of Pentecost in the year of the crucifixion of Jesus – the first public manifesto of the followers of the Galilean after they had found themselves bereft of his visible leadership. There was no need, in that early summer in Jerusalem, to talk about the crucifixion of Jesus; that was common knowledge. The news was not of his death but of his having been raised from the dead. Nevertheless, the crucifixion was not merely the factual presupposition of the resurrection; it was what gave meaning to it. And as the gospel, the good news, was taken out into areas remote from the events of Holy Week, it became necessary that the proclamation of the resurrection should be preceded by a preaching of the cross. Neither the one nor the other of these two events can be understood, religiously, in isolation. Each required theological interpretation. Together, they constitute what modern theologians call 'the Paschal mystery' – the mystery of the Christian passover, the Christian redemption from captivity.

Death is for every human being the end of history. Seen only within the limits of history, the death of Jesus was also the death of all that he stood for. It gave the lie to his own message and rendered vain his mission. He had proclaimed an imminent Reign of God, and it had seemed that in some way his own mission was intimately bound up with this coming. The claim had been rejected by those to whom he had been sent. They had shown what they thought of it by allowing him to be crucified. He had brought a message of salvation; he had not managed to save himself, and with his death the rejected message vanished into the void.

The crucifixion, seen in a Christian perspective but in abstraction from the resurrection, did not only disprove Jesus' gospel in and by itself, leaving things otherwise as they had been before his baptism by John. The gospel was presented, already by the Church of the New Testament period, as the fulfilment and the sublimation of the whole ancient covenant, and thus of the destiny of the People of God, that People for whom, according at least to later rabbinic teaching, God had created mankind as a whole: the People who were the very meaning of creation. Jesus was the epitome and representative of both human history and divine creation. His death – apart from his resurrection – signifies universal death. 'Then I, and you, and all of us fell down.' It is strange that some Christian scholars seem prepared to offer us a gospel without the resurrection.

How did the primitive Church see these things? We have two great and unmistakable Christian interpretations of the gospel from those days: the Pauline and the Johannine. They are not the only witnesses, but they are the most articulate and the most deeply and widely reflective. It has become so customary to treat the Pauline writings as evidence simply of his own individual genius that it seems worth while to point out that such is not our way in other fields, when a mind that is uniquely great gives expression to a tradition to which the mind's owner is deeply committed. We do not think we are being misled about Elizabethan England when we study Shakespeare. Nor do we feel that the funeral oration of Pericles, though probably in large measure an invention of Thucydides, has no light to cast for us upon ancient Athens at its apogee. Certainly Paul's mind is not the mind of Jesus of Nazareth, nor the mind of Peter or Andrew. But it is a Christian mind. And it is the mind of one who was totally given to the Christian mission and the building up of the Church, who lived in the midst of the Church at a period of high excitement and bitter controversy. Paul had to defend himself against those who thought that he had betrayed the Torah, the 'Law of Moses' as we call it; and he had to defend his converts against an incipient Gnosticism. Does he ever have to defend himself against the Christian mainstream for the place he gave to Jesus Christ in the divine economy of salvation?

I want to consider a passage from the Second Epistle to the Corinthians. The passage is embedded in a context in which Paul has found himself driven to a totally frank self-exposure to his readers; they know him well enough to be able to discover any insincerity in his writing here. Here we encounter Paul himself, as we do likewise in the Epistle to the Galatians, where again he senses that everything is to be gained or lost. And if his presentation of Christian truth had been alien to the accepted tradition, he would have been shown up at once by his opponents as heterodox. Here he is, then, writing to the Corinthians:

> Therefore, knowing the fear of the Lord, we persuade men; but what we are is known to God, and I hope it is known also to your conscience. ... the love of Christ controls us, because we are convinced that one has died for all; therefore all have died. And he died for all, that those who live might live no longer for themselves but for him who for their sake died and was raised. From now on, therefore, we regard no one from a human point of view; even though we once regarded Christ from a human point of view, we regard him thus no longer. Therefore, if any one is in Christ, he is a new creation; the old has passed away, behold, the new has come. All this is from God, ... God was in

Christ reconciling the world to himself, not counting their trespasses against them, and entrusting to us the message of reconciliation (2 Cor. 5:11, 14–19).

A paraphrase with some comments may not be out of place. 'The love of Christ controls (or, better, constrains) us.' Is this our love for Christ, or his for us? I suggest the latter, in harmony with Galatians 2:20: 'the Son of God, who loved me and gave himself for me'. In one sense, love can never constrain, for it asks for nothing less than a perfectly free response of answering love. Yet to know that one is loved is to recognize an appeal that can hardly be resisted. We are 'convinced that one has died for all'. That is our judgement (not just a theory but a considered affirmation), and it is the premiss for an important inference: 'therefore all have died'. Jesus, we are told today, was 'the man for others'. Paul says that he is the man for *all* others. He is the representative man. Elsewhere Paul will present him as a second Adam, both representative and source of a new and all-inclusive humanity. When the representative dies, all whom he represents die also in him.

Hence, if we live nevertheless, our life belongs henceforward not to us but to him in whom we died; in him whom God raised from the dead. Ours, then, is a risen life. And because we are risen, we see things in a perspective and a light that are not available to those who are not risen: we regard no one from a (merely) human point of view. Everyone now is different in our eyes; we see our fellow men for the first time as they truly are. Christ himself was never visible as he really was to men without faith. Perhaps we too were once without faith; but now we see Jesus as the disciples saw him: Blessed are the eyes which see the things which you see. Our old scale and scheme of values is overthrown. We are 'converts', and conversion involves a revaluation of all values. Conversion gives us a new horizon. In that new horizon everything is seen differently, and more truly. It is not just that a Christian has accepted opinions which he did not share before. Rather, his faith enables him to see things as they really are: 'I was blind, and now I see.' If one is 'in Christ', if – to put it simply – one is a believing Christian, then one is a 'new creation', for one is now 'in' the second Adam; and in Adam men became creatures. The old has passed away; we start from a new and higher beginning.[1]

There is an element of rhetoric in Paul's language in this passage. But rhetoric may be used to convey not only what is specious and false, but what is surprising but nevertheless true; and there can be no doubt of Paul's passionate dedication to truth as he dictates these sentences. No doubt we must also recognize that Paul is searching for language to express the inexpressible; the same is true of all theology, from the parables of Jesus to the *Summa* of Thomas Aquinas. But religious truth is not less, but more, than what can be articulated in language; we cannot attain it by evading the language.

Behind Paul's words here, there is the sober conviction that Christianity has introduced a new order of reality into human history – indeed, as we shall see, one must go further and say that it has introduced a new and higher order into creation. Paul is proclaiming that something that is novel is also true. His message is of course unwelcome to those who believe that to discover the ultimate truth about everything past, present and future it would only be necessary to reconstruct the 'big bang' with which the universe began. For Paul, creation remains open to new creation. We were living in an unfinished universe, and what had been lacking is given in the risen Christ.

The Pauline authorship of the Epistle to the Ephesians is seriously questioned by many modern scholars. For my present purposes, it is not necessary to take a position on this matter. Even among those who deny or doubt the Pauline authorship there are some who hold that the author of the Epistle 'was steeped in Paul's works and [his] ideas were only a slight development of those which Paul had expressed in his letter to the Colossians'.[2] Similarly, J. A. Grassi writes: 'Whatever the final judgment on authenticity is – if such is possible – *Ephesians* is certainly a mature development of Pauline thought and theology.'[3] It is also inspired Scripture. In what follows I shall, for convenience, refer to the author as Paul, without thereby wishing to pre-empt the question of authenticity.

Paul begins this epistle with a sublime sketch of the order of reality into which Christians have been introduced in consequence of a divine purpose accomplished and realized in the work of Christ. In the passage of 2 Corinthians discussed above, the divine causation, while of course presupposed throughout, is only mentioned towards the end: 'All this is from God, who through Christ reconciled us to himself and gave us the ministry of reconciliation; ...' Until that sentence, the passage had adopted a point of view within history and meta-history. But in Ephesians 1:3–14 the eternal purpose and the causal action of God are the leitmotiv, giving a kind of deductive colour to the whole exposition. Further, it is made clear that the new divine order in creation does not involve only believers. They have been caught up into a vast scheme: the final 'uniting' (summing-up) in Christ of the whole created universe. Into the sweep and dynamism of that divine plan, already in process of accomplishment,[4] the Christian believers have been really incorporated. Having made their act of Christian faith, they have been 'sealed' with the Holy Spirit, who – thus given – is the pledge of the consummation yet to come but eternally predestined.

This sublime panorama, it will be noted, finds its roots in an actual historical fact: the redemptive death of Jesus. Thus rooted in history, and through history in the created order, the divine plan (what the Fathers called 'the economy') remains historical also in its further development. We are deep in historically, though partially, realized eschatology. The post-historical, eschatological, *raison d'être* of all history (all creation) is already present and at work in history in the Christian fact.

We have to resist the temptation to think of this realized eschatology as a merely interior reality, a change of heart not actually incorporated in fully concrete historical fact, conditioning, and processes.[5] Redemption, according to New Testament theology, is of the whole man, and its fruits are to be seen in the actual historical order, just as the resurrection of Christ was a restoration (and glorification) of his whole self, soul and body, not just immortality for his human soul. Indeed, the eschatological reality is being actualized in and for the whole of creation: Christ must 'reign till he has put all things under his feet' (cf. vv. 20–22), and everything in heaven and on earth and under the earth is called upon to pay him homage.

Believers, then, precisely as such, are not sanctified souls but fully historical human beings; human beings, however, possessed by a new and splendid faith, itself a response to a new and tremendous self-disclosure and gift of God.

Birds of a feather flock together. Men who find themselves caught up and transfigured by a great and novel truth tend to associate with one another. It is therefore natural to expect that Christians will not be a mere number of believers but a real historical community – like what we call 'the Church'. And Paul tells us that the exalted Christ – exalted above every name that is named – has been given to be the 'head' of the Church 'which is his body, the fulness of him who fills all in all' (v. 23).

Plainly, the believers constitute the Church. The Church is not a mere Platonic idea, or a merely 'mystical' invisible union of believers, its extension and physiognomy known only to God himself. It is the fully historical and growing (hence developing) incorporation, embodiment, the preliminary historical realization, of the divine plan for the whole of humanity and the whole universe. That 'plan', in its essence the infinitely rich, eternal purpose of God, is to bring all things, in Christ, into union with God in a new order of reality based not on merely natural facts interpretable by merely natural reason but on a real but supernatural event apprehended by faith:

(The plan of the mystery hidden for ages in God was to be communicated by Paul to all men) that through the church the manifold wisdom of God might now be made known to the principalities and powers in the heavenly places. This was according to the eternal purpose which he has realized in Christ Jesus our Lord (Eph. 3:10–11).

Thus the redemption is no secret now. It is to be published not only to interested human listeners but to the powers that hold sway throughout the universe. And the Church is the mouthpiece of this publication. Is the Church less 'public' than its message? Is the Church less than an historical, concrete community, a flesh-and-blood reality? We may turn our attention to 2:11–22. In this passage Paul is addressing particularly Christians of Gentile origin, and is expounding the truth that 'we are [God's] work-manship, created in Christ Jesus for good works, which God prepared beforehand, that we should walk in them' (2:10).

Therefore remember that at one time you Gentiles in the flesh, called the uncircumcision by what is called the circumcision, which is made in the flesh by hands – remember that you were at that time separated from Christ, alienated from the common-wealth of Israel, and strangers to the covenants of promise, having no hope and without God in the world. But now in Christ Jesus you who once were far off have been brought near in the blood of Christ. For he is our peace, who has made us both one, and has broken down the dividing wall of hostility, by abolishing in his flesh the law of commandments and ordinances, that he might create in himself one new man in place of the two, so making peace, and might reconcile us both to God in one body through the cross, thereby bringing the hostility to an end. And he came and preached peace to you who were far off and peace to those who were near; for through him w᾿ both have access in one Spirit to the Father. So then you are no longer strangers and sojourners, but you are fellow citizens with the saints and members of the household of God, built upon the foundation of the apostles and prophets, Christ Jesus himself being the cornerstone, in whom the whole structure is joined together and grows into a holy temple in the Lord; in whom you also are built into it for a dwelling place of God in the Spirit.[6]

Here Paul begins by looking back to the time before the gospel. At that time there was a division in mankind between the Jews on the one hand and the Gentiles on the other. The Jews were an organized human community, a 'commonwealth', and from this commonwealth (which inherited the covenants) the Gentiles were excluded. In consequence, they were without hope, without the Messianic promise, without God.

All this has now been changed through the reconciling work of Christ and its prolongation in the preaching of the gospel. Elsewhere Paul says that God was in Christ reconciling the world to himself (2 Cor. 5:19). In Ephesians the work of reconciliation is described as taking place between Jews and Gentiles. Now, through the crucifixion, the two are reconciled and made one; and thus reconciled with each other, they are jointly reconciled with God himself and have access to him by 'one Spirit'.

Paul writes here as though there had been a total reconciliation between all Jews and all Gentiles. He knew very well that this was not historically true. The Christians – Jews and Gentiles in one body – were a tiny group in the world, though a recognizable group: in 1 Cor. 10:32 they are simultaneously aligned with and distinguished from the unconverted Jews and 'Greeks' as, in contrast with them, 'the church of God'. But Paul would argue that the process of reconciliation preached and accepted was still going on, and must continue till the gospel message had had its full effect. The Christian community is thus the germ, the nucleus, of a reconciled universe, of mankind and the world 'summed up in Christ'. The commonwealth that was God's people under the Old

Covenant has been replaced – or should we say 'transformed'? – in the 'one body' of a renewed humanity through the historical crucifixion of Christ. This new entity, the historical body of Christ, is universal in scope and range; and since that universality has not yet been factually realized it is dynamic and missionary in function, not to say in essence.

I think it is unreasonable to doubt that, for Paul, the 'Church', which is the 'body' of which Christ is the head, is the actual association of historical human beings, made concrete in a number of local 'churches' in Palestine and elsewhere in the Roman Empire, to various local embodiments of which he addresses his letter. Nothing in his writings suggests a distinction between this historical entity and the 'eschatological' Church which, for the author of the Epistle to the Ephesians, is an integral part of the divine economy of a consummated and supernaturalized creation. It is consonant with this conclusion that the eschatological Church is rooted in the historical flesh-and-blood Jesus Christ, actually crucified and actually raised from the dead, and that Paul appears to be speaking to his readers as to actual members of this eschatological reality.

Indeed, the notion of an essentially invisible, merely 'mystical', Church is not one that would have occurred to, or been welcomed by, main-line primitive Christians. Such a notion would perhaps seek its roots in a Platonic doctrine that man is essentially a soul, though burdened and restricted by the extrinsic encumbrance of a material body. But although here and there in the New Testament (and far more, of course, in the later Christian literature) we can find signs of the influence of Greek philosophy, the anthropology of Christianity has remained basically faithful to its Jewish ancestry, and man has been seen as essentially an historical, which is to say a flesh-and-blood, entity. When the Church broke away from the Synagogue (and this was happening before the date of composition of the Epistle to the Ephesians) it did not, after abandoning the institutional framework of Judaism, become a mere movement of ideas, or a set of theories. It took shape as an alternative historical entity, a community of historical beings, united in their faith and integrated into a real fellowship by the sacramental rites of baptism and the eucharist, which are signs (and in Christian belief effective signs) of a supernatural bond; signs which exist in the sphere of full matter-based history.

This is the community which received the name of 'the Church'.

Scholars dispute whether the term was originally applied to each of a number of local Christian groups, or was rather applied in the first instance to Christians as a whole, wherever they might live and worship. Is 'church', in the facts behind the New Testament, primarily a local group; or is it a universal association? My own view might be that the term was taken over from the Old Testament at a time when the one outstanding Christian group was that of the Christians in and around Jerusalem, but that from the first it had a flexibility which would allow it to be used in both a local and a universal sense. The Epistle to the Ephesians shows that, when a Christian's eyes were raised from local to universal concerns, the application of the term 'Church' to the universal body of believers was easy and could be taken for granted.

At this universal level Paul sees the Church as a unique, historical and therefore 'visible', fellowship or polity. Yet one cannot but be struck by the fact that he goes on to urge his readers to *preserve* the unity of the Spirit in the bond of peace; to 'put on the new man'; to be truthful in their dealings with one another 'because they are one another's limbs' – as though the body of Christ could be disintegrated by human moral failures; to be kind to one another and forgiving; in short, to 'walk in love just as Christ has loved us', and to be subject to one another in the fear of Christ (chs. 4, 5).

Such exhortations to unity and to behaviour conducive to unity raise an important question. Does the unity of the Church depend on the efforts of its members in such a way that (since every Christian remains a fallible and potentially sinful person) the Church's unity is precarious and may cease to exist as a reality in the world? Such is the contention of many Christian thinkers who argue that, just as the Church in history is less than perfectly 'holy, catholic and apostolic', so it may be less than perfectly united. They see the present divisions between Christian groups as evidence that this is in fact the case. They hope, indeed, that as the Church grows in holiness (but does it?), so it will grow towards unity, and many of them are of course devoted to the cause of unity as embodied in the ecumenical movement. They perhaps do not always bear in mind that since, in this world, the Church will never be perfectly holy in their sense of that term, the visible unity of the Church will always be precarious, and may have to be conceived not so much as an attainable and permanent goal but as an unrealizable eschatological hope or a Kantian regulative idea.

Before dealing specifically with the interpretation of the Epistle to the Ephesians with its powerful exhortations to preserve unity, let us remind ourselves again of what is fundamental to the nature of Christianity.

Unbelievers and those who adopt a neutral stance about religion naturally understand Christianity as one among the many alternative versions of the human quest for God or for 'the divine'. Christianity, according to them, is one more case-history in the long search of humanity for some transcendent underpinning of historical experience and of its unendurable relativism. Comparative religious studies, or the history of religions, can show us a host of such alternatives, from the religions of so-called primitives to the great world 'faiths' (a Christian word, but convenient). Man, Augustine observed, is made for God, and his heart is without repose until it comes to rest in this goal. Hence human history is pervaded and permeated by the quest; and the varieties of religion are in large measure to be explained by the varying cultural contexts in which the search has been conducted.

Christians reject this interpretation of their own religion as inadequate. Christianity is not, fundamentally, nothing more than a human quest for God. At a deeper level, it is God's quest for man. It springs from a divine initiative that is disclosed primarily in the utterly unprecedented, unpredictable, unique fact of the incarnation of the Word of God in Jesus Christ. Throughout the whole texture of Christianity this divine priority over human thought, aspiration and action is preserved. It is summed up in the doctrine of prevenient grace, the divine offer and enablement which precedes and effects our free human response. The priority of grace was affirmed when the Church rejected Pelagianism and semi-Pelagianism. It was strongly maintained by the leaders of the Protestant Reformation, but it is the shared conviction of all authentic Christianity. It is the analogue, in the supernatural order, of the fact that man and his universe did not create themselves: their very existence and their continuance in existence depend upon a totally free divine act. And Thomas Aquinas was not afraid to affirm that creation is an act not only of divine power but, supremely we may say, of divine love. From the beginning to the end of our relations with God, from our coming into existence to our ultimate introduction to the beatitude of God's reign in the 'absolute future', God's action always comes first and our response comes second. Augustine himself, elsewhere in the *Confessions* from which our previous quotation was taken, makes God in effect address him in these words: 'Thou wouldst not be seeking me if thou hadst not already found me.'

It follows, incidentally, that Christianity is not basically a system of ethics (even the ethics of 'Love God above all things and your neighbour as yourself'). Nor is it a moral exhortation: 'Do what you judge to be right'.[7] Man's ethical insights and moral strivings are secondary to something much more basic. They are response: response to an intervention, a relevation, and a solicitation of God's redeeming and transforming love. And even the response itself, to the extent that it is affirmative, is a divine grace. Only the deliberate refusal of offered grace can be seen as escaping from the priority of grace. God is man's only saviour; man himself is man's only destroyer.

There is, in consequence, no evading the conclusion that, if the historical and visible unity of the Church is a precarious thing, subject to the fallibility and peccability of the Church's members, and capable of disappearing for a time, or permanently, from among the realities of history, then this unity is not part of the divine *datum* of redemption.

This point may be still further developed. The Church is essentially, in the stage of probation, an historical reality and not a mere Platonic idea or an eschatological utopia. But a reality must have its own unity (*ens* and *unum* have an identical denotation). Hence, a reality that is essentially and 'visibly' historical will have its own historical and visible unity. If, then, this visible unity of the Church is not guaranteed by God but is only the uncertain reward for meritorious but uncertain Christian efforts, then the Church itself is not part of the divinely-given 'economy' of salvation.

The divine priority in the drama of redemption has its anticipation in the covenantal relation established between the Old Testament People of God and God the author of the covenant. The relationship was established by God's own act, and the gifts of God are without repentance. The covenant called for a fitting response from Israel; and the message of the prophets is that this response was far from perfect. But, despite warnings and threats, the conviction remained that God would not be unfaithful to his covenant, his commitment, or to the promise implicit in it. Even if Israel as a nation were to turn its back finally on the divine offer and promise, God would see to it that there was a faithful remnant to inherit both. Perhaps the suffering servant of the latter half of the Book of Isaiah is a personification of that remnant. The New Testament, it is true, depicts Christ as inaugurating a new covenant to supersede the old. But it should be remembered that this new covenant was already foreshadowed in the Old Testament – and understood not as something entirely different from, but as a renewal on a new basis of, the old covenant. The relationship with God remains, not because of man's fidelity nor subject to man's good will, but because God is faithful and his will must prevail.

Beyond question Paul sees the Church as part and parcel of the divine economy of redemption. The Church, we may say, is the People of God renewed and recreated on a new basis, the basis which is the Paschal Mystery of the resurrection of Christ crucified and the consequent mission of the Holy Spirit. Paul's vision is of the Church as the dynamic and growing anticipation of the redemption of the whole of mankind and the whole universe; the vision disintegrates if the Church itself is liable to disintegration, if the Church could cease to exist as an historical entity because of the infidelity of its members.

So what is the point of Paul's exhortations to preserve unity, if that unity is in any case guaranteed by God? The question is similar to that other question: If I am predestined to salvation, why should I put myself out to be good?

(1) The visible unity of the Church, being intrinsic to the Church's fully historical character, is a covenanted, that is to say a divinely guaranteed, reality. But no individual member of the Church, indeed no subsidiary group of its members, whether a strictly local church or a confederation of such in a national or regional collectivity, is assured of continual membership irrespective of his (or its) own personal or particular response to the continuing offer of divine grace. Any individual, any particular group (even a collection of dioceses or provinces) may defect, and is in danger of defecting, unless the effort is made to 'maintain the unity in the bond of peace'. Each reader of the Epistle to the Ephesians, and each local church to which the letter may come, needs therefore both warning and exhortation. Of each it is true that he – or it – has an obligation to 'become what he is'. Just as the Christian has died with Christ in his baptism and *therefore* must 'mortify his members on earth', so the Christian has been incorporated into the indefectible reality and unity of the Church

and therefore must labour to preserve that unity and union. After all, Judas left the koinonia, the fellowship; but the fellowship survived intact and the vacant place was filled.

(2) Nevertheless, the visible unity of the Church, while certain, is not a magic fact. It does, in a sense, depend on the faithful perseverance of the Church's members – or at least of some of them. What the covenant involves is that, by the grace of the Holy Spirit and as a result of God's infallible providence (which is not inconsistent with real human freedom, though a mystery remains), there will always be a faithful remnant that will respond, not indeed perfectly, but at least with such minimal adequacy that the polity, the divine commonwealth, the 'communion' of believers, will survive as a unique, visible, historical entity. By the word 'visible' we of course mean here 'concrete and recognizable'. Such visibility is essential. Not only is the Church an integral part of the divine economy of redemption (and this economy is itself historical); but the Church has precisely a duty laid upon it by God to proclaim the message of salvation. This message must therefore be preserved in the Church's teaching in its integrity, and it must be provided with adequate grounds for its credibility and must be discoverable by those in good faith who come in contact with it. All human creations, if they are merely human, are marked with that sentence of death that belongs to humanity itself. All merely human structures are built ultimately on sand. Sooner or later, when the storms of mortality beat upon them, they will collapse – whether we think of a Judaism which has failed to recognize its Messiah or of a Roman Empire which has deified its human ruler. Only the Church of Christ is built on rock and, despite the failures of its rulers, will survive.

Perhaps it is hardly necessary to add that the other so-called 'notes', or marks, of the Church are in the same case as the 'note' of unity. It is quite true that the Church is never as holy, as catholic, or as apostolic as it ought to be, just as it is never as 'one' as it ought to be. The fact that the Church's members are each and all in a process of development which , at the best, is from the less to the more perfect, and that each of them is fallible and peccable, makes such a conclusion statistically inevitable. But God's fidelity guarantees to our faith that the Church will never fail to be at least adequately holy, catholic, and apostolic. Similarly, it will never cease to be visibly one, with a unity that is not intrinsic to its nature but comes as a gift from God, a gift continually bestowed afresh: 'Behold, I am with you all the days, even to the end of the world.' But, I claim, there is no way for the Church to be visibly one, so as to be a recognizable option for the man who seeks religious truth, unless it remains a visible unity of actual communion.

*　*　*

The suggestion can of course be made that I have read into the Epistle to the Ephesians an ecclesiology which, being a Roman Catholic, I have foisted upon it; that I have performed an act of *eisegesis* rather than of exegesis. I therefore append some passages from authors who were not Roman Catholics.

Dean Armitage Robinson was an Anglican ecclesiastic and a distinguished scholar. He was an early supporter of the aspirations that took shape as the modern ecumenical movement. In a book entitled *The Vision of Unity*, he writes of Christ as understood by St. Paul:

> Christ died, Christ rose, Christ ascended, Christ is supreme in the unseen world; and the same Christ is still living and working in the visible world to-day. He is not bodiless; ... He sees and speaks, He comes and helps, in and through His larger and ever-growing body – that body into which His disciples are baptised, within which they are held united by the sacred food which is His body, ... [Paul] could never allow the possibility of a broken Christianity, which should admit of two churches – Jewish and Gentile. The Gentile was co-heir and concorporate with the Jew, or he was nothing at all; he was a member of the body, or else he was still an alien, still without hope. ... The unity of Christians, and therefore Christianity itself, was at stake in the controversy; ...[8]

In his commentary on the Epistle to the Ephesians Robinson shows clearly that at least he was not willing to acquiesce in Christian disunion. And, as he says, 'as we rouse ourselves to enquire afresh after the meaning of unity, we may hope that (the author of the Epistle) will speak to us afresh':

> The Apostle begins with the disclosure of the great purpose of God for the world – the gathering into one of all things in

Christ ... He showed that while hitherto (his Gentile readers) had stood outside the sphere of the special development of this purpose, they were now no longer outside it, but within. For a new beginning had been made: Jew and Gentile had been welded together in Christ to form God's New Man. The proclamation of this oneness of mankind in Christ was the mission that was specially entrusted to St. Paul ... That they should know and understand all this was his earnest prayer, as their knowledge of it was an essential preliminary to its realization. Having been given this unity, they must keep it ... Mankind had started as One in the original Creation. But in the course of the world's history, through sin on the one hand, and on the other through the revelation of God to a selected People, a division had come in. Mankind was Two and not One. There was the privileged Jew, and there was the unprivileged Gentile. It was the glory of grace to bring the Two once more together as One in Christ. A new start was thus made in the world's history.[9]

On Ephesians 1:4 ('he chose us in [Christ]') Robinson observes:

It has been said that in the word 'us' we have 'the language of charity', which includes certain individuals whom a stricter use of terms would have excluded. That is to say, not all the members of all the Churches to whom the letter was to go were in fact included in the Divine Selection. To this we may reply: (1) Nowhere in the epistle does St Paul suggest that any individual among those whom he addresses either is or may be excluded from this Selection.
(2) Unworthy individuals there undoubtedly were: but his appeal to them is based on the very fact of their Selection by God: 'I beseech you that ye walk worthy of the calling wherewith ye have been called' [4:1]. ... just as the Prophets looked more to the whole than to the parts, so St Paul is dominated by the thought of the whole, and of God's purposes with the whole. It is a new Israel that Christ has founded – a People of privilege.[10]

We may complement these extracts from Robinson by the following from the Anglican Bishop Eric Graham, whose com-

mentary on Ephesians forms part of the S.P.C.K. one-volume
commentary published in 1928:

> The essential place of the Church in the divine scheme of
> redemption ... is never absent from the mind of St. Paul ...;
> but nowhere else does he treat the theme so fully as in
> Ephesians, or make it so abundantly clear that redemption
> implies not merely a personal and individual reconciliation with
> God, but also membership in a corporate society of divine origin
> – the Church of Christ.
>
> What, then, is the Church? It is a visible society ... But it is
> more than a mere society, just as its origin is more than human.
> It is an organic union, answering to and manifesting the unity of
> God – Father, Son and Holy Spirit (4:3–6). ... But the most
> frequent and characteristic of St. Paul's metaphors in this
> connexion is that which represents the Church as the Body of
> Christ ...; i.e. it is His outward and visible manifestation; the
> organ of His self-expression; the instrument whereby He works.
> Moreover, it is an essential part of Himself, just as His 'natural'
> body was in the days of His flesh; without it He would be
> incomplete, not, of course, in His perfect Deity, but as the
> Incarnate Saviour of mankind.[11]

Combining these remarks from two Anglican scholars, we can
conclude that the Epistle to the Ephesians (which the Free Church
scholar Dr Mitton says has 'deservedly been regarded as the
quintessence of Paulinism') presents Christianity as a new
beginning in God's purpose of gathering all things together in
Christ. The Gentile converts had been given this unity of mankind
in Christ and must keep it. They had been called to be limbs of the
body of Christ. Into it they had been baptized and in it they are
held united by sharing in the Eucharist. This body of Christ is so
essentially one that Paul could not allow the possibility of *two*
Churches, one Jewish and the other Gentile. In the struggle to
prevent a visible division between Jewish and Gentile Christians –
such that there would be two 'Churches' – the unity of Christians,
and therefore Christianity itself, was at stake. The Church, this
'visible society' as Graham calls it, is not only the instrument with
which Christ works in the world; it is 'part' of him, so that without
it he, in his role as incarnate saviour of mankind, would be
incomplete. In that observation of Bishop Graham we may hear an

echo of Augustine's dictum that the 'whole' Christ *(totus Christus)* is not just Jesus Christ the head of the Church, but this head *and* his 'members', the members of the Church. The mystery of redemption is a single mystery, including both Jesus Christ and his Church.

Behind the Epistle to the Ephesians there lay the dispute, agonizing for Paul, of the terms of admission of Gentiles to the Christian community. He had insisted, against strong Jewish-Christian opposition, that Gentiles need not, so to say, become Jewish proselytes in order to qualify for membership of the Church. He had seen the victory of what he stood for ratified, in principle, at Jerusalem itself, according to the Acts of the Apostles (15:6–29). But schism and the threat of schism are recurrent phenomena in Christian history. In the Johannine literature, and particularly in the First Epistle of John, we see an inspired writer facing the actual fact of schism, and reacting to it in a way that is hardly distinguishable from that of Cyprian a century and a half later.

Chapter II

Communion

The Church is a fact and factor of history; it is what the French would call 'une grandeur historique'. As such it attracts the interest of historians, who are not themselves always Christians. From the nature of their craft historians approach their object, human history in the sense of what has actually occurred and the underlying causes and motivations, by way of documents and other memorials of the past. These constitute for them their data. They are only interested in mystery when, at the end of their researches, reflections and reconstructions, they have reason to believe that behind all this there is something more than meets, or could ever meet, the eye. What they are primarily seeking, at least at the first stage of their work, is 'the facts'.

Every fact, however, occurs within a context; the study of one fact leads the inquirer to another. Facts can indeed be recorded in chronicles; but the quest for intelligibility leads to the desire to make a story, a narrative, out of the chronologically successive facts. And the best stories have a plot, or at least some thread of intelligible continuity. The history of England can easily become for the historian the history of that continuing thing, the British Constitution, or of British government.

The historian of the Church is similarly drawn by the attraction of a plot. Hence the Church may come to be seen by him, and in consequence presented to his readers, as primarily, what indeed in part it is, an institution – or, as the *Concise Oxford Dictionary* (1925) defines that word: an 'organization for the promotion of some public object'. An institution requires, for its better functioning, a constitution, a body of regulations or law, a government and officers.

I have no difficulty in regarding the Church as an institution. Thus I accept that it is, among other things, an 'organization'; and that it exists for the promotion of some public object – the communication to mankind at large of the gospel of Jesus Christ. But there is some danger that the Church may come to be regarded, in some quarters, as nothing but an institution; as though it were adequately and fully classified as one specimen of this species of fact. The tendency to do so was encouraged in the Catholic Church by the revolt of the Reformation against the current Catholic institution and the consequent launching of theories of the Church of Christ which seemed to depreciate, if they did not altogether deny, its institutional aspect. It has been pointed out that the anti-Protestant reaction in ecclesiology was carried to such a point that Bellarmine could define or describe the Church in such terms that a community of human beings entirely destitute of grace and holiness would have satisfied his stated requirements for the Church.

In modern times, it is true, historians have become aware that the history of political institutions is only a small part of their field, and we have histories of social life, of economics, of culture. Nevertheless, the historian is bound by the limitations of his data, just as the physical scientist is bound by the limitations of his. The Church disclosed by the historian will remain an historical entity, and is in danger of being presented as nothing more than such. The mystery of the Church will at best be suggested rather than proclaimed.

The Second Vatican Council was offered for its consideration a draft document on the Church, and the first chapter of this draft was entitled: 'On the Nature of the Church'. The Council changed this title (and the contents of the chapter), preferring to take as the title of its own first chapter: 'On the Mystery of the Church'. The change was immensely significant.

If the Church is a mystery we have to resign ourselves to the fact that we shall never grasp it in its fullness in a single definition. A mystery is indeed an object of our intellectual curiosity; but it is one which we shall never fully encapsulate in human concepts and language.

Since the great theological reappraisal sanctioned by the Second Vatican Council, theologians are less inclined to offer definitions of the Church, and more likely to seek, elaborate and discuss 'models' of it. The notion of 'model' is taken not directly from the field of art but from that of the physical sciences. When the atomic theory was propounded, it was presented as a description adequately corresponding with reality. It involved, as the word 'atom' suggests, that the material world was built up out of units of matter that were severally indivisible: you could 'cut up' a pellet of metal, but an atom could not be 'cut up'. It was precisely the atom's indivisibility that made possible, so it was held, a material world such as our senses provided us with. In course of trial, the theory began to become questionable and at length it was found possible to 'split the atom'. The theory, as theory, was put out of court, although it may still have had its uses as a model. A model does not claim to give the full truth about one's object of inquiry. Thus it is possible, and no doubt convenient, to work with the model of a particle of matter when studying electrons. The model proves fruitful in many respects; that is to say, its use enables one to discover more about the electron than one knew before. But it does not explain all the relevant data: an electron produces effects which are more like those of radiation than those of a material particle. Thus science can operate with two models of the electron. Scientists of course believe that each of these models, being fruitful for discovery, enshrines truth about the electron. But they would no longer say that either model is capable of encompassing the whole truth about this object.

I think that in some respects a scientific model has the functions and character of what Plato would call an 'hypothesis'. Any hypothesis lives, for much of its time, a precarious life; one goes on using it until it is falsified by evidence or is proved to be incoherent. At that stage, Plato would have discarded his hypothesis. But one does not necessarily discard one's scientific model – if only because one has not yet conceived a model that will do justice both to the data that the model has failed to take into account *and also* to those that it has taken into account. So long as no completely adequate model of an electron is available, one will continue to operate with two models and will have to say that, up to the present, an electron remains something of a mystery.

The Church is a (supernatural) mystery; or rather, it is a constituent element in the one mystery of the divine economy of the redemption and supernatural elevation of the created order. A supernatural mystery is likely to be more formidable for our human understanding than natural 'mysteries' in physical science. Fr Avery Dulles, in his book, *Models of the Church*, writes:

> Mysteries are realities of which we cannot speak directly. If we wish to talk about them at all we must draw on analogies afforded by our experience of the world. These analogies provide models. ... The peculiarity of models, as contrasted with aspects, is that we cannot integrate them into a single synthetic vision on the level of articulate, categorical [*sic; categorial?*] thought. In order to do justice to the various aspects of the Church, as a complex reality, we must work simultaneously with different models. By a kind of mental juggling act, we have to keep several models in the air at once.[1]

Those who desire a clear-cut definition of the Church (such as Bellarmine offered), which would suppose an intellectual and conceptualizable grasp of the Church's 'nature' (an Aristotelian term, not much in favour with modern physical scientists) may be reminded that the Second Vatican Council, in the chapter referred to above, chose to present its object, the Church, not in a precise and comprehensive definition but by recalling some of the models of the Church that are thought to be found in the pages of the New Testament, especially in teaching attributed to our Lord himself.

Before the Second Vatican Council I wrote a book, *The Idea of the Church*[2] which was held by critics to emphasize unduly the model of the Church as an institution. In what follows I would like to try to view the Church in the light of a different model, that of 'communion'. That the Church is communion, or a communion, is often stated or implied in the documents of Vatican II, and the notion is also much used by the authors of the Statements (on the Eucharist, on Ministry and Orders, and on Authority in the Church) of the Anglican/Roman Catholic International Commission.

Dom Gregory Dix, celebrated for his work, *The Shape of the Liturgy*, wrote some important articles (recently reprinted in book form)[3] on *Jurisdiction in the Early Church, Episcopal and Papal.* In these articles he argues that, while evidence for papal jurisdiction in the first three centuries of the Church is slight, the same is also true of evidence for episcopal jurisdiction in the same period. It was, he suggests, after 'the Peace of Constantine' brought the Church into close and positive relations with the State, that the Church began, as it were inevitably and without any sense that it was doing something new, to emphasize notions of jurisdiction and of statutory Canon Law. And as it thus began to emphasize the jurisdictional character of bishops, it did the same with regard to the papacy: as bishops came to be seen as having their jurisdiction, so *pari passu* did the Pope come to be seen to have his. There had, in the earlier period, been very real notions of both episcopal and papal (or Roman) leadership, but these notions had been implicitly rather than explicitly juris-dictional in character. After Constantine they were gradually replaced by more explicitly jurisdictional notions; and the sacramental basis of leadership, so clearly seen in the earlier period, was to that extent thrown into the background. Dix appears to have thought that this change was irreversible. He did not live to see the Second Vatican Council and its efforts to restore in fuller vigour the apprehension of the sacramental foundations of episcopal and papal jurisdiction.

'Jurisdictional' is an institutional notion. 'Sacrament', on the other hand, is a notion that harmonizes well with the notion of a divinely guaranteed, established and sustained 'communion' in the 'body of Christ'.

The word 'communion' comes from the Latin word *communio,* which is the translation of a Greek word *koinonia.* The question is whether the concept of 'communion' can give us a helpful model of what the Church is.[4]

The word itself occurs several times in the New Testament, but with the exception of one, for me important, example in the First Epistle of John, these instances are not specially helpful for our present purpose.

Let me explain what I shall here mean by the word 'com-munion'. I am not referring specially to Holy Communion, but shall frequently have at the back of my mind the use we make of the word when we speak of 'the Anglican Communion' or 'the Eastern Orthodox Communion' – meaning the community of Christians who are, respectively, either Anglicans or Orthodox.

I take the word as meaning: (1) a relation or relations between persons, established through shared 'possessions', shared experien-ces or shared goals and hopes; (2) a community arising out of such established relations. The Greek word *koinonia* like its associated verb *koinonein* refers us back to the Greek adjective *koinon*. What is *koinon* is shared, as opposed to what is *idion*, private. Hence *idion* is used of private property or experience, *koinon* applies to shared, or public, property or experience. *Koinonein* thus means 'to share in common', and *koinonia* (a noun) means 'sharing'.

To possess something in common is in fact to be consequentially related with one another; whereas to hold something in private *(idion)* tends to divide the owner from others – hence, an idiosyncrasy is something that marks one off from one's fellows. The common field of a medieval village was the possession, not of a private owner, but of the villagers collectively; each of them was, along with the others, an owner of the field. Such common sharing inevitably created relations between the villagers; you will not be permanently and entirely unconcerned about those who have common rights with you over the same piece of property: common rights, and common interests. If common ownership does not lead to collaboration, at least it will lead to mutual controversy. Common ownership, then, is a foundation for relations between the owners – this is communion (meaning 1). And there can be little doubt that this common ownership, this sharing, was a positive factor in building up the village community, its sense of common purpose, its recognition of a common identity – this is communion (meaning 2).

The common field is common property in the most materialistic sense of that term. But property can be taken in a wider sense. Common parentage is something that turns brothers and sisters into a family. Family is objective fact, a fact of real relationship. It tends to create in its members a sense and recognition of relationship that is unique and can be very powerful: blood is thicker than water.

Similarly, a common citizenship binds the people of a nation into a unity and is the basis of the virtue of patriotism.

Besides common possessions, there are common or shared experiences. An example of communion based on shared experience is the solidarity among veterans of a battle or a campaign, a solidarity that creates a sense of fellowship. These veterans have been together in a situation that called forth the deepest emotions and passions; it has left a permanent mark on them, and when they meet – as they may contrive to do by means, for example, of annual reunions – they recognize that they are united through a bond which none other shares.

Communion, however, can be as brief as the brief experience that gives rise to it. A friendly exchange of smiles as two men pass on a road puts them, for the moment, into relationship with each other. It is a transient analogy, almost a foretaste, of that (eschatological?) kingdom of souls of which Kant speaks. Ships that pass in the night are changed thereby; each carries the other's mark upon it.

In other circumstances a smile can be the first, almost sacramental, moment of, and initiation into, a relationship which will last and grow through life and perhaps beyond. Virgil, in the Fourth Eclogue, signals the first smile of recognition directed by a baby towards its mother: 'Incipe, parve puer, risu cognoscere matrem.' The child's smile of delight is met, with moral if not physical inevitability, by the mother's responding smile. The child is no longer 'it' but 'he' or 'she'. Nothing will ever be the same between child and mother again. One is reminded of Paolo and Francesca in Dante's *Inferno,* who looked up from their book at each other, and were held in that gaze for the rest of the day.

The mother and child were related before that celebratory moment, and by the closest of biological ties, the child being flesh of her flesh. But the communion of and through the exchanged smile is something more than relatedness. It is real: ontological, one might say. But through the exchanged recognition it has become *inter-personal* communion. Communion based on common possession or shared experience is not always interpersonal communion, though it is always communion between persons. But always it contains a potency of interpersonal relations. I may never have met the man who, my newspaper tells me, has won the first prize in the recent lottery. But if we are both Englishmen this common nationality is already a bond between us and would, if we met and recognized the bond, establish a special interpersonal relationship between us.

Thus, we can enlarge on our preliminary description of communion. Communion is a system of personal relations built upon and flowing from common possession or common experience, and in potency to become interpersonal relationship.

Personhood has been much discussed in recent thinking. If at one time it seemed possible to define it in terms which made it nearly identical with conscious individuality, it now seems less possible to understand it without reference to relationship and to the possibility of personal development, largely through relationship: we grow by degrees into greater personhood, and that growth is to a notable extent a growth in relations with the world about us, and especially with other persons. Doubtless we should bear in mind that relations exist only if there are realities to be related. The Persons of the Holy Trinity are, tradition tells us, to be understood (with all due respect for the limitations of analogical talk) as 'subsistent relationships'; however, if we may venture the phrase, there is a divine nature identical and common to the three Persons, which are therefore never unsubstantial.

Human personhood grows towards its own perfection in the development of personal relations and particularly in the development from relatedness as a fact to interpersonal relationships in which that relatedness is more fully 'lived'. This is supremely true when we bring into our horizon of thought the element of the divine. Man grows more and more himself, more fully personal, as he grows in willed relationship with God. That is why prayer is a powerful element in the development of ourselves – although it should be obvious that its influence in this direction will be corrupted if we practise it with that end primarily in view. I should not love my friend primarily because I shall thus become more myself.

We have spoken of communion as relatedness based upon common possessions or shared experiences. We must not forget that it may also be founded upon common hopes or aspirations. A political party is a communion based upon the desire and hope to achieve a shared aim or aims. There is a Society for the Promotion of Christian Knowledge. Missionary societies exist not only to maintain existing missionary activity but also to convert those who are not already Christian believers. The Church conceives itself as existing to spread the gospel and to prepare, with God's grace, the conditions for the advent of the 'absolute future'. And doubtless the Church, like many other communions, is based conjointly on shared possession, shared experience, and shared aspirations.

Communion has been said to be a relatedness in potency to become interpersonal relatedness. A potency can profitably be studied in the light of that to which it is in potency. A piece of scientific research is to be understood by reference to the question which it seeks to answer. An acorn becomes more intelligible when we have examined an oak tree. That to which a potency is in potency is called by philosophers its 'act'. And Aristotle taught that process is a form of 'movement' from potency to act, a movement that is already virtually 'informed', given character, by the act towards which it is in process. So what are interpersonal relations, as distinct from relations with things and from those relations with other persons (or communities) where we either have no contact with them or treat them as though they were things rather than persons?

The baby's first smiling recognition of its mother is the moment at which the baby ceases to be 'it' and becomes 'he' or 'she'. It is also the moment when the mother becomes for the baby a real self. At the core of interpersonal relations is recognition of the selfhood of the other. It is a fruit of genuine attention to the other as other. There is an attention to the other that is too immature to amount to recognition of the otherness of the other. When we are half asleep we have 'experience', but it amounts to little more than a modification of our own sensibilities. When the baby 'recognizes' its mother, it has woken up from its primitive pure solipsism. But besides the immaturity that precedes attention, there is corrupt attention. By 'corrupt attention' I mean the effort to see the other as conforming to, or possibly subserving, our own requirements. Such corrupt attention is very frequent in polemical theology: we require that the other should see things from our point of view, in our perspective. Since he plainly does not so see them, we are angered and tempted to doubt his good faith, or at least his intelligence. He becomes an obstacle to us, something to be circumvented if not destroyed. So far as we are concerned he is not, or ceases to be, himself. And as there is corrupt attention so also, and in consequence, there is corrupt love.

At an early stage of my classical education I was introduced to the *Alcestis* of Euripides. Admetus has incurred the divine penalty of death, and his wife has consented to stand proxy for him, to die vicariously on his behalf so that he himself may survive. The play portrays Admetus' grief at the prospect of losing his 'beloved' wife. But it is very painfully obvious that his grief is totally self-centred. Fundamentally, he is not sorry for his wife but for the pain of loss that he will suffer through her death. He is one of the more revolting spectacles in literature. He has loved his wife, Alcestis, not as and for herself but as a source of benefits to himself. His very grief shows that he has made her an object for his own self-satisfaction. His love is a basic hypocrisy. He has never given her pure attention and he has never given her pure love. Love flows from attention; and on the other hand, attention presupposes love. As is the one, so is the other.

I here use 'love' as a convenient shorthand expression. Others might prefer to talk of respect. To my way of thinking, respect is incipient love. Respect shows its true inner substance when it flowers into love as it intrinsically tends to do. If Admetus had had a pure love for his wife he would never have accepted her offer to die for him.

Underpinning interpersonal relations there are relations based on shared possession, experience or aspiration. And below these, again, are things. Things are the earthy foundation, the presupposition, the milieu, and the support and instruments, of interpersonal relations. For we live in a real world, and human persons are flowers springing from the soil that is the object of the physical sciences. We have, as it were, a hierarchy of intercommunicating levels: things; common possession, experience, and aspiration; personal relatedness springing from such sharing; and interpersonal relations that show what personal relations are capable of becoming. And overarching this hierarchy there is the Absolute Mystery, generally called 'God', with whom eternally is his Word, mysterious and divine himself, incarnate for our salvation. Through and in the incarnate Word we have the potency and, please God, the actuality of interpersonal relations with God himself. Christ is the Mediator, because, being the Word of God and sharing with his heavenly Father in his godhead, he has become consubstantial with us, sharing in our human nature, and through it sharing in the world of things, in which we blossom and which is the first level of our communion through relatedness.

There is more than one form of attention that is given to things. One can have a tree within one's field of vision and yet fail to perceive it. When one begins to perceive it one may attempt to make it speak a message to oneself. A corrupt attention will see the tree as just material for the carpenter; it has failed really to see the tree for what it is. One can try to make the tree speak a message for oneself; but the tree refuses to be forced: it becomes an enigma, a dumb oracle. But one can offer it the homage of pure attention, entailing an act of self-abnegation on the perceiver's part, an act in which we surrender our claims. And when, without relaxing but rather enhancing our attention, we simply allow the tree to be itself in our perception of it, then at last the tree 'speaks' to us; and it speaks itself.

The same is true of a poem. Our unregenerate selves try to make a poem echo our own thoughts. To allow the poem simply to speak itself to us requires a sort of conversion – and a heightened attention. There is an asceticism of aesthetic appreciation. If you insist on reading the Sonnets of Shakespeare as autobiographical (or even as your own anticipated biography, which is still more corrupt), you miss the poems themselves, only discovering in them the raw material of an historical investigation. They must be allowed – and this supposes on our part not apathy but an attention that is deeply and purely willed – to be themselves and speak themselves. Then they will disclose their own inwardness; they will show themselves to us as things of beauty and a joy for ever.

Something similar can be said of all literature, including documents that are read specifically as data for historical reconstruction. How much scriptural exegesis, so called, has been the fruit of a determination on the part of the interpreter to get out of the documents what he demanded that they should contain. Few of us have been without blame in this respect. We can apply to ourselves the saying of Lichtenberg: 'A book is a mirror. If an ape looks into it, then obviously, what looks back out is not an apostle'.[5] Too often our own preoccupations have prevented us from 'hearing' what the biblical authors are actually saying, and what a religious world they are actually speaking out of. At a somewhat lower level, how much of biblical scholarship in modern times has been so concerned with questions of chronology, the mutual relations between documents, 'probabilities' based on a false understanding of historical reality (as though it were only another form of physico-scientific reality), that the meaning of the documents has been overlooked – until it has seemed more important to decide whether St Luke borrowed his Beatitudes from St Matthew, or both have used a common source, than to attend to the message: 'Blessed are you poor, for yours is the kingdom of God'. Spiritual poverty is the key to correct exegesis.

One cannot say everything at once. I have been speaking of attention as though it were the presentation of a mere mirror into which the object of attention might reflect and give itself. But in fact attention is always 'my' attention. To eliminate myself from the act of attention is to eliminate attention itself. I am impelled to attention by a question of my own; that question orientates and gives persistence to my attention. But in pure attention my question itself becomes flexible, open, subject to modification. And to the extent that my question is an expression of myself, the fruit of pure attention is not just that my question is answered in the terms in which it was originally formulated or in other terms developed in the act of attention, but that I myself have grown and developed. Henceforward my question will be somewhat different from what it was before; and the questioner will have been changed also. I have heard a monk say that the expectations and aspirations that took him to his religious vocation became changed by the very process of persevering in his response to them.

Here one may make the observation that ecumenical dialogue, or the quasi-ecumenical dialogue (so much more difficult) of inter-faith or faith-and-world convergence, is a process of mutual attention. The purer that attention, the greater the possibility that the dialogue will change both partners to the dialogue, enrich both their traditions by mutual information, and ultimately, it may be hoped, allow both traditions to flow into a common synthesis richer than either by itself.

A human life is never really solipsistic. Each of us lives in a 'world', without which we are nothing. Or rather we live, or come to live, in two concentric worlds. There is the world which we know and which, as known by us, is a vast construction founded on our experiencing, inquiring, understanding, judging, and evaluating selves: the world of our home and country, of our friends and relations, of Shakespeare and Paul and Plato and Newton and Einstein and Newman and Heidegger — as known by us. And beyond that known world there is the not-yet-known world into which we sometimes stumble by accident, and which ever lures us on to further exploration, experience, and understanding — for the desire to know is impatient of all limits. Each of these worlds, the known and the not-yet-known, is centred in ourselves. We know that this makes it a highly 'relative' world and we are never satisfied with this relativity; we ever seek to transcend it.

I have spoken of pure attention to the other as other, and have said that its fruit is a recognition of the selfhood of the other. Selfhood spells consciousness. Hence pure attention in interpersonal relations is a recognition of the other as the centre of a world that is other than our own — though not so entirely other that it is not revealed to us indirectly through our attention to the other person. And when pure attention and pure recognition pass over, as by nature they do, into pure respect and eventually pure love, there is a fusion of two worlds springing from the union of our two selves. The beloved is our *alter ego*. We sympathize, which is to say that we feel with him, rejoicing with his joy and aching with his suffering. Christians speak of the passion, the suffering, of Jesus Christ. Catholics also speak of Mary's 'compassion'; and the word is meant in its strong sense. The love of Christ, as we heard St Paul saying, constrains us so that the death of him who has become our Beloved is death for us also; and his being raised from the dead is our resurrection. Attention, respect, love, mystical identification (which yet preserves selfhood intact, and indeed deepened and enlarged) are moments of transcendence.

We have been speaking of interpersonal relations, and I have maintained that they are the development of relations between persons that are established through common possessions, shared experience, or common hopes. Interpersonal relations are consciously experienced as such. The relations out of which they develop may be facts before we become conscious of them as such. A common citizenship actually relates all who share it; but each citizen is only conscious in the full sense of the interpersonal relations which develop between him and some of the other citizens.

Interpersonal relations are a development of personal relatedness. Another possible development is community (communion in sense 2). Communities are based on a substructure of things, experiences or ideals shared in common, and these shared realities exercise a magnetic attraction, drawing those who share them towards common action and social unity. I have already spoken of the medieval common field and its tendency to create or rather in this case, no doubt, to reinforce community. We can expect that this community will need some body of custom, some record of its past transactions, some recorders of community tradition, some assembly or representative body to deal with new questions that arise for the community. The community will need officers and it seems usual for it to provide itself with a representative figurehead. Thus equipped, it will be able to have and to carry into practice a community policy. And observers of such communities will be able to recognize, alongside features that they tend to have just because they are communities, a particular character or ethos that is unique to each of them. Two Benedictine monasteries, each living under the same Rule and Constitutions, may have a quite different 'feel' about them, so that no one who really knows either could mistake the other for it.

A community need not be locally based, though the name 'community' is especially reserved for such locally based communions. It is possible for a number of people to have, and to discover that they have, a common interest in postage stamps; they are philatelists. Philately is their shared 'possession' or experience. How natural that someone should propose the establishing of a society of stamp-collectors; and the society will come to need a secretary, a treasurer, a board of management, and probably a chairman of the board. It will need funds and these funds will need administration. It will produce minutes of meetings and annual reports. It may well sponsor a philatelic magazine. It will thus begin to produce a literature and will soon be enriched with a tradition of its own past. In other words, communion will have created community, and community will have embodied itself in institution.

There is nothing intrinsically legalistic, authoritarian or 'institutionalistic' in such developments; although experience shows that all these vices can arise upon them. One may hazard the generalization that every aspiration tends to generate a movement, and every movement tends towards institutional embodiment. A Marxist aspiration towards human justice and economic rationalism produces a Communist movement. A Communist movement produces a Communist party and eventually establishes itself as a Russian government with a political constitution and a set of political objectives.

As community tends towards institution, so one looks, in an institution, for the spiritual force that gives it life, coherence, and effectiveness. Recently, Mr Bernard Levin has argued: 'A state system which is so deeply soaked in ideology as the Soviet one must live by ideology alone.'[6] Doubtless this simplified unduly the problem of Russia. Russia, and indirectly her state system, lives by something deeper and older than Communism. Many have observed that in her international role Russia today is in many respects Tsarist Russia *rediviva*. Today she is remembering her historical past and, if not building the tombs of her earlier prophets, at least preserving their monuments as national heirlooms. What really gave Russia her will to survive in the Hitler war was a very primeval love of 'mother Russia' rather than a passionate adherence to the philosophy of a nineteenth-century

German thinker. Years ago a Catholic Polish layman agreed with
me that Marxist-Leninist Communism is so unnatural that –
provided the cold war never erupted into a hot war, which would
revive basic patriotism – the Russian Communist system was
inevitably doomed; it would wither away.

> ... a mighty power [Levin continues] which claims to speak for
> all history, and to speak, moreover, in the name of an infallibly
> scientific system of thought, cannot long survive the death of the
> spirit within. ... the rulers of China, and millions of their
> subjects, are still convinced of the theory by which they profess
> to live; in the Soviet Union it is clear that nobody has seriously
> believed any of it for years. ... (And as regards the rulers of
> Russia, he comments) ... to *speak* in disbelief, and try to be
> convincing while doing so, is utterly impossible.[7]

I am not here concerned with the correctness or otherwise of Mr
Levin's analysis of the Russian scene. But I agree with his
contention that even the most powerful human institution draws its
life from shared conviction. When that conviction decays and dies,
the institutional corpse may seem to be still alive, but decom-
position has already set in and will in the end produce total
distintegration. A gospel or an ideology needs and, given pro-
pitious circumstances, will create for itself an institution; and an
institution depends in the end on a gospel or an ideology. So much
so that sociologists now discuss the sociology of belief. A 'crisis of
authority' in a church may have various causes; it may, for
instance, be the result of the misuse of their position and
opportunities by those who exercise authority in the church. But it
may also be an effect, and it is likely to be a cause, of a crisis of
faith – or at least of belief or of theology. Without faith the
Church cannot survive; and indeed it has been called 'societas
fidelium', the community of believers.

We have to hold on to two complementary truths. A community
will create for itself its institutional structures and through them it
will institutionalize its policies. But a community is not to be
simply and exclusively identified with its institutions. Historians
make a distinction between a state and the nation of which it is the
state. The nation is the civil community. It has its own national
ethos, spirit, purposes and memories. It seeks to express itself in
institutional organization as a state. But in the end the life-blood

of both nation and state is in the soul of the people, or rather in their whole humanity; and government, in the longest run, is dependent on the consent of the governed. On the one hand, a nation that fails to find self-expression in institutions and with a government cannot function as a nation; and it will probably find itself enslaved to the will of a nation better equipped institutionally. On the other hand, a government that is basically at odds with the spirit of the nation can survive for a time as a tyranny. But it is built on sand and when the storms of history blow and beat upon it, its foundations will collapse.

I shall shortly be moving on to a consideration of Christianity as a gospel, a message and a hope, creating from the community in which it is embodied its own institutional self-expression. Before I do so I must warn the reader against supposing that I wish to present the Church as a simple equivalent, in the religious sphere, of a secular state. There are analogies, and they may be helpful. I have already used a religious term, 'faith', to describe the inspiration – another religious term – of the state. But the analogy is, like all analogies, dangerous.[8] If we want a secular analogy, it will be better to think less of the state and more directly of the nation – although one enters the nation normally by birth, while entry into the Church is, in theory at least, by free adhesion to its gospel and by the sacrament of baptism. Better still, perhaps, to concentrate on our own less political and not necessarily secular word, 'community'. We should, however, beware of accepting without qualification a meaning that might be read into Mr Clifford Longley's article in the *Tablet*.[9] Mr Longley suggests that we might consider Christianity as a 'movement' rather than as an institution. The suggestion is important and may prove valuable. But we must not take Mr Longley as meaning that the Church is in no sense an institution, or even a community.

Can an insight, a doctrine, an ideology, a gospel live on in the world and influence history without embodying itself in community and institutional forms? The question is of some importance, because there have always been voices claiming that the institutionalizing of Christianity has been a mistake and a misfortune from the beginning.

We might begin by considering Plato and Platonism. Plato, while deeply indebted to a philosophical and scientific tradition, was a highly individual thinker and poet. His influence on subsequent history has been enormous; indeed, it has been said that everyone is in the last resort either a Platonist or an Aristotelian. Although Plato founded the Academy, which survived him, and propagated and developed his doctrine, Platonism has for many centuries been handed on and its influence diffused without the help of a specific Platonic institute. As for Shakespeare and the poets, they have not as a rule given birth to institutions; although one has heard of a Robert Burns Society.

There are, then, recognizable spiritual forces in our culture that have continued to exist without their own institutional embodiments; perhaps because they were not apt to give birth to communities. Yet even these are not exempt from the general law, since they have been, so to speak, parasitic on communities and institutions embodying other purposes. Poets live in nations and spread their influence through and across the boundaries of nations. Nations and other communities have their own traditions, out of which are born both poets and philosophers. Philosophical and poetical (or other artistic) novelties are expressions of, or reactions to, existing community traditions, and it is within such traditions that thought and art develop their own traditions, even though they may not create a community of their own for that purpose.

Thus we are led to speak of traditions. When common possession, experience, or aspiration has led to the creation of community, there grows up in the community a system of agreed custom and the germs of what may become 'laws' of the community, together with shared memories of past emergencies and past decisions that may be relevant for the continuing life of the community; and the appeal to precedent is thus made possible. A common stock of information, values, practical skills, ethos and orientations is formed and transmitted in and by the community to its new members. This is tradition: an interior reality not devoid of external expression, whether oral, ritual or written. Tradition is to the community (for example, a village community with its common field) what memory is to the individual: a principle of its interior life and of the unity of that life. In due course tradition will expand to include a treasury of heroic and unheroic anecdotes, even perhaps of local sagas and ballads. This growth and vitality of tradition in a local community will happen in wider scope and possibly greater depth in the greater community of the nation. It happens also in the community that is the Church.

Sir Karl Popper has written of the rational and scientific

tradition as an example of the function of tradition in social life. Tradition, he argues, exists in and is carried forward by community: it is a social tradition.

I shall come back to Popper later in this essay. For the moment, let us turn, for an old but moving statement of tradition in Christianity, to Newman:

> Prophets or Doctors are the interpreters of the revelation; they unfold and define its mysteries, they illuminate its documents, they harmonize its contents, they apply its promises. Their teaching is a vast system, not to be comprised in a few sentences, not to be embodied in one code or treatise, but consisting of a certain body of Truth, pervading the Church like an atmosphere, irregular in its shape from its very profusion and exuberance; at times separable only in idea from Episcopal Tradition, yet at times melting away into legend and fable; partly written, partly unwritten, partly the interpretation, partly the supplement of Scripture, partly preserved in intellectual expressions, partly latent in the spirit and temper of Christians; poured to and fro in closets and upon the housetops, in liturgies, in controversial works, in obscure fragments, in sermons, in popular prejudices, in local customs. This I call Prophetical Tradition, existing primarily in the bosom of the Church itself, and recorded in such measure as Providence had determined in the writings of eminent men. ... This is that body of teaching which is offered to all Christians even at the present day, though in various forms and measures of truth, in different parts of Christendom, partly being a comment, partly an addition upon the articles of the Creed.[10]

Tradition is a natural development of communion and more particularly of communion as it finds expression, stability and continuity in community. Even when the original basis of communion was a possession as material as a shared field, we saw how the shared possessions come to include shared memories, shared emotions, shared loyalty. Belonging to the community is a value shared in common by its members, and in various degrees and modes the innumerable and accumulating bonds which bind them together become the basis of interpersonal relations, of mutual respect, even of love. The horizons of the 'worlds' of the several members become enlarged, and the community itself acquires a quasi-personality. Community can thus become an immensely powerful factor in human history. We have only to think of the city states of ancient Greece or of medieval Italy. To re-read the funeral oration placed by Thucydides on the lips of Pericles is to become aware of a strength of loyalty and (sometimes rather narrow) idealism which, despite our rational reservations, fills us with admiration. In our own days we witness the strength of community feeling and loyalty in the Jewish people or again, admittedly at a lower level, in the 'old boys' of a great school or the members and former members of a university.[11]

To love another is to discover in him one's *alter ego*. With varying degrees of intensity the members of a community make this discovery about one another. And this is the stage in our reflections at which it may be useful to say a word about representation.

The word 'represent' can carry various nuances. In a weak sense, it means to offer or convey a likeness of its original which is, however, conceived to be other (and less) than the original. In a strong sense, on the other hand, to 'represent' someone is to bring his influence and authority to bear in a situation in which he is not physically present: an ambassador represents his sovereign in a foreign court and speaks with that sovereign's authority. He can, if a plenipotentiary, commit his sovereign, within the limits of his own role, to decisions of which the sovereign has no previous detailed knowledge; and on the other hand, his person is invested with the sacredness of his sovereign in such a way that an insult to the ambassador as such is an insult to the sovereign. It is in this stronger sense that I am here speaking of 'representation' and 'representatives'. The fact is that any member of a community *ipso facto* represents his community. He not only symbolizes it but in some sense embodies it – literally 'makes it present' by his own presence. In the days when boys wore school caps, they could be told by their masters that they must be careful, when wearing their caps, to behave in such a manner as not to bring disgrace on the school of which they were representatives. They might even be told, though the phrase may seem slightly rhetorical, that they carried the honour of the school with them. It is indeed a fact that the public misdemeanours of a schoolboy in the outside world may bring discredit on his school, just as his positive achievements are seen as achievements of the school – it may be noticed that a newspaper, when publishing first-class honours gained at a university, will mention not only the student's university college, but his school. More seriously, when a British citizen is apprehended by the police of a foreign state, the British consul or ambassador will promptly take cognizance of his plight and will watch with anxious care to see that justice is done to him. The apprehended citizen really embodies Britain, and wrong done to him is rightly conceived of as wrong done to his country.

Thus, every member of a community represents the community. The community is in a real sense epitomized in each of its members; and every member feels for every other member as for his *alter ego*.

Representation, even in this strong sense, has of course its gradations. If every citizen represents his country, this is true in a higher sense of one who in a notable way has expressed or embodied the ideals or interests of his country. A great Englishman, as distinct from a great man, is one who notably and loftily embodies England and what England 'stands for'. There are those who regard St Thomas More not only as a saint and martyr in a general sense, but more specifically as a great Englishman. Again, but in an official sense, one who wears 'the queen's uniform' represents his country not merely in his personal qualities nor merely as any one member of the national community; he is an 'official representative', and the queen is the official representative *par excellence*. In Shakespeare's *Julius Caesar*, Mark Antony, speaking of the dead leader whether as a man or as an official, says of his assassination:

> Then I, and you, and all of us fell down,
> Whilst bloody treason flourish'd over us.

In a sense that is more than merely rhetorical, the leader embodies his community (and hence it is common in Shakespeare for a sovereign to be referred to by the name of his country: the king of England *is* 'England'). And as he represents his country in this strong sense, when he dies his country dies; and should he rise again, his country, his community, would rise with him to a new life. Modern biblical scholarship has coined the term 'corporate personality' to refer to this very meaningful fact of representation. The People of God is epitomized in its representative head; and the leader *is* that People. It is not easy to determine whether the

Suffering Servant in the Book of Isaiah is an individual or a community; perhaps the composer of the 'Suffering Servant' songs could only have said: 'he is both'.

Communion, especially when it takes shape as community, is highly flexible and capable of being actualized at different, and sometimes hierarchical, levels. England is embodied not only in the nation as a whole but in a typical English village. The Church – if, as I shall argue, it is a communion – is embodied not only in the 'universal' communion of the faithful the world over and down the ages, but also in each local community that remains in 'communion' with the universal Church.

> (The) Church of Christ is truly present in all legitimate local congregations of the faithful which, united with their pastors, are themselves called churches in the New Testament. For in their own locality these are the new people called by God, in the Holy Spirit and in much fullness (cf. 1 Thess. 1:5) ... In these communities, though frequently small and poor, or living far from any other, Christ is present. By virtue of Him the one, holy, catholic, and apostolic Church gathers together *(consociatur)*[12]

The local church, within the universal communion of the faithful, represents both the universal Church and its Master, the Representative at once of his heavenly Father and (as a second Adam) of the whole human race, which he came to redeem and whose burdens he bore.

It remains to point out that a community can exert its influence far beyond its own boundaries. It can do this, it is true, in egoistic and destructive fashion. But it can also radiate its own values which will be reflected in those who are not members of the community but thus become in some way its debtors. Christianity has spread its own influence far beyond the limits of the 'churches', and the flame which is its expression burns in communities and individuals who would not recognize or wish to acknowledge the origin of this light by which nevertheless in large part they live.

Chapter III

Earthen Vessels I

At its heart, Christianity is a gospel: a message of good news. It is a message received by men; and is only fully 'gospel' to the extent that it is received by men: by men who in so receiving it are representative of the whole material creation of which they form part. The message is from the Absolute Mystery that we call God.

The First Epistle to the Thessalonians was written about twenty years after the crucifixion of Jesus the son of Mary of Nazareth. It is thought by many scholars to be the earliest extant Christian document. In it Paul addresses his Thessalonian converts in these terms:

> ... we thank God continually, because when we handed on God's message, you received it, not as the word of men, but as what it truly is, the very word of God at work in you who hold the faith (2:13).

What the Thessalonian converts heard with their ears was a flow of human words, the words of Paul. What they apprehended by faith was 'the very word of God' with which Paul's words were in some sense instinct.[1]

It is this 'word of God' which is, it would seem, meant when, in the Epistle to the Galatians and elsewhere, Paul speaks of 'gospel'. Thus:

> I am astonished to find you turning so quickly away from him who called you by grace, and following a different gospel. Not

that it is in fact another gospel; only there are persons who unsettle your minds by trying to distort the gospel of Christ. But if anyone, if we ourselves or an angel from heaven, should preach a gospel at variance with the gospel we preached to you, he shall be held outcast (Gal. 1:6–8).

This word of God is to be sharply distinguished from the findings of human philosophy (and, as we should today add, of physical science or historical research). It differs as regards its contents, since 'What no eye has seen, nor ear heard, nor the heart of man conceived', ... God has revealed to us through the Spirit' (1 Cor. 2:9f.). And it differs also from the fruits of human investigation because, though humanly transmitted, it comes from God himself, and is therefore as true as he himself is. It is what in theological language is called 'revelation'.

The contents of this 'revelation' came to be seen as identical with Jesus Christ himself. The Fourth Gospel makes this point explicitly: 'the Word', which was in the beginning with God and was God, 'was made flesh, and dwelt among us, and we beheld his glory'. Jesus Christ is himself the Word, the message, from God; he is the gospel, the good news.

A word is a communicated message. A divine word reveals something of its author, God himself, in a way analogous to that in which a poet is disclosed in his poems.

As a word addressed by God to men, the gospel only accomplishes its purpose, reaches its goal, becomes what in essence it is, namely a communication, when it is received *as* a divine communication. Until it is thus received it is in potency rather than in act. Only as received is it a word. Words spoken into a vacuum are not communications.

Who, then, are the intended recipients of the Word of God? The Word is sent to all men indifferently and so its aim is universal. Whoever rejects the Word is not in the same condition as he was before the Word was presented to him; he 'will be condemned' (Mark 16:16). This universal aspect of the Word is important. The Word is no secret communication from God to some chosen souls. It is God's Word, his final Word within the historical order, to all who are men. It is not only a final Word; it is a total Word. St John of the Cross, the sixteenth-century Spanish writer on the spiritual life, sometimes called the 'mystical doctor', after conceding that under the Old Covenant it was proper to seek revelations from God, continues:

> But now that the faith is established through Christ, and the Gospel law made manifest in this era of grace, there is no reason for inquiring of (God) in this way, ... In giving us His Son, His only Word (for He possesses no other), He spoke everything to us at once in this sole Word – and He has no more to say. ... since He has finished revealing the faith through Christ, there is no more faith to reveal, nor will there ever be.[2]

This teaching is not of course peculiar to St John of the Cross. It is central to Christianity, and is stated equivalently in the Epistle to the Colossians:

> ... the secret ... now disclosed to God's people ... is this: Christ in you, the hope of a glory to come. He it is whom we proclaim. ... I want ... the Laodiceans ... to come to the full wealth of conviction which understanding brings, and grasp God's secret. That secret is Christ himself; in him lie hidden all God's treasures of wisdom and knowledge. I tell you this to save you from being talked into error by specious arguments (1: 26–2:4).

Language used by Christians has sometimes suggested that the word of God is addressed to the soul of man rather than to the whole man. This is not the teaching of the New Testament, where the anthropology remains, on the whole, basically Jewish. One can read Plato as maintaining that the real self is the soul, and the body only its temporary prison. The biblical idea is rather that man is an animated body. Jesus spoke not just to men's souls but to men themselves in their wholeness and historical concreteness. He is depicted in the Gospels as feeding them in their hunger, restoring sight to the blind, hearing to the deaf, even historical life to the dead. He surrounded himself with real human beings; he did not create a *phrontisterion* (a 'reflectory', as Rogers so aptly renders Aristophanes' word). His followers were more like a communist cell than an academy of souls. More importantly, he was himself a human being in the full sense of that term. He felt hunger and, according to the Fourth Gospel, thirst. He slept. Above all, he redeemed mankind in the agonies of the crucifixion.

The word of God is addressed, then, to human beings in the fullness of their body-and-soul humanity; it came as and in a fully human being; it is given as a public revelation on the stage of fully human history. It is a word intended for reception by men of flesh and blood, by man in the social complexity of his life on earth; and it is only fully communicated if it is thus received.

Man is an historical being; Heidegger has even said that his existence is a becoming. Each man comes to himself in relations with others and in community. The message of God, therefore, as received, will itself be historically conditioned; and we may expect that, since community is part of our historical conditioning, that Word will find its true being in community: it will become a community possession.

Hence the Word given by God becomes, in transmission, a communication made by man to man. It is only by faith that the Thessalonians could apprehend by and through and in the 'words' of Paul the Word of God. Paul's words, so to speak, embodied God's Word. We can even say that the Word of God has to become a human word in order to become an effective communication, to all mankind, from God. As communicated, the Word takes on a human conformation. But as divine, it will exercise a continuing normative influence upon the human language in which we seek to bring it to expression. And there will be occasions (cf. the 'different gospel' so vehemently denounced by Paul in the Epistle to the Galatians) when a soi-disant conveyer of the Word is in fact trading spurious goods.

Meanwhile, the Word was originally given, as was inevitable if it was to be communicated to man in his full concrete historicalness, at a particular moment in universal history: Jesus Christ 'suffered under Pontius Pilate'. But although thus given in a particular moment, it was intended for all mankind, and at once the issue of its transmission arises:

... 'everyone who invokes the name of the Lord will be saved'. How could they invoke one in whom they had no faith? And how could they have faith in one they had never heard of? And how hear without someone to spread the news? And how could anyone spread the news without a commission to do so? And that is what Scripture affirms: 'How welcome are the feet of the messengers of good news!' (Rom. 10:13–15).[3]

Who was the first communicator of this divine message? The New Testament is clear enough that Jesus himself proclaimed a message from God: the good news of the advent, actual or imminent, of the Reign of God. There is continuity and also a certain discontinuity between the gospel preached in words by Jesus and the gospel preached by Christianity. The discontinuity arises from the fact that between the two preachings there intervened the resurrection of Christ. But of course there is a deep continuity also. Jesus is the incarnation of the Word preached by the Church. He proclaimed his own gospel not in words only but in action, suffering and death; it was this whole gospel that the Church proclaimed in the light of his resurrection. The original communicator, Jesus, is identical – not alone in his words but in himself – with the message which he conveys and the Church continues to convey.

The word communicated by Jesus was, in the deepest sense, not his word but the word of his heavenly Father. As the matter is put, in the Fourth Gospel, on the lips of Jesus: 'The teaching that I give is not my own; it is the teaching of him who sent me' (7:16). He is not the word of himself but the word of God. He was 'sent' by God with a message, a message that he had received, not invented. He was the original human communicator of the word; he was its original content; and he was the first recipient of it.

At this level of reflection, we are of course thinking of the *human* Jesus. Modern theology is being driven to a consideration of the human consciousness of Christ. 'No modern Christology could evade the question of the development and the limits of the human consciousness of Jesus'.[4] It is a difficult subject. The historical materials, as distinct from the theological indications, for its adequate treatment are exiguous or disputable. But scholars are laying more emphasis today than hitherto on the prayer of Jesus and on the invocation that characterizes that prayer: 'Abba' (the tender, respectful term used by a son, young or old, in directly addressing his father). It is a fact that, while the Gospels depict Jesus as referring, in speech to his followers, to God as 'your Father', he never associates them with himself in calling God 'our Father'; the point is brought out strikingly in the Johannine saying: 'I am now ascending to my Father and your Father, my God and your God' (John 20:17. Note: not 'our Father and our God'). A Christian will find it easy to believe that there was an implied uniqueness of relationship in Jesus' use of 'Abba' in his prayer.

How did the *human* consciousness of this unique relationship to God arise? I think that it arose by God's disclosure of the relationship, its revelation, to Jesus. In other words, the very heart of Christianity, as revelation, is that self-disclosure of the Father to Jesus. Of course, an inference inevitably follows. If God makes himself known to Jesus as uniquely his Father, then Jesus is God's son, and uniquely so. And only one who is ontologically God's son can receive the historical revelation: 'You are (uniquely) my Son'.

The man Jesus was an historical being like all his fellow men, a being whose consciousness developed with time. It is natural to suppose that there was a gradual, step-by-step, awakening to full consciousness of Jesus' realization of God as his Father and of himself as uniquely God's son.

As regards Jesus' knowledge of himself as the co-equal Son of the divine Father, Rahner makes use of a notion which he has widely employed in other contexts, that of a pre-conscious or 'unthematic' self-awareness on the part of a spiritual being which is quite distinct from, and is antecedent to, the knowledge which it can have of itself as an object in acts of introspection. ... Something like this view is found in Dr Pannenberg's great work *Jesus, God and Man,* ... . Fr Louis Bouyer describes this view approvingly ...[5]

Our direct knowing moves inexorably 'outwards' towards objects which are other than ourselves, and, in an important sense, other than the actual process or act of knowing them (and this despite the fact that in knowledge the known becomes in some, also true, sense one with the knower). 'I know' is a transitive verb and is incomplete without an object. We can, indeed, having known an object, proceed to reflect upon this act of knowing; we can make our knowing, in its turn, our object; and in thus knowing our knowing we can become imperfectly conscious of ourselves as knowers. But behind all this, and concurrent with every act of conscious knowing, there is an immediate awareness which is implicitly a self-awareness. And as I become gradually conscious of myself as knowing, so my self-awareness (which is to be distinguished from my self-consciousness) is heightened. Life is a process of, among other things, self-discovery, not primarily by introspection but primarily by serious attention to our environment, including God, the Absolute Mystery that is the ultimate 'environment' of every creature.

The upshot is that, if we are talking about Jesus as a human knower, we can reasonably hold that from the first his awareness and self-awareness included an awareness of his divine sonship, an awareness enfolded in his awareness of God. But, applying the distinction between awareness and consciousness, and that between consciousness of 'the other' and self-consciousness, we can affirm that Jesus only gradually came to realize with full self-consciousness that relationship. We can say this, while remaining in full agreement with Dr Mascall that 'it is ... futile for us to try to guess what it feels like to be God incarnate'.[6]

The classical formulation of Christological doctrine, the Formula of Chalcedon, reiterates the teaching of the Epistle to the Hebrews that Jesus, in his humanity, was like us in all things, sin only excepted. True, this was a formulation concerning Christ's human 'nature' rather than directly about his human knowing and consciousness. But if we accept the thesis that behaviour expresses nature ('agere sequitur esse') we can make a bridge between the Christology of Chalcedon and these modern speculations on the human consciousness of Jesus.

Is all this discussion mere irreverent curiosity? I do not think so. Our subject is the Church as part of the mystery of redemption and supernatural elevation. My thesis, throughout this book, is that this mystery is an 'incarnate' mystery, a mystery incorporated into human concrete history and the very material texture of the world. But the Church is nothing without Christ. It therefore matters that we should be able to see Christ as both fully divine ('and the Word was God') and fully human, in the unity, to use the Chalcedonian term, of a single hypostasis. Unless he is fully divine, the whole Christian economy collapses. Unless he is fully human, he is not fully humanly-historical; and, as was argued against Apollinaris, 'what was not assumed in the incarnation was not healed': unless Jesus is fully human he cannot be fully our Saviour. But to be human in history is to grow in knowledge by accumulating and developing experience.

How did this primordial revelation of God take place in Jesus, whether as an event or a process? It is the religious event *par excellence* in human history. Hence it is more appropriate, if we wish to understand it in some measure, to turn not to the lowly experience of *l'homme moyen sensuel* or that of the philosopher or scientist, scholar or artist, but to religion in its most highly developed form.

At its heart, religion is communion. Supremely, it is communion with God. My argument in this book is that it is a communion with God which creates and depends on communion with one's fellow men. But if communion is a mode of experience we are forced to admit that it is ultimately personal; and groups are only personal inasmuch as they are made up of persons. Hence the classical masters of the spiritual life suggest themselves for consideration. I have mentioned St John of the Cross above. Has he anything with which to enlighten us here?

We have to bear in mind that the religious experience of even the greatest of these spiritual writers is to be distinguished from that of Jesus as being (*a*) the experience of mere men, (*b*) the experience of fallen men for whom redeeming grace is logically subsequent to their natural existence, whereas through the hypostatic union Jesus was conceived and born in the fullness of grace.

Religion in this life is determined in its character by the goal to which it is directed. To understand it we need to meditate upon the full communion of the saints in heaven. In *The Spiritual Canticle*, Stanza 38, St John of the Cross has his attention fixed upon this final consummation, and projects his thought to the perspective of heaven attained:

> The soul's aim is a love (for God) equal to God's (love for her). She always desired this equality, naturally and supernaturally, for a lover cannot be satisfied if he fails to feel that he loves as much as he is loved. Since the soul sees that through her transformation in God in this life she cannot, even though her love is immense, equal the perfection of God's love for her, she desires the clear transformation of glory in which she will reach this equality. ... Just as the soul ... will know then as she is known by God [1 Cor. 13:12], so she will also love God as she is loved by Him. ... Besides teaching her to love purely, freely, and disinterestedly, as He loves her, God [through the gift of the Holy Spirit] makes her love Him with the very strength with which He loves her. ... Until attaining this equality of love the soul is dissatisfied, ...[7]

St John of the Cross points out that, though he is here describing a perfection of religion that cannot be attained in this historical life by us, still, in the case of some great saints, 'there is nonetheless a living and totally ineffable semblance of that perfection'.[8]

It will be observed that this love of God which is both the heart and, eventually, the consummation of religion is an activity of the human being, but an activity that has God as its ultimate 'agent': 'God makes her love Him with the very strength with which he loves her'.

I suggest, then, that revelation is closely bound up with 'communion'. In the case of the original revelation the communion in question is the loved communion between the man Jesus and his heavenly Father. That communion will have been within the perspective established by the primordial, but pre-conceptual and in principle 'pre-conscious' awareness of Jesus the incarnate Son of God. As we 'know' in a primitive awareness that we are intelligent creatures, so Jesus 'knew', with a similar awareness, that he was more than a creature.[9] Earlier, however, I have put forward the theory that communion is a relationship (and, at its highest, an interpersonal relationship) between persons, and is based on common possession, experience or aspiration. What was the 'possession in common' underlying Jesus' communion with his heavenly Father?

At the deepest level, there is the totally divine communion between the Persons of the Holy Trinity: an august communion, the very archetype and antitype of all communion. The common possession, if we may speak in such terms (and obviously we are speaking analogically), which is the basis of this communion is the divine nature itself: a 'possession' not divided out between the Possessors but possessed in its totality by each.

At the creaturely level, we may make distinctions. (1) Jesus is consubstantial with us intelligent creatures. As this creaturehood is a gift of God, this very status of being a creature simultaneously distinguishes him from, and unites him to, the Creator. (2) Jesus was born into, and grew up in, the pre-Christian People of God; and this gave him a link with the Author of the Covenant which constituted the People of God as such. (3) Jesus is the Son of God, the second Person of the Holy Trinity. His human nature was therefore hypostatically united with that Person. Thus, and precisely in his human nature thus hypostatically united, he had a unique 'common possession' with his heavenly Father. We may never know how this link operated in the historically developing relationship of Jesus with his Father. But we cannot forget it, and I have in fact suggested that it founded a unique pre-conceptual and indeed 'pre-conscious' awareness.

Chapter IV

Earthen Vessels II

The communion of the man Jesus with his heavenly Father was as fully historical as his humanity was genuine. It was, moreover, a communion that was to be communicated to us others, so that we might 'come to share in the very being of God' (2 Peter, 1:4). It was a communion founded in common possession, and creating relationship between persons and the possibility of consequent community. How does this relationship function within the stream of history?[1]

Man communicates with man in a variety of ways, but particularly by language. Behind language there are concepts; I agree with Lonergan that language is 'the expression of mental acts'.[2] And behind concepts there are 'insights', flashes of understanding when we 'see the point' – whether the point is the point of a joke or the implication of evidential data, or the meaning of a hypothesis. Most of us have had such an experience of insight, whereby we emerge onto a new level of understanding. The insight has priority, in principle, over its conceptualization. Who has not had the experience of feeling about for concepts and for words in which to give some, perhaps rough-and-ready, expression or formulation to the truth given in an insight? Poets and lovers spend lifetimes in trying to find, indeed to invent, the language they need.

Language, then, is an expression of concepts, and exists for the 'communication' of insights. And some insights are so original that current language is inadequate for their expression and communication. We know how modern physical science has taken over, charged with new meaning, 'technicized' the speech of every day, so that those who already know the meaning of 'a mass' as a 'dense aggregation of objects' (*Concise Oxford Dictionary*, 1924) have to learn afresh what physicists mean by 'mass'. The language of physical science is a monument to the power of 'mental acts' to mould language. This technical language goes beyond, yet without losing contact with, ordinary language. It is necessary if the insights and discoveries of the scientists are to find expression and eventually become public. But what is true of language in this respect of adequacy and inadequacy is true also of the concepts underlying the language. Inherited concepts, like inherited language, will be inadequate, as inherited, for the expression and finally the communication of genuinely original insights.

Jesus was fully human. He was born an infant, like the rest of us; that is to say, he was born without language. He grew not only in stature but in wisdom. This process of education of the man Jesus will have been through the reception of the current culture, and more particularly the religious culture, of his home, country and people. The evidence of the New Testament, as of subsequent Christian history, shows that the language of this culture, and the concepts clothed in that language, were in the end insufficient to carry the new revelation. It is not in language or in concepts but in insight that we can find a model or analogy of the act in which the primal revelation, that made to Jesus himself, was received.[3]

Jesus was 'related' to his Father through his divinity. He was related to his fellow men through his humanity. His mission was to transmit to them the primal revelation of which he himself was the original recipient. Hence the need for him to grow in wisdom in a particular historical environment, thus learning to use the language and concepts of that particular Jewish milieu for communication with his immediate fellow human beings.

We may pause to ask, in our greatly evolved cultural situation, whether Judaism was in fact an apt matrix for Christianity. I have already suggested that it was inadequate for this purpose. It is remarkable, to take a simple instance, how the proclamation of the imminent advent of 'the Reign of God' was apparently central to Jesus' own mission, yet the term, 'Reign of God', tends to drop out of the language of the primitive, post-resurrection, Church as that is set before us in the New Testament books.

Nevertheless there are reasons, both *a priori* and *a posteriori*, for holding that the Jewish religious-cultural matrix was, though ultimately inadequate, a good milieu for the first transmission of the new revelation. Lonergan has pointed out that a divine redemption of man, if it is to be real and not a cosmetic operation, will take man as man historically exists and address itself to him in that historical context.[4] Within the story of that universe, man, says Lonergan, is an emergent probability that has been actualized: things reached a point at which the emergence of man was a 'live option' and the option was actually taken: man appeared on the scene, a new and higher species of life, and the first emergence, within the material scheme of things as known by us, of an intelligent animal. The leap from the sub-human to the human is enormous; so much so that, whereas previous leaps took shape as the emergence of new and higher species of life, further progress, now that man has entered the scene as an intelligent agent, takes place not by the formation of new, superhuman, species but by ever-ascending achievements of human intelligence, disclosing wider and wider horizons of being, truth, value and practical possibility. Such 'leaps' are simultaneously continuous with the situation within which they occur, and discontinuous since they introduce something genuinely new into the situation and thus transform the human condition.

Christianity is a religion of redemption. Redemption is necessary because man has not only progressed; he has also fallen. But if redemption is to be real, and not merely mythical, it will have to be something engrafted into the situation for which it is the remedy. It will have to find and take man where he is and lift him out of his predicament without dissociating him from his world. It may be expected to take advantage of fortunate (which Christians will truly call providential) historical antecedents. It will have to find a particular situation – since to take man as he is to take him in his historical particularity, and every historical situation is unique – a situation in which it may hope to appeal to a human grouping not altogether unprepared for it. The 'scandal of particularity' of which some theologians speak when discussing the Christian claim is not really a scandal at all, but an inevitable result of historical conditioning.

Seen from within an historical perspective, Christianity is a step forward in the evolutionary process. Long before Darwin, Aristotle had something to say about what is presupposed by the evolution of species. A new species is a higher form of life. Aristotle maintains that the emergence of a higher form requires a properly disposed 'matter'.[5] A penultimate disposition will make possible, even practically probable (though the probability may be great or small), the achievement of the ultimate disposition of the same matter without which it is quite impossible for the new form to supervene. The ultimate disposition – and here is Aristotle's remarkable insight, overlooked, I venture to maintain, by nearly all theoreticians of evolution – will be the result of the capacity of the new form to transform the penultimate into this ultimate disposition. The new form, for its historical realization, needs the ultimate disposition; the ultimate disposition, for its constitution, needs the new form. The ultimate disposition and the new form are casually correlative; the new form is not simply 'produced' from the matter; it 'arrives' from 'elsewhere'.

Thus it seems that, granted that man is redeemed by Jesus Christ, we should expect *a priori* that the historical existence of Jesus will have occurred not just anywhere in the time and space of human history but at an apt point: at a time and place and within a culture where men were particularly prepared to receive him.

Such an apt situation was undoubtedly that of Judaism, the one religious culture in which full ethical monotheism, with a profound sense of the divine dimension of history, had established itself and had built up for its maintenance and defence an immensely strong set of inner supports and outward siege-works. Judaism was a highly structured religion, fiercely intransigent in face of the counter-claims of various forms of paganism threatening it from without.

Christianity has ratified this understanding of Judaism, as a providential preparation for the religion of the incarnation, by identifying the God of Jesus Christ with the God of the Jews and by incorporating into its own Bible the sacred books of the Old Testament Canon.

The New Testament shows us, in broad outline and somewhat fragmentarily, how the divine revelation, in and as Jesus Christ, sought to express itself in Jewish thought-forms, language, imagery and ritual, while at the same time profoundly modifying its borrowings so as to adapt them to its own substance and intrinsic requirements. At the centre of this process are such symbols as the Covenant, the People of God and its *ecclesia*, the Messiah or Christ; and the concept of the creating – and revealing – word of God.

In short, Christianity is a religion rooted in humanity and the conditions of humanity, in historical culture, and in that physical world in which men live out their lives and from which they draw substance and sustenance. The Christian religion is as concrete as it is universal.

Being thus fully historical, Christianity cannot escape from the fact and implications of 'communion', since it is a divine communication to all mankind: to man in his personal uniqueness and to man in that social dimension which is necessary for his personal development. There will therefore be a Christian contribution to human communion. Christianity will take shape in historical relations between men and will reach its full flowering in interpersonal relations. We should expect that a Christian community would result. But it is essential to bear in mind that this human communion, inaugurated by the incarnation, will itself be subordinate to man's communion with God, actualized in Jesus Christ and so made possible for the rest of mankind.

The process of incorporating the relevation in images, concepts, language, symbol, ritual and culture is not easy or automatic. It is not the sort of process that can be handed over to a computer. It is more like the work of a poet or a painter. It requires what, in a general sense, we call inspiration and 'genius'. The New Testament leads us to believe that Jesus himself, as man, had such inspiration, an inspiration that was genuinely divine. At his conception, we are told, his Mother was overshadowed by the power of the Most High and 'the Holy Spirit came upon her'. 'God's favour' was on the child Jesus. At his baptism 'he saw the heavens torn open and the Spirit, like a dove, descending upon him' and 'thereupon the Spirit sent him away into the wilderness'. The Church sees Jesus as the one plenarily endowed with the gifts of the Holy Spirit, those gifts which are offered, to all his brethren, and are received in measure by those of good will.

Jesus, in turn, is represented as promising to his disciples an outpouring of the Holy Spirit for the task that was laid upon them. In the Fourth Gospel he is depicted as saying that the Holy Spirit would bring to the remembrance of his disciples all that he had said to them, and would lead them into all the truth. We have to bear in mind that the truth in this context is not merely theoretical knowledge; it is the truth that is identical with the 'way', truth that is carried out into practice.

It is by the action of the Holy Spirit that the revelation is fully incorporated into human history by becoming a revelation not only offered but accepted, expressed and proclaimed. The Christian tradition has not confined the period of original revelation to the limits of Jesus' historical life. How could it? The coping-stone and consummation of the whole revelation, as offered, was the resurrection of the crucified Jesus, and thus fell outside the limits of his historical life. The period of revelation, when seen most fully and profoundly, is the period of revelation offered and revelation primitively received – first by Jesus himself and then by the eyewitnesses of his mission and his risen self. So Christianity has marked off the 'apostolic age' from all subsequent ages of the Church. It is this uniqueness of the age of original revelation which helps us to understand why the quality of inspired Scripture is assigned to authoritative books written in the apostolic age (broadly conceived), the books namely of the New Testament Canon.

Nevertheless, we must not so emphasize the uniqueness of the apostolic age as to overlook a very important complementary truth.

We have seen that Christianity is in a special sense an historical religion: at its heart it is a revelation accorded to and embodied in an actual historical human life, that of Jesus of Nazareth, and it was directed to man, individual and collective, in his full historical reality.

But from the first it was a religion of *transmitted* revelation. Jesus was not a hermit, hugging to his breast the revelation of his Father's redeeming love. He proclaimed this good news; and he made disciples. It is in his own life and mission that we find the origins of what has come to be called tradition: the transmission of the revealed Word and the consequent building up of a treasure of the truth thus transmitted. The parables and the Sermon on the Mount are themselves parts of tradition in this fundamental sense of the word.

As a sad result of controversy among Christians it has become common practice to distinguish Scripture and tradition as two distinct realities. Hence I must make it clear that in speaking here of tradition I am speaking of something of which Scripture itself, and particularly the New Testament books, are part and parcel. Tradition means the transmission of a divine revelation originally received by one who, though he preached, is not the human author of any written work. In tradition, revelation becomes revelation transmitted. Whether the transmission is by word of mouth, by written (even inspired) documents, by cultic acts or unofficial gestures, is for our present point irrelevant.

Revelation, it may be repeated, must be conceived as taking place in two 'moments', though these moments need not be regarded as moments distinct in time. There is, first, revelation offered; and secondly there is revelation received. Revelation fully becomes itself only when it is received. A lover may seek to communicate his love to the beloved one, to 'reveal' his love. But unless the communication is received and assimilated by the beloved, the communication has failed to be a *communication*; what has occurred is a failed attempt at communication. Similarly, if divine revelation offered did not become revelation received, we should have to say that it had failed to be revelation: a divine 'attempt' at revelation would have failed. I have pressed this general principle back to the very act of divine revelation to man in Jesus Christ. In order that the Word of God might achieve its goal in and for humanity, it was necessary that Jesus in his humanity should himself receive, in the historical way that is the only human way, the revelation. I now add that it was necessary that he should both receive and assimilate it. And since in fact the revelation was the incarnate Word, Jesus Christ himself, it was necessary that, in coming to know his heavenly Father through the Father's self-disclosure, he should *pari passu* come to know himself as the unique Son of God.

The divine revelation, however, was not merely for Jesus himself. He was 'sent' to proclaim the 'good news'. This mission of Jesus was not an extrinsic addition to the incarnation. On the contrary, the incarnation was an act of divine universal love and was therefore intrinsically self-transcending.

The revelation to Jesus could only effectively become a revelation to all men and to every man through a process of transmission of the Word. This process is what I call the process of tradition. It was going on before any of the New Testament books were written. The Synoptic Gospels indicate (*a*) that Jesus conducted a public work of proclaiming the gospel, (*b*) that in particular the transmission of the good news was made to those whose positive response to the proclamation made them disciples, (*c*) that already during the lifetime of Jesus some at least of the disciples were commissioned by Jesus to carry the good news to others to whom he himself had not yet directly spoken. While scholars may raise the question whether the commissioning of the Twelve narrated in Mark 3:13ff., 6:7ff. was for a permanent or only a transitory occasion, it is probable that the evangelists themselves tell the story as legitimizing the role of the apostles in the primitive Church. In any case, the process of transmission was resumed under different conditions after the resurrection of Christ and the 'sending' of the Holy Spirit upon the primitive Church. The New Testament documents are part of that process of transmission: they are written and inspired tradition.

The process of transmission of the gospel did not cease with the end of the apostolic age. Had it done so, revelation itself would have disappeared from history, and the universal object of revelation would not have been actualized.

This is the point at which we are able to qualify the statement that revelation 'ended' with the end of the apostolic age. The statement is true in the sense in which it is intended: there can be no additions to that revelation that is the Word incarnate as Jesus Christ in his life, death and resurrection. This revelation is being continually offered to the world as the Church continues her mission of proclaiming it, and this continuing proclamation we call tradition. But revelation offered in tradition becomes fully itself only to the extent that from place to place, from generation to generation, from culture to culture, and from person and group to person and group, it is actually received and assimilated by its hearers and so becomes fully alive, fully itself, throughout the whole range and compass of historical humanity. The sending and gift of the Holy Spirit were not a transient phenomenon. They are something that is going on all the time. This continually enables the Church as a collectivity, each individual believer and, in principle and intention, every human being and the whole of humanity in its collective life and experience, to assimilate (which means also to understand), in measure but never fully, the revelation transmitted by tradition: Christ himself, in whom 'lie hidden all God's treasures of wisdom and knowledge' (Col. 2:3). Thus revelation is continued in the propagation of faith.

I have emphasized the historical character, and therefore the historical context, of the revelation to Jesus. We have seen how this revelation was both continuous with the Old Testament religion and also, in its novelty, discontinuous. Modern scholarship has come to see the religion of the pre-Christian People of God as a progressively more profound and more extensive understanding of the revelation to Moses. The late Professor Butterfield, for instance, was struck by the evidence that, in the apparent disaster of the Babylonian captivity, prophecy plumbed greater depths of religious reality than were disclosed in earlier times less humiliating for Israelite pride.

When we turn to the New Testament we again find a process of progressive understanding of the Word incarnate. It is of the highest importance to realize that a growth in understanding does not mean a growth in the revelation itself. On the other hand, we cannot *a priori* dismiss a later and more developed understanding because it brings before us aspects or depths of the tradition which are not evident in earlier documents. The Fourth Gospel may be the latest of the Gospels and one of the latest books of the New Testament; but we cannot reject the Johannine interpretation of Christianity just because it is late (nor because it may be thought to have utilized cultural aids to interpretation that were not available to the Synoptic evangelists). It is by degrees that the Church comes to penetrate and to unfold the riches of the original revelation and, in so doing, comes also to understand itself better.

Such considerations, applicable in the first instance to development within the Bible itself, are legitimately applied also to the post-apostolic Church. The Church of the Fathers may in certain respects have understood the revelation better than the inspired writers of the New Testament books. Post-apostolic Christian life and literature are not merely a translation of New Testament concepts and language into terms adapted to changed cultural situations. From the Fathers, the saints, the spiritual writers and the theologians we can be brought to see further into the revelation than a mere reading of the inspired texts would have enabled us to do.

On the other hand, our own contemporary interpretations of the tradition are not necessarily and in all respects superior to those of Augustine, Cyril, Aquinas or St John of the Cross. In the continuing 'dialogue' between the Christian present and the Christian past there can be genuine 'give and take'. Yet we have to remind ourselves that the Christian past can speak to us in this dialogue only to the extent that we allow it to do so and give it a voice through our honest attempts to interpret its records.

To sum up this long discussion: Christianity communicates to mankind and to every man God's final message to us in history. The message is clothed, as it is communicated, in human 'language', but it is not for that reason less divine. The humanizing of the message is the very expression of a divine love that bridges the gulf between the Creator and his creation. The message is ultimately a revelation of God himself and of his redeeming and transforming action towards mankind and the world. It is a message expressed not just in the teaching but in the historical actuality of Jesus of Nazareth, who is the message, the Word of God, incarnate. As incarnate, Jesus was fully human. It appears reasonable to hold that he was himself the recipient of the revelation. This, in turn, means that he grew in the knowledge of his heavenly Father. And precisely as he came to know him better as uniquely *his* Father, so he came to know himself better as uniquely the Son of God.

The divine revelation, thus given in the first instance to Jesus and perfectly received by him, was given for transmission to others, and ultimately for the enlightenment and redemption of the whole of humanity and of every man. The transmission of the revelation is called tradition (though this word may also be applied to the content of what is transmitted, in which case it means 'the revelation as transmitted'). The process of tradition began already during the earthly life of Jesus. It was continued, after Christ's resurrection and the outpouring of the Holy Spirit, in the evangelizing work of the primitive Church, including particularly that of the 'apostles'. Tradition received written embodiment in the New Testament books, though these show no sign of any human intention to produce a complete written record of the tradition.

Tradition, being a process of communication, entails finding the right 'words' to convey the message in various cultures and to differing individuals; it inevitably involves a work of interpretation. If this process of interpretation and communication is to remain faithful to the original revelation – if, that is to say, the purpose of God in the redemptive 'economy' is to be fulfilled, as Christians believe it will be – there is required the assistance (which becomes, in the case of the Scriptures, the inspiration) of the Holy Spirit.

In the process of communication we can expect that there will occur deeper and more extensive understandings of the original revelation. The notion of a 'development' of doctrine has aroused suspicion in some quarters, but development is of course going on all the time, not least in the sermons that are preached week by week in Christian churches. Development does not add to the original revelation but explores, illuminates and applies it to man's ever-changing condition. The early Church had to interpret the gospel to the Graeco-Roman world and to the representatives of Greek philosophy. St Thomas Aquinas interpreted it in terms of a Platonized Aristotelianism. Today the immense enlargements of secular knowledge and understanding that are typified and expressed in the physical sciences, modern concern with history as fact and as intelligent activity, and the 'human sciences' in general, call for new, deeper, but abidingly faithful, interpretations of the gospel received in tradition.

Note: The question whether Scripture in some sense 'contains' every item of the 'truths necessary to salvation' is an extremely complex one. The Council of Trent has often been thought to have canonized the notion that some of these items are to be discovered only in tradition and are not represented in Scripture. Today this interpretation of the meaning to be attached to Trent's pronouncement on the subject is controverted. On the other hand, impressive patristic evidence is adduced by those who claim that *all* the revelation given by Christ is deposited in the Bible. If it could be proved that there is a real patristic unanimity on this point (and that the Fathers understood the issue in the way in which it has been understood since Protestantism made itself the champion of the *sola scriptura* thesis), then it could be argued that the matter is already decided – and in the opposite sense from what Trent had been thought to teach.[6] I have the impression, however, that all these matters are still to some extent *sub judice*. I am anxious not to mutilate the fullness of the revelation by a hasty and 'fundamentalist' acceptance of the *sola scriptura* principle; and, on the other hand, not to do violence to sound principles of exegesis by attempts to 'discover' in Scripture evidence of things which, at least to educated common sense, would appear not to be there. There are discussions of the 'Scripture and Tradition' problem in Yves Congar, *Tradition and Traditions* (The Macmillan Company, New York, 1967) and Louis Bouyer, *L'Eglise de Dieu: Corps du Christ et Temple de l'Esprit* (Paris, 1970), pp. 422–36. The least one can say is that nothing that contradicts the inspired basic meaning of Scripture can be an authentic expression of divine revelation.

Chapter V

Koinonia in the Fourth Gospel

Communion is not just a notion or concept. It is a fact deeply embedded in our human condition. It is itself the condition required for the flowering of the personality of each human individual. I have argued that it is a relatedness, or relationships, arising out of common 'possessions', experience or aspirations. I have further argued that it has the potentiality of further development, on the one hand into interpersonal relationships where communion becomes more fully actualized in mutual knowledge, respect and love; and on the other hand into community.

Communion seems to be a useful model in our attempt to understand, as possibly also to identify, the Church. My supposition, then, is that the Church is itself a communion.

A Christian need feel no *a priori* objection to this hypothesis. Despite the theological distinction between grace and nature, the God of gracious redemption is at the same time the Creator of the natural world. In redemption he comes to find us by himself entering into history: by becoming man. To become really man is to become one for whom communion is of the essence of his condition. If he assumes human nature we can expect that he will consecrate human communion. Communion thus Christianized will in these pages be distinguished from communion in general by giving it the name *koinonia*, borrowed from 1 John 1:3: '... that which we have seen and heard we proclaim also to you, so that you may have fellowship *(koinonia)* with us; and our fellowship is with the Father and with his Son Jesus Christ'.

I propose to see what light may be thrown by this hypothesis on the Farewell Discourse in the Fourth Gospel (chapters 13–17). In what follows I am not supposing that this discourse (or discourses) is a kind of taped record of actual conversation between Jesus and his disciples.[1] I read it as a theological reflection from within the Church with a considerable history of such reflection preceding it. The date of the Gospel as we now have it is quite uncertain, though it will hardly be later than about 100. Whatever date we assign to it, we can ask ourselves about the author's intention in writing it; and the later we put the composition, the more pressing this question becomes. If there is a strong contrast with the first three Gospels, there is a profound similarity of thought and language with the thought and language of the author of the First, if not of all, of the canonical Epistles of John; and the author writes with the same sort of authority as that assumed by the writer of the Epistle. If the Epistle is not the work of the evangelist, they come from the same Christian milieu. I shall use the Epistle to throw a light, I hope not misleading, on the Gospel.

If the Church is a koinonia, that is to say a particular, divinely established and guaranteed communion, what is the common possession, experience or aspiration that underpins it and makes it distinct from all other communions? The answer to this question is as simple as the issues it raises are complex and profound. The 'common possession' of the koinonia, which is also capable of becoming experience and of establishing a unique hope, is Jesus Christ himself.

(1) In his godhead Jesus Christ, with the Father and the Holy Spirit, shares the indivisible 'nature' of God. The three persons of the Holy Trinity are subsistent relations and the 'medium' of relationship is godhead commonly and totally possessed. The relatedness that constitutes every communion is here actualized perfectly in interpersonal relations between Father, Son and Holy Spirit, in so supereminent a degree that here communion exists in its primal and transcendent form. Just as all fatherhood takes its name and nature from the divine Fatherhood, so all communion finds its archetype in the Holy Trinity.

(2) As the Word of God incarnate, this same Jesus Christ, the Son of God, is God self-communicated to man. In the incarnation God gives himself to mankind as a new 'common possession'. And from the alternative point of view, here in the incarnation man is in perfect communion with God because in this man Jesus

manhood exists only as assumed by the Word who is God. Jesus Christ 'belongs' to God by his godhead; and he belongs to us by his manhood. He is a 'common possession', founding a koinonia that is not merely between men but includes, and primarily, God himself: our communion, as we are told in the First Epistle of St John, quoted above, is 'with the Father and with his Son Jesus Christ'. If the Church is koinonia, it has depths that a natural sociology can never plumb, for its roots are divine.

God is love in perfection; as the Epistle says, summing up the Good News, God is love. Love is essentially self-communicating. In this connection Aquinas quotes the philosophic dictum: 'the Good propagates itself' *(bonum diffusivum sui)*. We have to remember that divine love propagates itself in the created order not automatically nor in virtue of a necessity imposed upon it from without, but by free decision, electing its recipients; and this notion of election is characteristic of the New Testament literature.

The incarnate Word is therefore incarnate love; love 'propagating itself', love for ever transcending itself and rediscovering itself through transcendence.

It is thus no accident if incarnate love tends from the first to establish an ever-widening koinonia in which the common possession is precisely Jesus Christ, incarnate love itself. The Gospels show us Jesus as one conscious of a 'mission' from his heavenly Father. This mission is not something extra to the incarnation itself; it is the incarnation freely, by personal decision and wholly, giving, that is to say diffusing, itself.

Already within the lifetime of Jesus on earth the koinonia was in process of formation (or perhaps we should say pre-formation), as men and women responded to the invitation of divine love incarnate. A 'little flock' began to take shape, the heir to all the divine promises. Within this little flock there was an inner core of persons specially chosen by Jesus to be communicators of the Message that was himself.

As is well known, the actual word 'church' *(ekklesia)* does not occur in the Gospels, except in two passages in St Matthew's Gospel. Nevertheless I suggest that the Johannine Farewell Discourse can be read as containing an informal ecclesiology, and one that is largely understandable by use of the model of koinonia.[2]

Jesus knows that his hour has come to depart out of this world to the Father (13:1). Jesus is a man, a human existent, a *Dasein*, as Heidegger would say. He is therefore historical, for man lives in history. He is historical in such a profound sense that we can apply to him Heidegger's paradoxical dictum (false if we were talking the language of classical metaphysics): 'The essence of *Dasein* lies in its [historical] existence'.[3] But historical existence entails finitude, 'and the most obvious mark of human finitude is death'.[4] Death 'marks off the *Dasein*, as Being-in-the world, from the nothing into which he disappears when he ceases to be in the world; ... death [is] one's ownmost possibility'.[5] 'All existence may be considered as a Being-toward-death, an existence in face of the end.'[6]

Death is what faces Jesus now; and he in turn faces death. Death for him, as for us, merits all the awesome realism accorded to it by Heidegger. It is indeed a disappearance into that 'nothingness' which Heidegger once proposed as a fit subject for philosophy – the 'nothingness' that remains when every science and all the humanities have exhausted their subject matters. But for Jesus death itself, like life, has a divine aspect. *His hour has come*, and this is not a mere question of neutral chronology; an 'hour' in the Fourth Gospel is a particularly significant moment in the working-out of divine providence – a man's hour is also God's hour. And Jesus is not passing into nothingness – unless nothingness is a fit name for God,[7] for he is departing out of this world *to his Father*.

His hour has come, but he is not yet dead. In view of death's proximity there is still something for him to do in this world: *having loved his own who were in the world, he loved them to the end.* Like the rest of us, Jesus grows with the passage of time. So his love for his disciples grows also. The time has come for him to complete his self-giving to them – for love is a self-giving – and in so doing to give them, with final completeness, that communion with his Father which is his own inalienable possession.

Jesus and his disciples are not, of course, a 'perfect society' if by that we mean a communion that has achieved all that communion means. Judas is one of them, and the cancer of disloyalty is already at work within him: *the devil had already put it into the heart of Judas ... to betray him.* This makes what follows all the more significant. He who has *come forth from the Father* and is now returning to his Father, he to whom the Father has entrusted all authority (has *given all things into his hand*) displays his love for his brethren in a gesture that spells total forgiveness; a forgiveness that, like every advance of love, can be refused. *If I do not wash you, you have no part in me ... You are clean, but not everyone of you. For he knew who was to betray him.*

The gesture of love, pure of all self-assertion, is also a pattern; for the love has to be still further diffused. *I have given you an example, that you also should do as I have done to you ... He who receives any one whom I send receives me; and he who receives me receives him who sent me.* So the koinonia will not end with the death of Jesus in whom it finds its foundation. He will die, but it will continue (cf. 1 John 1:1–3).

Forgiving love is efficacious – but it can be refused; this is the negative correlative of the fact that love offered can only freely be accepted. *One of you will betray me.* And at the moment when the gift of brotherhood, the 'morsel' of this basically religious meal, is received, *Satan entered into* Judas *and he immediately went out; and it was night.*

The author of this Gospel is at once simple in his language to the point of naïvety and clumsiness, and profound in his thinking to the point of exquisite irony and sophistication. According to the Epistle, *God is light.* And in the Gospel Jesus says, *I am the light of the world; he who follows me will not walk in darkness but will have the light of life* (8:12). Judas is an historical figure but may be interpreted as a type. In departing from the koinonia he turns away from the light and goes out into the only alternative; it was night out there beyond the lighted table of the meal.

Shall we be wrong in turning again to the Epistle and its warning about the antichrists? *Many antichrists have come ... They went out from us* (as Judas *went out*), *but they were not of us.* Externally, of course, they had been 'of us', for they had been members of the koinonia in its external visibility. But even then they had been like Judas, Judas into whose heart the devil had already put the thought of treachery before Satan finally took possession of him. Had the antichrists really been 'of us', in heart as well as externally, *they would have continued with us. But they went out, that it might be plain that they all are not of us* (1 John 2:18ff.). Real communion with Christ and with his heavenly Father does involve external communion with the Church. But external communion by itself is not enough; though voluntary cessation of visible communion *is* enough to prove that the interior communion has been lost.

The koinonia, in other words, is a highly complex unity of external 'visibility' and inward spiritual reality. Neither aspect is sufficient without the other – just as neither 'heart' nor 'body' suffices to make a historical man. External communion is a *sine qua non*; but it is an empty sham unless it is the condition of interior communion, a unity of hearts. On the other hand, spiritual or interior communion is a non-historical Platonic ideal unless it is combined with external communion.

The Gospel, it may be suggested, is anticipating all this in the Judas episode. Alternatively put, the antichrists, those archetypal schismatics, were playing out the role that Judas had chosen for himself. He *went out* into the night. They too had gone out into the darkness where there is no koinonia, no Christ the light of the world. It is only after laying down this formal truth, this 'short way with heretics' *(compendium adversus haereticos)* that the author of the Epistle goes on to mention the error, basic though it was, that had become the new principle of communion for the antichrists in their self-chosen separation. The same short way was taken by Cyprian in the middle of the third century, when he tells a correspondent that it is unnecessary to know what error Novatian propagates since Novatian is proved wrong by the very fact that he is not in the koinonia of the Church.

Not that the members of the koinonia can afford to be complacent. To belong to it is to be summoned to a lofty ideal: *A new commandment I give to you, that you love one another; even as I have loved you, that you also love one another.* Communion is relatedness, and koinonia is relatedness founded in the shared possession of Christ. But communion is a potency of community and of interpersonal relations of respect and love. This potency is to be actualized in the koinonia, and will be its 'note' in the judgement of the world: *By this all men will know that you are my disciples, if you have love for one another.* The ideal, it is true, will not be attained. The disciples will not even love Jesus himself – let alone love one another – sufficiently to carry out their admirable intentions: *I say to you* (Peter, their leader) *the cock will not crow, till you have denied me thrice.* The difference between Peter and Judas is that the former's fall was mere weakness and was promptly repented of.

Treachery, then, there will be and lapses due to human weakness (which, we gather, are not at all the same thing as deliberate treachery); but *let not your hearts be troubled.* In this last short time that Jesus is with them, he is concerned to cheer them and give them courage.

Would it be self-deception to think that, with the departure of Judas, the conversation takes a more intimate tone? In chapter 14 we are again considering the koinonia. Jesus is going away, but the koinonia will not cease to exist. His disciples know that 'way' which will take them to the Father in his footsteps. For that way is himself. He is not only the way; he is *the truth and the life.* And if they truly know him they know his Father. For he is 'in' his Father and his Father is 'in' him; the communion between Jesus and his heavenly Father is complete, the complete mutuality of love in its perfection. So complete is this communion, this union, that *he who has seen* Jesus 'has seen the Father' – and this although 'No one has ever seen God' (1:18). The communion between Son and Father is so complete that the Father can endorse Jesus as his perfect representative. What Jesus says and does is his Father's word and work: *the words that I say to you I do not speak on my own authority; but the Father who dwells in me does his works.*

In Jesus, then, his Father's work is inserted into the world and history. This insertion is not to cease with his death. On the contrary, the believer will *do the works* that Jesus does *and greater works than these.* It is wholly true, and Protestantism has been right to emphasize the fact, that the redemptive work of Jesus, precisely as redemptive, was complete in his passion and nothing can be added to it. Yet it is also true that the work of God which he initiated will go on. It will go on through the instrumentality of those who believe in him – of, we may say, the koinonia of the believers.

So at the very moment when the prospect of Jesus' death would seem to write *Finis,* the end, to the whole of the economy of grace, a note of victorious hope enters into the discourse. Certainly, Jesus is going to his Father; his death is now inevitable, and Judas' departure has already lighted the fatal fuse. But the work will go on and will increase. Christ himself will be active in another dimension beyond but subsuming this world's history.[8] Thérèse of Lisieux promised to spend her time in heaven in doing good on earth.

He will do whatever his disciples *ask in his name.* How will he do this? By intercession with his Father, which will result in the sending of *another Counsellor, to be with you for ever.*[9]

We may be correct in thinking that it is through this sending of the Holy Spirit that Jesus himself will *not leave* them *desolate* but will *come* to them. He will still be visible to the eyes of faith though not, henceforward, to the (unbelieving) world. Thus Jesus will manifest himself to his disciples even after he has departed to his Father. And we are asked to understand that the underlying condition of such 'coming', such 'visibility', such 'manifestation' is love. *If a man loves me he will keep my word*; and the word of Jesus is the word of *my Father who sent me. In that day you will know that I am in my Father, and you in me, and I in you.* It may at first be confusing that the language here moves between Jesus as a person, knowledge or apprehension, and love. But the teaching of the Fourth Gospel is that Jesus Christ *is* his Father's Word, is therefore truth embodied, and at the same time is the Father's gift of love. Our last quotation ('I in my Father, you in me, and I in you') is exactly comparable to the koinonia of 1 John 1:3 ('that you may have koinonia with us; and our koinonia is with the Father and with his Son Jesus Christ'), although in the Gospel the word 'koinonia' is absent. For all this we have, the Gospel implies, the promise of Jesus. One question may here be raised. 'If a man loves me'. So is the whole promise conditional on the precarious good will of believers? The answer, as regards individuals, is presumably, (while allowing for God's prevenient grace,) yes. But can it be supposed that good will will ever so universally and collectively fail that the promise is rendered futile? The same question arose when we were considering the exhortations to preserve unity in the Epistle to the Ephesians. Doubtless a similar answer would be correct here also in the Fourth Gospel setting. But the issue will recur later.

The Holy Spirit, when he comes, will not be inactive. He will be the envoy of the Father, but sent in Jesus' name. Hence his action among the disciples will be within the horizon of the revelation given in the incarnation: *he will teach you all things, and bring to your remembrance all that I have said to you.* We may suppose that this bringing to remembrance will comprise more than a mere triumph over amnesia; it will involve an understanding of the Word incarnate in the light of ever new circumstances; it will guide the hermeneutical process, the continual 'saying the same thing in other words' which is necessary if the Gospel is to speak to men in every age and every culture. *He will take of mine and declare it to you* (16:15; the word translated 'declare' means 'report'). The revelation once given, therefore, will not become a dead letter of the past, but will be for ever new as it is repeated in and to the Church by the Spirit of God who is the Spirit of Christ. The shared possession of Christians which is the basis of the koinonia will always be Christ as he made himself known to his disciples during his ministry; though of course it will be this Christ crucified and risen. We could therefore say that the life of the Church is a continual 'coming' of the unique, historical, incarnate Word; it is a kind of second advent, a *parousia*. It is a *parousia* distended across the ages of history, yet new and complete at every moment of that history. All this does not, on the other hand, mean that we can dispense with the doctrine of the final Second Coming of Christ.

Chapter 14 had begun with the words, *Let not your hearts be troubled.* Now, after the foretelling of the Counsellor, Jesus (v. 27) puts his consolation in a positive form: *Peace I leave with you; my peace I give to you*; and so, again, *Let not your hearts be troubled, neither let them be afraid.*

If we take the Farewell Discourse as a literal record of Jesus' conversation with his close disciples at the last supper, there is something deeply touching about this concern of his, despite his own approaching passion, to console those who, because they love him, are on the brink of despair at his departure. A similar theme recurs in chapter 16 (vv. 20ff.) where Jesus, throwing his mind forward to the time when they will actually have been left behind by him, says:

> Truly, truly, I say to you, you will weep and lament, but the world will rejoice; you will be sorrowful, but your sorrow will turn into joy. When a woman is in travail she has sorrow, because her hour has come; but when she is delivered of the child, she no longer remembers the anguish, for joy that a child is born into the world. So you have sorrow now, but I will see you again and your hearts will rejoice, and no one will take your joy from you.

Moving as it is to see the Discourse as a literal record, we cannot forget that the author of the Gospel, writing perhaps fifty or more years after the crucifixion, will have had in mind the needs of the Christians of that date. The promises to the disciples, particularly the promise of the Holy Spirit who will *bring to your remembrance all that I have said to you* are, we can conclude, meant for these Christians of the second or third generation (or later); and for those who will follow them. In other words, a Christian will infer, the promises are valid for the whole history of the Church; both the promises and the comfort: Do not be disturbed at heart, do not play the coward. For Christ is for ever coming, coming in the coming of the Holy Spirit sent by the Father – coming as he came in the historical incarnation, which was a piece of actual history ever being renewed in the life of the Church.

Chapter 15 is largely about the individual and his task of fidelity: *If a man does not abide in me, he is cast forth as a branch and withers.* But the thought moves further. The believers have a task not only of 'vertical' fidelity to Christ but of mutual love. The koinonia, a divine and human thing, is a fact which should develop (is it too much to infer?), through the free willing of its members, into a historical love-charged community: *this is my commandment, that you love one another as I have loved you.* The demands of love are great – as great as Jesus' own self-giving in death: *greater love has no man than this, that a man lay down his life for his friends.*

He calls them friends. The word in this passage is to be taken in a strong sense. It is contrasted with the word 'slave': *no longer do I call you servants* (the Greek word is 'slaves') *for the servant does not know what his master is doing: but I have called you friends.* Slaves, according to Aristotle, are animated instruments of their owners, existing not to carry into act any thoughts of their own but only to execute their masters' intentions. They are not privy, says Jesus here, to their masters' mind. But Jesus has held nothing back from his disciples of all that he has received (by revelation) from his Father. The Word, fully incarnate, has been fully communicated to others. The Father's mind is now present in history not solely in his Son but in those whom the author of the Epistle will call God's children. Clearly, the incarnation is a self-transcending reality; and its radiation, like itself, is fully historical not now in one sole person but in all the believers who are summoned to love one another and therefore, presumably, to stay together in community.

The initiative, of course, in all this has been that of Jesus (and his initiative is his Father's). The disciples did not choose him; he chose them. In their turn, they are to *bear much fruit, and so prove to be his disciples.* We may presume that part of this fruit will be seen in the propagation of the gospel and the recruitment of the koinonia. And, in the divine intention, the fruit is *to abide*. True, they will be persecuted as Jesus was persecuted. But the Counsellor will nevertheless be bearing witness, as will the disciples; and doubtless the Spirit's witness will be embodied in the witness that they will give; they will be his mouthpiece.

I pass on now to chapter 17, the so-called 'high priestly prayer'. *Father, the hour has come*; we are reminded of the opening words of the Discourse in chapter 13. The 'hour' is the dénouement of a fully historical life, and Jesus can say, now, *I glorified thee* (my Father) *having accomplished the work which thou gavest me to do*. What the Church Fathers will come to call the 'economy', God's redeeming purpose in Jesus and the Holy Spirit, has been completed. On the cross Jesus, in this evangelist's re-presentation of him, will be able to say: It is completed.

In this completed work the Father is glorified. He is glorified precisely in the glorification of the Son: *Glorify thy Son that the Son may glorify thee*. And the Son's glorification is achieved in the transmission to others of what the Father has given him: *Thou hast given him power over all flesh, to give eternal life to all whom thou hast given him. And this is eternal life, that they know thee the only true God, and Jesus Christ whom thou hast sent.*[10]

This glory, historically actualized in the passion and resurrection of Jesus Christ, is in truth *the glory which I had with thee before the world was made*.[11] The author here is faithful to the doctrine of his Prologue: the Word which became man and, thus, became the Word of God in history and for history, 'was with God and ... was God'.

What, then, is this work in which the eternal glory of the godhead has been 'incarnated' in history? It is a work of communicated revelation: *I have manifested thy name to the men thou gavest me out of the world ... and they have kept thy word.* The revelation, the Word incarnate, has thus become the common possession of the Father, the incarnate Son and the disciples. The revelation, then, is the basis of the koinonia of which 1 John speaks. It is 'on offer' in Jesus, and its acceptance is contained in the acknowledgement by the disciples that Jesus is indeed God's incarnate Word: *... I have given them the words which thou gavest me, and they have received them and know in truth that I came from thee; and they have believed that thou didst send me.*

Through this triumph of faith the disciples can be distinguished from 'the world'; they have become the object of the divine predilection: *I am not praying for the world*, although 'God so loved the world that he gave his only Son', *but for those whom thou hast given me, for they are thine; all mine are thine, and thine are mine, and I am glorified in them.* Here the note of 'glory' enters in again. Glory belongs primordially to the Father and is shared eternally by the Word in the unity of the godhead. This glory is given to the Word in his incarnate insertion into history. And the incarnate Word, in turn, has given this same glory to the disciples: *The glory which thou hast given me I have given to them* (v. 22). Thus the divine self-giving, the eternal act within the godhead through which the Three are One, is communicated to Jesus in history and by him is transmitted to the members of the koinonia. The Church is not an extraneous appendage to the redemptive incarnation. Rather, we can say, since the Church itself is commissioned to proclaim the gospel to all mankind, it is, with the incarnate Word, the anticipatory summing-up of the whole of creation, the preliminary actualization of God's purpose in creating the world and man.

For a new phase in the whole majestic unfolding of the eternal plan in historical terms is now about to begin. Jesus is leaving the world, and the believers are not yet leaving it: ... *now I am no more in the world, but they are in the world, and I am coming to thee.* But the work, initiated by Jesus himself, has to be continued. So he utters the prayer: ... *keep them in thy name, which thou hast given me, that they may be one, even as we are one.* He prays that his disciples may be one (the Greek is: 'one thing', a unity). So it is not just a question of a number of individual believers. The commonly possessed revelation is to become the basis of a real historical koinonia. Hitherto, this unity has been preserved through the presence and action among them of Jesus in his historical life and work; or so I infer from verse 12: *I have guarded them, and none of them is lost but the son of perdition* (doubtless, this is a reference to Judas); we saw that Judas was 'lost' – though the word was not then used – when he went out from the koinonia into 'the night'.

The contents of chapter 17 of the Gospel are formally a prayer. The question may properly be asked: Is that which Jesus here asks from his heavenly Father, the unity of his disciples (or the permanence of the koinonia), guaranteed to us by the fact (if it is a fact) that Jesus prayed for it? Despite the assurance in 16:23

(Truly, truly, I say to you, if you ask anything of the Father, he will give it to you in my name) it is a common experience of Christians that what we pray for is often not given to us, at least in the form in which we asked for it. And if the reply is made, Yes, but the prayer of the incarnate Word must have privileges beyond those accorded to mere Christians, then we cannot forget that Jesus prayed in agony that the cup of the passion would pass him by. It did not pass him by. The prayer was no doubt conditional: 'Not what I will but what you will be done' – but could there not be an implied condition in the prayer of chapter 17?

I suggest that one can approach an answer to this question from two complementary standpoints.

Assuming that we are dealing with an actual prayer of Jesus and not simply with a prayer put upon his lips by the evangelist, we can say: If *this* prayer is not granted, then God's purpose in the redemptive 'economy' is unfulfilled. The whole affair of the incarnation of the Word becomes a futility. For the Good News was given to Jesus for communication. The communication was effected in and by the establishment of the koinonia, whose 'members' are not only the believers but Christ himself and his heavenly Father; and to this koinonia the glory of God has been given. Through this koinonia salvation is to be offered to the whole of mankind; indeed (if we may here borrow some thoughts from St Paul and the Epistle to the Ephesians) this koinonia is the germ and pledge of the unification of all mankind and the whole of the created order in the new and higher order of God's finally accomplished purpose. The koinonia not only will but must survive, and this not conditionally upon the precarious fidelity of its human members taken by itself, but rather because God himself has committed his whole purpose in creation and redemption to this koinonia.

There is an alternative standpoint. Whether or not this prayer was actually spoken by 'the historical Jesus', it is recorded, or perhaps composed, by the author of the Gospel. He is writing, we may think, for second- or even third-generation Christians. He must be supposed to be not merely regaling them with stories of unfulfilled hopes of his divine Master, but endowing them with strength and guidance for their own Christian life and behaviour. What could this prayer signify for them if it either were or could be unfulfilled? How could it help, for instance, in the sort of situation indicated in the First Epistle of St John, where a group or groups of Christians have broken away from the visible unity of the Church and constituted a new fellowship on the basis of (erroneous) doctrine? In the Epistle the bare fact of the 'schismatical' condition of these dissidents is given as a proof that they are in the wrong. But the argument will not work if the unity of the koinonia is precarious.

The purpose of the redemptive economy, I repeat, is that the eternal Word of God should be communicated in temporal form to men living in 'the world', that is to say in the ambiguities of human history. The communication takes place through a koinonia that is for ever mission-directed. Indeed, if we take seriously the doctrine of the incarnation – that the Word of God is not some message from God that Jesus brings but is identical with himself, the very Word of God who is with God and is God – then the koinonia will be seen to be not merely the vehicle of this message, but in some way an incorporation of the message. The Church is called by St Paul the body of Christ. We have heard the author of the Fourth Gospel telling us that the glory which Christ 'had with his Father before the ages' is given to his disciples, and that discipleship means membership of the koinonia. What is the glory of God but divine love itself? It is this divine love, which underpins the whole created order, that is brought into historical actuality first in Jesus and then, through him and the outpouring of the Holy Spirit, in the koinonia. We have heard St Paul (and/or the author of the Epistle to the Ephesians) telling us that the passion and resurrection of Christ have introduced a new order, a superior dimension, into history, so that as a result we live in what we can only call a renewed world. This new order is incorporated, given in living germ, in the koinonia. Thus it is true not only that the message from God must be preserved in its integrity for all men and the whole course of history, not only that the koinonia must be preserved for the transmission of that message, but that the message and the koinonia are in some sense, if not identifiable (for only in Jesus is incarnation fully itself), at least so closely interwoven that the fate of the one depends on the fate of the other.

So Jesus prays: *Sanctify them in the truth; thy word is truth. As thou didst send me into the world, so I have sent them into the world. And for their sake I consecrate myself, that they also may be consecrated in truth.*[12] The purpose of Jesus' self-consecration, about to *be consummated* in death, is that the disciples also may be consecrated in truth. This is vital. The koinonia exists by the truth it has received – that truth which is the incarnate Word of God. That truth is transmitted by Jesus not immediately to 'the world' but to the koinonia. If the koinonia collapses, then the truth is 'gone with the wind' and the purpose of the whole economy, the very value of Jesus' death, is lost.

Now the thought of the prayer is turned explicitly towards those who will be converted *through the word* of the disciples. Reminding ourselves once again that the evangelist is writing at a period when, probably, the last of the 'apostles' was dead or near death, we should not restrict these words, as endorsed by the evangelist and included as relevant for his readers, to a generation contemporary with the apostles, that is to those who owed their conversion immediately to the apostles' preaching. The words are surely applicable to all successive generations of the koinonia – for all of us owe our faith at least indirectly to the missionary movement inaugurated after the resurrection by the Twelve and their associates. The prayer at this point, then, can be applied to all generations of Christians 'till the end of the age' as St Matthew would put it. The prayer is that all these believers should be one (the same prayer as that offered more immediately for the disciples a little earlier): *that they may all be one; even as thou, Father, art in me, and I in thee, that they also may be in us.* (It is possible that in the last clause here cited we should read, with some manuscripts, *that they also may be one in us.* With or without the addition of 'one', the meaning is presumably the same.) Jesus prays that the Christians may be one and may be 'in' him and his Father, *so that the world may believe that thou hast sent me.* Jesus has, in fact, given to the Christians (presumably in giving to his disciples, as above) the glory which he has himself received from the Father. And this glory is to ensure their unity. And the purpose of the unity is the mission that is transmitted by Jesus through his disciples to the Church: *so that the world may believe that thou hast sent me.* We, who live in a world where there is a variety of Christian Communions, each separated from the others, need to ask ourselves what sort of unity among believers would be apt to persuade 'the world' that Jesus is more than a deluded prophet, that he is indeed the One sent from God to introduce the final economy of salvation.

* * *

Questions may properly be asked about the validity of the experiment contained in this chapter: the attempt, namely, to find in the Farewell Discourse of the Fourth Gospel an implicit ecclesiology that can be restated in terms of koinonia. Have we not been building an improbability (of a particular ecclesiology in this Discourse) upon a prior improbability (the use of koinonia as a 'model' for the Church)? An objector can point to the fact that the word 'koinonia' is absent from the whole of the Fourth Gospel. I have, indeed, referred to the use of the word in the First Epistle of St John, but modern scholarship is not agreed that the Gospel and the Epistle come from the same pen. And in any case, is not the evangelist a 'mystic', obsessed with the direct personal relationship of the individual believer with God in Christ? And can one suppose such a mystic to have any ecclesiology at all?

Something may here be said in answer to such arguments.

As I have made clear, in using the word 'koinonia' I have been referring habitually to the Church. But the word is a transliteration of a Greek word; and the English equivalent of the word is 'communion'. If the word is applicable in ecclesiology, it is as a word borrowed from general usage and then given a more particular (and, if need be, modified) meaning for a special purpose. This borrowing, with particular application and modification, is characteristic of the way in which the physical sciences have evolved their technical vocabulary.

Communion, I have argued, is a relatedness between persons that (a) has its foundation in shared possession, experience, and aspiration or hope. I have based this understanding of the word on its etymology (*koinonia* from *koinon*, something shared). The notion of communion, thus understood, seems to me to gain a clarity that is sometimes lacking from its usage – particularly its use by theologians. (b) This relatedness based on sharing has a twofold potency. It can develop into community; in community the relatedness of the sharers to one another, and each to all, founds a network of common thought, speech and action, and this network is sustained through 'institutions'. (c) But communion can also develop into 'interpersonal relations', in which the objective fact of relatedness blossoms in personal mutual knowledge, respect and love. It would seem that such interpersonal relations habitually require or presuppose some foundation like the shared possession, experience, or hope that, in my view, founds communion. If I am reproached for my lack of friendship for another, I am apt to reply: 'But we have nothing in common with each other'.

I have further argued or implied that communion, thus understood, is a universal condition of human existence. I accept the modern contention that personality depends, for its development and full actualization, on relations with other persons; and I should be prepared, if challenged, to maintain that such relations are not possible without some basis of sharing.

It is the faith of Christians that Jesus of Nazareth, in his life, passion and resurrection, and as 'interpreted' to us by the Holy Spirit, is the incarnate Word of God, a Word eternally 'with' God, a Word eternally God, eternally (to introduce a necessary precision) Son of God or God the Son. Godhead is thus the 'shared basis' of the communion of Jesus with his heavenly Father, alike in his eternal existence considered in abstraction from the incarnation, and in his historical existence as a man among men.

The man Jesus was fully human. This is the faith of Christians, affirmed in the Formula of Chalcedon but implicit of course in the faith of the Church before that date: docetism, the denial (or quasi-docetism, the depreciation) of this doctrine, has been steadily rejected by the main Christian tradition – at least in its formal self-expression.

I have therefore argued that Jesus experienced, from his birth onwards, the conditions and development that are natural to our humanity. His development therefore involved communion: the communion of the home at Nazareth, the communion of the Jewish religion, and eventually the communion of his disciples.

I have argued that upon this basis of common human conditions Jesus became the fountainhead of a new and specifically Christian communion, to which I have dedicated the particular term 'koinonia'.

This term occurs, as we have seen, in the opening paragraph of the First Epistle of St John. I do not pretend that it is there used in a technical sense, but I have endeavoured to see what the term may mean in the particular context in which it there occurs. It is quite true that scholars are not agreed about the common authorship of the Epistle and the Fourth Gospel. But there is something more to be said, which may justify my use of this paragraph as a help to the interpretation of the Farewell Discourse. A recent Commentary on the Fourth Gospel, published in

England in 1971 but written a few years earlier, is the major two-volume contribution to the Anchor Bible by Raymond Brown, a Roman Catholic scholar. It has been described by Professor C. K. Barrett as 'one of the most helpful contributions to Johannine studies in this century'. It is profoundly erudite, and cautious in its conclusions. Fr Brown thinks that 'the source of the historica' tradition' underlying the Gospel is John the son of Zebedee. He thinks that John had a group of 'disciples' whose relationship to him was 'much closer than Peter's relationship to Mark'. These disciples would include the author of the Gospel and the author of the Epistle – if indeed these two works are not from the same hand. He holds that the Gospel, the Epistles, and Revelation (the Apocalypse) 'share a distinctive theological milieu'. 'If one is inclined to posit different writers for the Gospel and the Epistles, their closeness would seem to indicate that their writers belonged to the same school of thought'.[13]

In particular, Brown calls attention to the resemblances between John 14 and 1 John (sc. the Epistle). Hence I revert to what seems to be a kinship between John 14:20 and 1 John 1:3:

John 14:20	*1 John 1:3*
In that day you will know that I am in my Father, and you in me, and I in you.	... that which we have seen and heard we proclaim also to you, so that you may have fellowship *(koinonia)* with us; and our fellowship is with the Father and with his Son Jesus Christ.

In the Gospel passage we note the reciprocity of the relationship that links Jesus and the disciples: *you in me, and I in you.* Such reciprocity is not here asserted between Jesus and his Father; but it is stated in John 17:21: (I pray) *that they may all be one; even as thou, Father, art in me, and I in thee, that they also may be in us.* True, the meaning in John 17 may be not that Jesus and his Father are reciprocally 'in' each other, but that they are *one* in each other. See, however, John 10:38: *that you may know and understand that the Father is in me and I am in the Father.* Similarly, it is not directly stated in John 14:20 that there is reciprocal 'indwelling' of the disciples in the Father and of the Father in them. Doubtless, for the evangelist and for the Christian, this reciprocal indwelling is entailed by the reciprocal indwelling of Jesus and the disciples. In 1 John 4:16, however, the matter is made explicit: *God is love, and he who abides in love abides in God, and God abides in him.*

My immediate point is that in John 14:20 there is mentioned a close association between Jesus and his Father on the one hand, and Jesus and the disciples on the other; Jesus, to borrow a term from elsewhere in the New Testament, is represented as a mediator, a bridge, between God and the disciples. The same is very plainly true of the passage in 1 John 1: Jesus is the link between his Father and the Christians and there is thus constituted a 'fellowship' between all three, involving incidentally a fellowship between the Christians themselves.

In line with my suggested understanding of 'communion' we shall ask: what is the 'common possession' that establishes this communion? The answer that I propose is, that it is Jesus himself. He possesses both the godhead which he shares with the Father and the Holy Spirit and the manhood which he shares with us. His heavenly Father 'possesses' him by every title: their one godhead, the eternal generation of the Son, his manhood which, like the whole of creation, belongs to the Creator. Do *we* possess Jesus? We do, since he is his Father's gift to us for our redemption. But is this Johannine doctrine?

According to 1 John, the purpose of the proclamation of Jesus to the readers of the Epistle is that they may have fellowship 'with us' – doubtless with those who already believe that gospel, whether as eyewitnesses of the life and resurrection of Jesus, or as enlightened by those eyewitnesses, that is to say as believing members of a Church that is 'apostolic' in its faith. One may therefore suggest that, once the readers have accepted the gospel (as, of course, they already have), the gospel serves as a 'common possession' between the writer and his readers. But the content of the gospel is the incarnate Word, Jesus Christ; and it would appear to be the New Testament teaching that the very preaching of the gospel is instinct with Jesus himself. Thus, in 1 Thessalonians we read of the gospel coming not only in word but in power and in the Holy Spirit. In Colossians the gospel is 'bearing fruit and growing in the whole world'. Another name for the gospel is God's word; and in Hebrews the word of God is described as 'living and active'. Again, the object of faith is the gospel of God revealed in Christ's redemptive work, and the prayer of the author of the Epistle to the Ephesians for his readers is that Christ may through faith dwell in their hearts. It was John and/or his disciples (cf. Brown cited above) who drew all this together in identifying Jesus as the incarnate Word of God. And Jesus is God's gift to men, the 'true bread' of real life given by his Father from heaven.

Finally, is the author of the Fourth Gospel too much of a 'mystic' to care about the Church and to have an, even implicit, ecclesiology? One obvious answer to this is that if he is a 'mystic' then so also, surely, is the author of the First Epistle; and the latter (whether or not he is identical with the evangelist) is certainly a 'churchman' and, as his treatment of the 'antichrists' shows, has a very clear idea of the Church as a 'visible communion' – to use a modern phrase: these schismatics are proved to be *anti*-christs precisely because, like Judas, they have 'gone out from among us' instead of 'remaining with us'. More generally, it is a mistake to suppose that Christian mystics are not also men who value the Church. On the contrary, the great tradition of Christian mystical spirituality, from Origen to St John of the Cross and beyond, is also profoundly 'Catholic' in its foundations and its loyalty. And what definition of 'a mystic' would succeed in excluding from that category Paul himself, an 'ecclesiastic' if there ever was one? Personally, I should wish to regard Christian mysticism as an eminent flowering of that interpersonal relationship (in the case of mysticism, the relationship with God that is founded in the incarnation) that is a typical and deeply valuable development of communion.

Admittedly, there is a danger in constructing a notion like communion as I have understood it and imposing it on an ancient writer. I do not, of course, claim that the author of the Gospel had thought out the idea of communion, or more particularly that of (Christian) koinonia, and was consciously operating with this elaborated concept; a notion may be implicit in a man's thinking without his conscious and reflective advertence to it. Nor would it be safe to try to compress the whole thought of this great religious genius into the straitjacket of any one notion. In any case, throughout this essay I am using the notion of koinonia not in order to embody it in a scientific definition of the Church but rather as a model to be tested and accepted so far as it proves fruitful. Doubtless, there are other useful models for ecclesiology. And I have earlier suggested that it may be advisable to accept simultaneously, as Fr Dulles proposes, more than one model of the Church, that mystery in which the mystery of Christ is made actual in our here and now.

Chapter VI

The Apostolic Age

Christianity, according to the New Testament, is the representative, the inauguration, and the vital germ of a new and divine order of created reality. It is not a new but merely subjective way of apprehending reality. Rather, it is a new and definitive epoch of history, although one to which, without the light of faith, we would be blind.

The proposal that I am pursuing in this essay is that integral to this new order of reality is a 'communion' in which God, Christ and believers are linked together into a unity, transcendent (since it includes God) and yet fully historical: believers are actual human beings rooted in inanimate nature and creating history itself as they continue to exist. The foundation of this communion, which I have called the koinonia, is Jesus Christ himself. Its sustaining and controlling force in history is the Holy Spirit.

Jesus Christ, born, crucified and raised by his heavenly Father from the dead, 'reigns until he shall have put all his enemies under his feet'. He is God's definitive intervention into creation and history. The new order that springs from the incarnation will have no successor until its implications are finally actualized in what Christians call his second coming. And since the koinonia is integral to the working out of those implications during this interim between his resurrection and his second coming, it is certain that the koinonia survives and will survive. This truth may be presumed to underlie the words with which St Matthew's Gospel concludes: 'Lo, I am with you always, to the close of the age'.

Inevitably, then, one turns to the history of the world subsequent to the crucifixion of Jesus to discover this historical koinonia, this communion of which human beings are the historical component, and to follow its course. It should be discoverable, the more so since it was established not as an introspective group but as a body with a mission to the whole of mankind, a body whose unity would itself be a recommendation of the truth of its message ('The glory which thou hast given to me I have given to them ... that they may become perfectly one' – the Greek says: 'that they may be perfected into unity' – '*so that the world may know that thou hast sent* me and hast loved them even as thou hast loved me': John 17:22f.).

For the earliest history of this koinonia we naturally turn to the New Testament and to what it has to tell us about the Christian movement and mission in the days when apostles were still alive or recently dead. The Epistle to the Ephesians, as we have seen, identifies the germ of the new order with the Church: 'that through the church the manifold wisdom of God might now be made known to the principalities and powers in the heavenly places' (3:10). What have our records to tell us about the Church in the apostolic age?

The records, good as they are in comparison with those of some comparable historical matters, are tantalizingly fragmentary and incomplete. Apart from information that we can glean from the Pauline Epistles, the First Epistle of Peter, and the opening section of Revelation (the Apocalypse) we have little direct evidence except what we can find in the Acts of the Apostles.[1] Unfortunately, the Acts devotes half its space to the missionary activities and life of St Paul, about which we have already some information from the Epistles. What is the historical value of the narrative of Acts?

In my view, there is at present no reliable consensus among scholars as to the historical truth of that narrative. As regards the date at which it was written, the dominant view seems to be that it is a rather late composition, perhaps about 85–90; but Robinson thinks that a strong case can still be made for putting it twenty years earlier. The author is almost certainly the same as that of the Gospel of St Luke, and there is really no substantial reason for denying that he was Luke the physician, the companion of St Paul. Despite the strenuous efforts of some critics, I think there is a very strong presumption that the author is the man who, in the 'We' passages, appears to claim to have been Paul's companion over a fairly large portion of the period of Paul's career covered in the narrative. Judging by the treatment of the text of St Mark's Gospel in the Gospel of St Luke, I should hazard the opinion that this author is really rather meticulous (not to say scrupulous) in his use of his sources, though he can blur the vividness of the material he borrows and of course, like every author, subordinates it to his historical and theological themes. An honest man, I am inclined to think; one who tried to write history but was perhaps somewhat lacking in critical acumen and not fully aware that his theology might be distorting his narrative. At the very least, one will be inclined to say that his story is one that reflects Christian presuppositions, with regard to the Church and its past history, that would have commended themselves to believers of about the year 90. Considered simply as a monument of the Church at that period of its growth, the book is of inestimable worth. We must, however, admit that – if indeed its composition was so late – there had been time for the growth of legend about the earliest days of the Church in its country of origin and at a time well before the destruction of the Temple of Jerusalem.[2]

There is a profound irony involved in the incarnation of the Word of God who is God. It is the act of God's love for his creation, taking shape, as genuine love always does, in self-identification with the beloved. As a medieval English spiritual writer puts it, '... this is the true condition of a perfect lover, only and utterly to spoil himself of himself for the thing that he loveth, ... and that not only for a time, but endlessly to be enwrapped therein in full and final forgetting of himself'.[3] This author is careful to point out that the lover does not covet 'for to un-be – for that were madness and despite unto God – but for to forgo the knowing and the feeling of [his] being'.[4] So the Word of God does not cease to be divine in becoming human and in self-identification with humanity. Nevertheless, this identification is 'full and final' – Christ did not cease to be human when he was raised from the dead, nor will he ever so cease.

But the creation, the humanity, with which the Word of God identifies himself in incarnation is a fallen creation, a fallen world and a sinful human race. The men and women whom he gathered into his koinonia already in his earthly life were as fallen as the rest of us – though his Mother had been radically redeemed 'as a result of the foreseen merits of her Son'.[5] Perhaps it is not a mere literary device when the Gospel of St Mark displays the disciples as continually failing to understand their Master, and when we read of disputes among them as to who should be 'first' in the Reign of God. The incomprehension is again portrayed in John's Farewell Discourse; and according to Luke (though here it may be a literary arrangement) the squabbling was still going on at the Last Supper. We have seen that it was as a member of the koinonia that Judas was tempted, even if his yielding to that temptation coincided with his (voluntary) self-'excommunication'. We speak of Judas; but at the end 'they all forsook him and fled' (Mark 14:50).

Hence it is not surprising to find that the history of the koinonia after the resurrection – and already in the apostolic age – has been a chequered one. It follows, however, that the religious inter-pretation of its development is not easy.

An added and practical difficulty in following this development in its earliest stages arises from the primitive Church's relative lack of reflection upon itself. What is true of man individually is also true, in due measure, of man in communion and community: we are orientated to the objects of our experience, and primarily to direct objects. Reflection upon experience comes later, and it is through such reflection that by degrees we come to attend to and be interested in ourselves.

Jesus was not concerned primarily about himself. He was, if we may dare to say it, 'God-intoxicated', totally attentive and self-committed to his Father. It is not surprising that some modern scholars think that few, if any, of the New Testament 'titles' of Jesus ('Christ', 'Son of Man', 'Son of God' and so on) were claimed by him in his own teaching. The Church, in its turn, overwhelmed by the resurrection of Christ, and filled with a passion for the propagation of its own faith, had at first little time or desire to elaborate an ecclesiology. It lived ecclesiology, it did not – on the whole and at first – write books about it. What is true of the apostolic Church is true also, in large measure, of the Church in the age of the Fathers. The great Councils of the first seven centuries were preoccupied with Christology and with its consequences for Trinitarian doctrine. Yet, as we shall see, some urgent crisis might provoke a Cyprian, an Optatus, an Augustine to reflect upon the Church. But all the time the Church was expressing its being, if not in theory, at least in the practice of its own living.

What is Luke's story of the first days of the koinonia after the resurrection of Christ? It can be divided into three sections. In the first, Christ, before his ascension, tells the apostles to wait for the promised Spirit of God, offers no blueprint for the Christian future, but says that, empowered by the Holy Spirit, they will bear witness to him to the ends of the earth.

The second, short, period between the ascension of Christ and Pentecost is a time of common prayer; the occasion is taken to replace Judas by Matthias and so restore the number of the apostles to twelve.[6]

The third period is constituted by the day of Pentecost itself. As they had prayed together after the ascension and had deliberated together about the replacement of Judas, so once again they (not just the Twelve but the more extensive koinonia) are together on that day. Their ears and eyes are assailed by preternatural phenomena 'and they were all filled with the Holy Spirit and began to speak in other tongues, as the Spirit gave them utterance'. The rumour of strange happenings spread in Jerusalem; men were astounded to hear these Galileans speaking in the various tongues of the members of the crowd, assembled in a Jerusalem that was full of pilgrims for the Jewish festival. There was natural perplexity, though some had a facile explanation of the surprising event. This gives Peter (who throughout the first half of Acts is plainly the leader of the koinonia) his chance to preach the gospel for the first time, it would seem, since the crucifixion of Jesus.

In reflecting on this Pentecostal scene one's mind is drawn to the 'theophanic' episodes in the Old Testament, which are paralleled by similar scenes in non-Christian literature. Bernard Lonergan has some interesting remarks on the problem of indicating divinity in the terms of primitive language and primitive conceptualization. The divine, he remarks, 'cannot be perceived and it cannot be imagined. But it can be associated with the object or event, the ritual or recitation, that occasions religious experience'.[7] A believer should not be disturbed at an inclination among biblical scholars to 'demythologize' a scene like that of the first Christian Pentecost. It is more important to reflect on the religious meaning that Luke is trying to convey, a meaning that he doubtless received from the Christian tradition and that had fastened upon the first explosion of Christianity in public, an explosion that was also the birthday of the Church.

The four evangelists associate the beginning of Jesus' public ministry with his baptism by John. Each of them refers to the Holy Spirit descending on him on that occasion. John (through the lips of the Baptist) speaks of the Spirit descending and *remaining* on Jesus. And Luke says that, as Jesus went on from his baptism and retired into the desert, he was 'full of the Holy Spirit'. We may compare Acts 2:4 where we are told that at Pentecost 'they', that is to say the Christian community, 'were all filled with the Holy Spirit and began to speak' – just as Jesus, filled with the Holy Spirit after his baptism, began to preach. The Church is in continuity with its Founder. What is the meaning of this insistence on the Holy Spirit, found both here and elsewhere in the New Testament books?

The koinonia is a historical reality, a soul-and-body affair, with its roots in inanimate nature. For the sociologist it is just one among a number of historical groupings, communions, or communities. But for faith it is a historical reality in which (as in its originator, the incarnate Word of God) God himself, the absolutely transcendent and supra-historical, becomes supernaturally operative in human affairs and so in the created world. The integrity of the koinonia and its permanence are assured by God; but they have to be worked out by human instruments according to the modes of contingent reality.

Every merely human grouping is doomed to decay and disappearance, just as every human being is born under sentence of death. Only the divine Spirit can ensure that the koinonia will survive; and only that same Spirit can bring it about that the operations of the koinonia will be not merely historically human but also eschatologically divine. Luke is telling us, then, that the Church is under the emprise of the Holy Spirit, and that accession to the Church means coming under that emprise: 'Be baptized, each of you, in the name of Jesus Christ for the remission of sins; and you will receive the gift of the Holy Spirit' (2:38). Not for nothing has Acts, our only 'history' of the primitive Church, been called the Gospel of the Holy Spirit; and it is only fitting that, after describing the result of Peter's Pentecostal sermon, the conversion of 'about 3,000 persons', Luke tells us that 'they devoted themselves to the apostles' teaching and fellowship (koinonia), to the breaking of bread and the prayers' (2:42).

Luke's first introduction of the word 'Church' to designate the koinonia is apparently casual. After the death of Ananias' wife,

Sapphira, 'great fear came upon the whole church and upon all who heard of these things'. Once again, we may remind ourselves that Christianity was conceived without a vocabulary of its own. We cannot even be sure that Jesus ever applied the word 'church' (*ekklesia* in Greek; its Hebrew equivalent would have been *qahal*) to the group of his disciples; his *ipsisima vox* may be heard more clearly in the designation of the disciples as the 'little flock'. But after the resurrection the group came to be known as the Church, a title which recalls the sacred assembly of the Israelites in the desert of the Exodus. Presumably this identification, and the new application of the title, occurred in Jerusalem in the very early days of the koinonia's activity there.

Luke only once mentions Christians as living in Galilee ('the church throughout Judea and Galilee and Samaria had peace and was built up': 9:31). His scheme of literary and theological composition had taken him in the Gospel from Galilee to Jerusalem, where everything is thenceforward concentrated until the great expansion takes place and the Church moves out into the rest of Judea, to semi-pagan Samaria, and then to the Greek world and finally to Rome. A great deal had to be omitted through compliance with this literary scheme. We know hardly anything from Luke about the particular achievements of most of the individual apostles; and even Peter is eventually left to depart into some anonymous place (possibly – cf. Edmundson, p. 51 cited above[8] – Rome; but to mention this would have spoilt the climax of Acts in the arrival of Paul at that city). But there must have been Christian groups in Galilee and, as we have seen, Luke at one point admits as much. We should have liked to know more about them (especially as this might have checked some ingenious scholarly speculation in our own time), just as we should have wished for better and fuller information about Palestinian Christianity generally in those primitive days. There will have been in Galilee (and in Judaea outside Jerusalem) unorganized sympathizers with the Galilean 'prophet'; and of these some, perhaps a considerable number, will have heard and accepted the good news of his resurrection. It may well be that several of the apostles, Galileans themselves, undertook the task of linking up their believing compatriots with the main group in Jerusalem, which plainly had its affiliates elsewhere in Judaea.

We thus have to think of a number of local incorporations of the koinonia. At all times, but especially in ages of poor transport and

meagre systems of communication, communion flourishes particularly in local groups: for instance, the geographical break-up of
a family imposes a great strain on its cohesion. And if it became
customary, practically from the first, for Christians to unite for
the commemoration bequeathed to the koinonia at the Last
Supper, this will have given still greater emphasis to the local
group; for a sacred meal is essentially a local celebration,
especially when it is frequently repeated. Not only *a priori*
considerations but the evidence of the Pauline Epistles shows that
in fact Christianity came into existence in local groups in the wake
of the efforts of the early missionaries and evangelizers. It has
been argued that in Paul's own writings, or at least the earlier
ones, the word 'church' designates in the first instance a local
group of believers (the church at Corinth, the churches in Galatia,
the church of the Thessalonians). But among the local groups the
church of Jerusalem was eminent for its temporal priority over the
others, for being in the place where the crucifixion had occurred,
for its status in the Jewish religion and polity which were the
matrix of Christianity, and for the concentration there of a
number of influential believers, which at first included the apostles
and later that 'brother of the Lord', James, who became the leader
of the Jerusalem Christians and held a position not unlike that of
later bishops. 'Universal Church' and 'local church' were, for a
brief but important period, identically perceived as the Church of
Jerusalem.

What was to prevent the substitution, for the single koinonia
that took shape around Jesus during his ministry, of a number of
local communities whose relationship with one another, if such
there was to be, would have to be worked out on a merely human
and contingent basis? But had this occurred, it would have spelt
the abandonment of the original notion of a single human
fellowship with a mission to the whole human family, finding its
unity in the Word of God incarnate.

We have argued above that the Holy Spirit was sent, and
indeed that he is being continually sent, to effect the survival of
the original single koinonia. But God works in history by means of
secondary created causes and agencies. Everything suggests that
the Church found itself, from its first appearance in public, at the
time of Pentecost in the year of the crucifixion of Jesus, already
possessed of leaders, the Twelve who became known as the
apostles. Arguments from silence are dangerous, but at least it is

interesting that Acts nowhere suggests that an apostle settled down to become the head of a single local Christian community.[9] And although Cullmann argued that the assumption by James, the Lord's brother, of the leadership of the Jerusalem community involved some sort of abdication on the part of Peter, the leader of the Twelve, it is in the first place to be remarked that this James was probably not one of the Twelve. Secondly, I conceive Peter as finding the source of his leadership not in the eminence of the local church of Jerusalem but in a commission given to him by Jesus himself, and as preferring to be free from this particular local tie in order to pursue an apostolic work which, while entailing the general direction of a number of local communities, would eventually, and perhaps sooner rather than later, take him to Rome. My suggestion, then, is that the unity of the universal koinonia was assured by such a more-than-merely-local leadership of the Twelve, and of any others who came to be associated with them as of comparable authority.[10]

The apostolic ministry would thus have been the historical bond of unity between the local churches, and logic requires that the apostles should have recognized some bond of unity among themselves – presumably the leadership among them of Peter, so amply attested in the New Testament as derived from Christ himself.

Merely to mention a primacy of Peter among the apostles is to raise the question of development in and of the koinonia. Claims are made today for the Pope as successor to the Petrine primacy that would have sounded strange to the first Christian generation. This therefore seems the place to observe that the koinonia, being in the full sense an historical reality, is obviously a developing thing. There has been strong Protestant reluctance to admit the possibility of a divinely guaranteed development of Christianity. Protestants have often preferred to place a quasi-fundamentalist reliance on the text of Scripture, read (if I may so put it) in a two-dimensional way. Thus, for example, if Scripture does not speak explicitly of a succession to the Petrine primacy, then such succession cannot be regarded as more than a human and contingent development, incapable of justly requiring the assent of faithful Christians. Catholicism has been similarly 'fundamentalist', to the extent that it – or its advocates – has sought to maintain that everything that it now considers irrevocable in the Church was already present in a kind of blueprint going back to

Jesus himself in his earthly ministry or his post-resurrection appearances. Are we really committed to either of these fundamentalist positions?

Analogies are dangerous. But we may ask ourselves whether the future history of an oak tree could in theory be discovered by a scientific analysis of the acorn out of which it was destined to grow. In an article entitled 'The Concept of Life' E. W. F. Tomlin speaks of 'preformation' as 'the idea that the entire adult structure pre-exists *in parvo* in the fertilized egg'.[11] The question is, however, whether the continuing living organism can be permanently affected and changed by the various environments into which it moves, without detriment to the genuine integrity of its real being. Certainly, in the case of man, the child is not committed as a human being to marriage; but if, in adulthood, the man enters into matrimony the entailed commitments become part of his genuine historical being, and he cannot renounce them without detriment to his true humanity.

Somewhat similarly, we can ask whether the future history of the physical world, in all its detail, could have been predicted by a diabolically clever intelligence from an examination of the state of the universe at the moment of the 'big bang' (supposing that the theory of the 'big bang' is acceptable). Such a supposition would raise grave difficulties for anyone who believes in human freedom of choice.

Karl Rahner has interestingly proposed[12] that decisions taken by the Church may in some instances have been genuinely 'free', in the sense of not having been determined *a priori* by the original 'blueprint', and yet – by virtue of their enactment under the guidance of the Holy Spirit – may have been either strictly irreversible or at least guaranteed, while they continue in force, as expressions of 'divine law'.

In any case it would seem as if the first major crisis (possibly the greatest of all crises so far) in the Church after the first Christian Pentecost was resolved by a step for which it was difficult to find clear warranty in the actual words of Jesus. I refer, of course, to the Jewish-Gentile crisis which, according to Acts, was the occasion for a decision at a 'Council' in Jerusalem in favour of the Gentiles. For what it is worth, the 'decree' of that Council, as given in Acts, makes no reference to any words of Jesus; the Council is content to appeal to its own authority and that of the Holy Spirit: 'It has seemed good to the Holy Spirit and to us ...' The Church, in fact, was becoming more itself[13] not by a conservative appeal to the past but by a bold adventure into an uncharted future, under the guidance of the Holy Spirit. The decision thus taken was of course extremely vulnerable to the criticism of conservatives.

Criticisms were not wanting, nor were they easily met. The letters of Paul show how his own missionary work in particular was harried by the opposition of the irreconcilable Judaizers.[14] It has been argued that his great collection from his Hellenistic churches for the impoverished Christians of Jerusalem was an effort to reassert the universal koinonia and its unity in face of the hostility still existing in the homeland to the Gentile mission and its principles. Even Luke, who does not like exposing the existence of disharmony in the Church, has to admit that Paul's visit to Jerusalem on the occasion of the collection was held to raise most awkward and delicate problems in public relations among the Christians themselves. When, some years later, the whole situation in Palestine was radically altered by the destruction of Jerusalem and the Temple, it is not unlikely that Palestinian Christianity began gradually to lose contact with what was by then predominantly a Hellenistic Church. This slow process of dissociation may have been further assisted by the growing unreflective sense of the inadequacy of the terms and concepts of Jewish-Palestinian thought for the expression of the new Christian insight. The 'conservatives' in the Hellenistic churches would have suffered alike from the loss of their strong Palestinian bases of support and from this obsolescence of their theology. The future in the koinonia lay with those who accepted the findings of the Council of Jerusalem and were prepared to work out their consequences.

Meanwhile, the first fruits of the enormously dynamic missionary enterprise of the first Christian generation were taking shape in the often turbulent, but presumably not entirely unordered, life of numerous local churches from Antioch and Damascus to Rome. There is evidence of a strongly 'charismatic' or 'pentecostal' element in the life of the primitive Church. We seem to be presented with a body or a movement in which enthusiasm was intense and sometimes uncontrolled. Luke's account of the first Christian Pentecost may be coloured by the memory of such enthusiasm. It seemed natural, as men looked back from the last decades of the century to the origins of the

Church, to suppose that these origins were accompanied by preternatural marvels: '... a sound came from heaven like the rush of a mighty wind, and it filled all the house where they were sitting. And there appeared to them tongues as of fire, distributed and resting on each one of them. And they were all filled with the Holy Spirit and began to speak in other tongues, as the Spirit gave them utterance'. 'Many wonders and signs were done through the apostles' – Luke's instinct is to connect these marvels with the governance of the Twelve (Acts 2:43), and he particularizes: a crippled man is cured by Peter's word and hand; and the man 'entered the temple with them, walking and leaping and praising God'. A little later there is a sort of repetition of the Pentecost experience: 'And when they had prayed, the place in which they were gathered together was shaken; and they were all filled with the Holy Spirit and spoke the word of God with boldness' (4:31). Miracles abounded, including the somewhat macabre miracle of the deaths of Ananias and his wife; and people flocked to the apostles and found healing – not least through Peter, whose very shadow was, it was hoped, capable of curing illness. We seem to have here a mixture reminding us at once of the strangeness of modern pentecostalism and the memories of the epic days of the beginning of some great new social-political enterprise like the start of the Communist revolution.

Nor were such phenomena restricted to the once-for-all beginnings of the koinonia. Judging from the First Epistle of Paul to the Corinthians, they were apt to occur elsewhere, when a new local church was founded. Paul's chapter on charisms (1 Cor. 12) is revealing; and Paul is writing as a contemporary, not, like Luke, picking up stories that had circulated about a period which was passing away, one may surmise, already before Luke's own conversion. The phenomena are those of folk religion and are of course, in a general sense, not limited to the apostolic age of the Church, nor indeed to Christianity itself. But already in Paul's letter to the Corinthians we see how Church authority and common sense came to react to all this, to attempt to place some control over the exuberance, and (at least in Paul's case) to take up the underlying – and by him accepted – assumption of the energetic working of the Holy Spirit in the koinonia and to transmute it into a glorification of the basic Christian doctrine of love: 'If I speak in the tongues of men and of angels, but have not love, I am a noisy gong or a clanging cymbal. And if I have prophetic powers, and understand all mysteries and all knowledge, and if I have all faith, so as to remove mountains, but have not love, I am nothing'. Nay, 'If I give away all I have' like the Christian commune of Jerusalem in those first days as depicted by Luke, 'and if I deliver my body to be burned' (the early Christian passion for martyrdom is vividly exemplified in St Ignatius of Antioch in the early second century), 'but have not love, I gain nothing' (1 Cor. 13:1–3).

The primitive Church was already a thing of considerable complexity, and it would be false to depict it either as 'merely pentecostalism' or as a sober anticipation of a well-ordered bourgeois Roman Catholic parish of today. Above, and surveying, the enthusaism were the apostles, and Luke not only lays quiet emphasis on their own immediate authority but (in chapter 6) exhibits them as commissioning others to exert authority in the koinonia. The occasion of the appointment of 'the Seven' was, indeed, not the alarming exuberance of charismatics but a more mundane complaint about equal distribution of this world's goods:

> The Hellenists (sc. Greek-speaking Jewish converts to Christianity) murmured against the Hebrews because their widows were neglected in the daily distribution. And the twelve ... said: 'It is not right that we should give up preaching the word of God to serve tables. Therefore, brethren, pick out from among you seven men of good repute ... whom we may appoint to this duty. ... And what they said pleased the multitude, and they chose (seven men) ... These they set before the apostles, and they prayed and laid their hands upon them.

This passage is sometimes appealed to as the inauguration of the office of deacons (as in our present threefold ministry). The word for 'to serve' tables is indeed the verb corresponding to 'deacon' (Greek *diakonos*, a server). But Luke does not here (or anywhere else in his two books) use the noun. It is surely more important that the passage may indicate Luke's sense that office in the Church is ultimately derived from the apostles, themselves directly commissioned by Jesus Christ.

We may compare his account of Paul's return journey on his first missionary expedition into Asia Minor (Acts 14). Paul and Barnabas 'returned to Lystra and to Iconium and to Antioch' in Pisidia, 'strengthening the souls of the disciples ... And when they

had appointed elders *(presbuteroi)* for them in every church, ...
they committed them to the Lord in whom they believed'. Here
again, if we can trust Luke, we have good evidence of both the
primitive Christian sense (which was also common sense) that a
continuing community must have officials, and the equally
primitive sense that all such authority in the Church must have an
apostolic origin and an ultimate derivation from the authority
entrusted to Paul and the Twelve by Christ. The Church was not
to be abandoned to charismatic anarchy – nor, indeed, to mere
democracy; though it is interesting to note that 'the Seven' were
selected by the multitude before having hands laid on them by the
apostles.

Acts does not state that 'the Seven' had any authority from the
apostles that would extend beyond the limits of the local situation.
Nor are we given to understand that the 'presbyters' appointed by
Paul in Asia Minor had more than a local sphere of duties. The
local churches were the great exhibition of the power of the gospel,
and it was to be expected that much of the energy of the Christian
movement should be expended on the nursing of, and caring for,
these communities. But the apostles were growing old and dying.
What was to become of the concept and reality of a single
universal Christian communion?

We need not doubt that there was a very strong sense of
more-than-local unity among the adherents of a movement that
had first to express its identity in difference from Judaism, and
then came under the fires of persecution. The abiding coherence of
the great Eastern Orthodox Communion, and nearer home the
survival of the Anglican Communion as a world-wide brotherhood,
show that such sentiments of identity and loyalty can hold
together groups separated both geographically and culturally
without an overarching unitary authority in daily exercise of its
functions. But was everything left, and to be left, to such interior
sentiments of sympathy and mutual allegiance in a new religious
movement that had only the shortest separate history behind it in
which to develop a strong particular tradition?

We have seen, in the case of Paul, that an 'apostle' could
continue to exercise authority over a number of local churches, for
example those that looked to him as their founder. The same may
be inferred from the First Epistle of Peter, at least if the author of
this Epistle is held to have been in some sense genuinely Peter. *A
priori* considerations would lead us to suppose that the same might

be true of others of the Twelve whose individual history is unknown to us.

The Epistles to Timothy and that to Titus (referred to collectively by modern scholars as 'the Pastoral Epistles') show a similar oversight of several local communities by one man; but here the one man is not an apostle but is represented as holding an apostle's commission: George A. Denzer describes Timothy and Titus as Paul's 'legates' in the regions of Ephesus and Crete respectively.[15] In the case of Titus, it is clear that the sphere of authority entrusted to him was wider than a single local church: 'This is why I left you in Crete, that you might ... appoint elders *(presbuterous)* in every town as I directed you' (1:5). It would seem that originally the several local churches were each managed by a group of functionaries named presbyters.[16] They were not wholly autonomous, since – at least if they were of apostolic foundation – each local church looked beyond its own membership to the authority of its apostolic founder. In the Epistle to Titus this supervision over a *number* of local Christian communities ('in every town') is delegated or transmitted by the apostle to Titus, who was not himself an apostle.

The Pauline authorship and the dates of the Pastoral Epistles have been hotly disputed in modern times. Denzer states the arguments on both sides, and makes out a case for placing these Epistles in the first rather than the second century. My impression is that they (at least the Epistle to Titus) delineate a stage in the evolution of office in the Church that is anterior to that which the Epistles of Ignatius of Antioch (first or second decade of the second century, if they are authentic) take for granted.

A similar stage of evolution to that evidenced by the Epistle of Titus is suggested by the Johannine Epistles. Here, again, questions of authorship and dating are disputed. Bruce Vawter *(Jerome Biblical Commentary)* says that 2 and 3 John are addressed 'to individual churches of a single town or area. The "Lady Elect" who is the recipient of 2 John can only be one of the local churches within the author's jurisdiction'.[17] Similarly, Vawter says: 'The character of 1 John is that of an epistle to several churches of a given area'.[18] He also thinks that all three Epistles are from the same hand and adds: '... the literary relation of 1 John with the Gospel of John makes it ... likely that the same secretary-disciple of John the Apostle is responsible for the writing of both the Gospel and the epistles'.[19] For our purposes, it is more important to infer that a date towards the end of the first century for the writing of these Epistles is quite defensible.[20] As in the Pastoral Epistles, we appear to be presented with a state of affairs in which above the 'local churches' (whether of a town or of an area) there is the authority of some major personage who, if not an apostle, has (in the case of Titus) or can be thought to have (in the case of the author of the Johannine Epistles) an authority deriving from an apostle or from personal standing in relation to an apostle.

We may now turn to the uncanonical document known among scholars as 'The First Epistle of Clement to the Corinthians'. Scholars usually date this Letter to A.D. 95–6, though Robinson claims that 70, the date proposed by Edmundson, merits 'the most serious consideration'.[21]

In this Epistle the author (whether as leader of the local church of Rome or, if not yet such, as Edmundson thought, then its secretary) is trying to heal a state of conflict in the church of Corinth, due not (as when Paul wrote the First Epistle to the Corinthians) to the threat of charismatic anarchy, but to rivalry about office-holding in the local community. The importance of his letter, for our present purpose, is that it strongly confirms the view that office in the early Church (what today we should call 'the ordained ministry') was seen as deriving its authority from the historical (or resurrectional) Jesus Christ through the apostles, commissioned by him and commissioning others in their turn. Clement writes:

The Apostles received the Gospel for us from the Lord Jesus Christ: Jesus Christ was sent forth from God. So then Christ is from God, and the Apostles are from Christ. Both, therefore, came of the will of God in the appointed order. ... [The Apostles went forth, and,] so preaching everywhere in country and town, they appointed their first fruits, when they had proved them by the Spirit, to be bishops[22] and deacons unto them that should believe. And this they did in no new fashion: ... for thus saith the Scripture in a certain place: 'I will appoint their bishops in righteousness and their deacons in faith.' And what marvel, if they which were entrusted in Christ with such a work by God, appointed the aforesaid persons?

Then, referring to Moses' appointment of the tribe of Levi for the priesthood, he continues:

... that disorder might not arise in Israel, he did this, to the end that the Name of the true and only God might be glorified. ... And our Apostles knew through our Lord Jesus Christ that there would be strife over the name of the bishop's office. For this cause, therefore, ... they appointed the aforesaid persons, and afterwards they provided a continuance (or better, gave a further injunction), that if these should fall asleep, other approved men should succeed to their ministration. Those, therefore, who were appointed by them, or afterward by other men of repute with the consent of the whole Church, and have ministered unblameably to the flock of Christ ... these men we consider to be unjustly thrown out from their ministration.

I have borrowed the above translation from H. F. Hamilton, *The People of God.*[23] Clement's line of argument is worth considering as evidence for a conviction which was surely not confined to himself. Hamilton remarks:

'... if St. Clement contemplated a class of presbyters who might be described as not from the Apostles, the whole sequence of the argument is destroyed: still more, if St. Clement had thought that the Corinthians would be able to point to a regular class of presbyters in any part of the world, who were not from the Apostles, then he must have realized that his argument from the divine order and sequence could carry no weight. ... the usurpers [who apparently had the authority of the Corinthian church behind them but not that of the apostles] 'must submit and withdraw entirely [Ep. Clem. 54f.]. And if we ask why, the reason given is because the new arrangement is not in accordance with the order appointed by the will of God, which involves a sequence through Christ and the Apostles. ... The casual, not to say incidental, way in which the fact of Apostolic appointment is mentioned, although the whole decision rests ultimately upon this fact, shows how completely the Roman Church assumed unquestioning acquiescence in the fact. ... This letter has the value of contemporary evidence on the question of appointment of clergy by the Apostles.[24]

Hamilton also notes that, since for Clement the words 'bishop' and 'presbyter' were still synonymous, he had no special word for 'men authorized by the apostles to appoint presbyters' – hence he calls these simply 'men of repute'.[25]

The Epistle of Clement is concerned with order in a local church. It offers a solution to the problems raised in the church of Corinth by appeal to the practice of the universal Church, a practice which it represents as a carrying on of arrangements made by the apostles (and ultimately, by way of the source of apostolic authority in Christ, by God himself). The Epistle implies that there is a universal Church order; and it tacitly assumes that the universal Church is 'prior' to the local church. Clement, in other words, is in no doubt that the koinonia is a super-local reality. Nor does he doubt that it has a structure which, because it is divine, cannot be rejected by any local realization of the koinonia on its own authority. His reference to 'the consent of the whole Church' is important, and has lessons for us today; but Clement does not derive the authority of the special group of officials, who are the pivot of his argument, from this consent, but from their role as successors of the apostles. There is no hint in the Epistle of Clement that these officials have (yet) assumed the position of heads, each of one local church. But they can be taken as the links between the apostles and the 'bishops' in the more modern sense of that term. They would seem to fall into the same class as Titus (and Timothy?) in the Pastoral Epistles, and perhaps as the 'Presbyter' who is the author of 2 and 3 John.

The course of our investigation has taken us from the charismatic excitements of the Church in its first origins to something approaching the institutional, hierarchical, model of the Church with which we have become familiar in later ages. It would be a pity if 'charismatic' and 'hierarchical-institutional' were to be regarded as mutually exclusive. But a phase of stabilization is to be expected in any human grouping after the first, fine, careless rapture of its inspired beginnings; and experience shows that without structure no such grouping has much chance of prolonged survival. The charismatic element of course did not die out of the Church. It may be that under the fires of persecution it tended to become canalized in the mystique of martyrdom, exemplified for instance in the Epistles of Ignatius of Antioch – though in the case of Ignatius something must surely be ascribed to his ebullient Syrian temperament.

Chapter VII

The Church in Antiquity

The purpose of this chapter is not to offer a sketch of early Church history. Rather it is to pursue a hypothesis and to seek support for it in the witness of Christian antiquity. The hypothesis concerns the koinonia which, I have argued, is integral to the mystery of a new divine order, involving an 'elevation' of the created order to a higher level. This new order was established in the resurrection of Christ and, being an historical order, is subject to the growth and development that characterize every historical movement.

But the new order is not only historical and therefore developing. It is eschatological, in the sense that its consummation and goal are in the post-historic dimension of that heavenly glory into which Christ by his ascension has already entered. This post-historic goal gives the new order its orientation and indeed is already implicit in its historical development; just as the glorified Christ was truly anticipated in his earthly and historical existence in Palestine two thousand years ago. Everything in Christianity as it makes its way through time is thus at once marked with the pledge, and actuated by the germ, of eternity. But it remains in a true sense provisional, inevitably imperfect, and only not precarious because the Holy Spirit at all times sustains the new order in existence and preserves it from the ultimate threats of temporality. This is true of the koinonia itself. In history it is imperfect, always falling short of the ideal which it incorporates. It is part of human history, and humanity, though redeemed, is on the whole not yet either inerrant or impeccable. Thus, from the first Easter onwards, there will always, here on earth, be something wanting to the credibility of the koinonia; and those who demand a Utopia or an earthly paradise will always be able to turn away from the koinonia as failing to measure up to the standards they have set it. It is in keeping with the mercy of God, however, that he does not abandon those he has redeemed because they fail to attain on earth a perfection which is promised to them in heaven. The Second Vatican Council has some wise words about the 'eschatological nature of the pilgrim Church':

> The Church ... will attain her full perfection only in the glory of heaven. Then ... the entire world, which is intimately related to man and achieves its purpose through him, will be perfectly re-established in Christ. ... the promised restoration which we are awaiting has already begun in Christ, is carried forward in the mission of the Holy Spirit, and through Him continues in the Church. ... The final age of the world has already come upon us. ... The renovation of the world has been irrevocably decreed and in this age is already anticipated in some real way. For even now on this earth the Church is marked with a genuine though imperfect holiness. However, until there is a new heaven and a new earth where justice dwells ..., the pilgrim Church in her sacraments and institutions, which pertain to this present time, takes on the appearance of this passing world.[1]

I have suggested – and this is the hypothesis in question – that the koinonia is to be identified with what Christians call 'the Church'. There are reasons for this hypothesis. In the first place, it is intrinsic to the idea of the koinonia that it propagates its Message and, in so doing, propagates itself. In order that the Message may find acceptance, it is necessary that the koinonia should be itself a recognizable entity in general human history. As Jesus was a person taking his stand in public history, so too must the koinonia be something publicly recognizable. Hence it is right to seek in history for the continuing life of the koinonia. One consequence follows immediately: a human grouping that has ceased to exist has, by that very fact, lost its right to consideration as a credible claimant for the role of the koinonia. For it is intrinsic to the divine purpose in Christ and in the koinonia that the koinonia shall survive to the end of history. Thus, to take an example, in the third century there was constituted, under the aegis of Novatian (a claimant to the See of Rome) a body of

Christians who claimed to be the true Church and denied that title to those who preferred to acknowledge the claims to the See of Rome of Novatian's rival, Cornelius. The Novatianist Church survived into the fourth century, but has long ceased to exist. We can therefore infer with certainty that its claim to be the koinonia was false. The body of Christians, in and outside Rome, who aligned themselves with Cornelius still exists and all modern Christian churches derive their descent from the apostolic age of Christianity through this body which the Novatianists rejected.

I am of course aware that this appeal to the death of a group as a proof that it was not the koinonia sounds brutal: *les absents ont toujours tort!* But the proof follows inevitably from the fact that the koinonia has a continuing existence guaranteed by God: the gates of hell will not prevail against it.

All existing Christian groups derive from the Great Church of the early fifth century. They include, along with groups whose separate existence does not antedate the Reformation, the Roman Catholic Church, the Eastern Orthodox Communion, the group that derives from those who rejected the decisions of the Council of Ephesus (431), and the churches who have not accepted the Formula of Chalcedon (451). Any existing Christian group could claim to be the koinonia. At a later stage we shall have to consider the suggestion made today that none of them by itself is the koinonia, but that – in some way or another – the koinonia maintains a disintegrated existence in all of them taken together.

If none of these claims or hypotheses is accepted, we are reduced to saying (since the koinonia must exist) that the koinonia carries on an existence that is not visible to the naked eye. But such a proposal can I think be rejected out of hand. If the koinonia is not historically visible, it cannot be presenting the divine challenge to humanity and it has no credibility; and credibility is of the essence of the Message and of the koinonia to which the Message is entrusted. It follows that, at least up to 431, the koinonia is to be identified with the only Christian body that has not disappeared from the stage of history: the 'Catholic Church' which was established by Theodosius I in 391 as the religion of the Roman Empire.

1 Clement of Rome

The fragmentary nature of our evidence for the apostolic age of Christianity has already been noted. The same is true of the subapostolic age. The Church only comes into the full light of general history with the Peace of Constantine in the fourth century. Our historical reconstruction of the early Church and of its fortunes is necessarily, therefore, comparable to the scientists' reconstruction of a dinosaur or of primitive man from incomplete skeletons. On the other hand, it must be dangerous to base arguments on the *lack* of evidence. In this connection, some remarks of Hamilton are important:

> ... the closer one examines the literature of the early Churches, the more one is surprised at the constant intercourse which was kept up between the most distant parts of Christendom. As examples one may cite the frequent references to hospitality in the New Testament and the activity of the travelling missionaries. 'Whether as the bearers of letters from one Church to another, or as living letters read of all men, the Apostles, Prophets, Evangelists, Pastors, and Teachers kept the life-blood of the Church in circulation ... It is to them that we owe the fact that there is one Bible everywhere received in the Church, one Creed, one weekly holyday, one Baptism, and one Eucharist.' So writes Dr. Wordsworth. And so also Sir William Ramsay: 'From the first the Christian idea was to annihilate the separation due to space, and hold the most distant brother as near as the nearest.' ... it is of course one of the commonplaces of Roman History that intercourse between the capital and every part of the Empire was direct and easy.[2]

With this background in mind, we shall often be justified in generalizing from particular authors of items of information. Thus Hamilton argued that Clement's confident appeal to the principle that official authority in the Church is only legitimate if derived via the Apostles from Christ is strong evidence that such was indeed the conviction and normal practice of the Church of his day.

Clement's letter was prompted by the news of dissension and what he sees as a contravention of due order in the church of Corinth: legitimate presbyters have been extruded from their administration, and men who are not in the legitimate succession have replaced them. But the local church of Corinth is a local representative of what Clement calls 'the nation', that is to say the Church, chosen by God. The members of the Church are 'in all the world'. The local church, therefore, cannot decide things simply by itself without reference to the general order of the universal Church. (One is reminded of Paul's 'knock-down' argument against women appearing unveiled in the local church assembly: 'We have no such custom, neither the churches of God').

Thus Clement views the Church as a universal reality transcending its local manifestations, and held together by common practices and principles, in a divine ordering which controls legitimate local diversity. He is fond of military metaphors: Christians are like soldiers; and soldiers must follow the lead of their officers. The legitimate presbyters are like officers in the Church. The result of due discipline, says Clement, will be *homonoia* – agreement in mind, or concord. *Concors* and its derivatives will be favourite words in the third century with Cyprian. Cyprian uses this word-group to refer to the harmony and mutual agreement which should characterize the relations of bishops throughout the world. It is obvious that, if common possession (e.g. a common faith) produces relatedness, and if these 'ontological relations' need to be developed into personal relations, then 'concord' assumes a place of primary importance. When it is impossible to attain concord, either the community will break up or it will be necessary to have some court of appeal or arbitration which can impose a decision on conflicting parties.

The Epistle of Clement takes it for granted that, although Corinth is a Pauline foundation and Rome is not, the local church of Rome has a perfect right to intervene in the affairs of the church of Corinth, when events in the latter church threaten internal concord and even seem to disregard the general order of the universal Church. This signifies that no local church is an island. However autonomous a local church may be (a modern word would be 'autocephalous'), still no such church is entitled to regulate its own affairs in its own way when that way would be basically different from the way of the universal Church. The particular example in this Epistle is the official status of the presbyters: a local church must have presbyters who are in what today would be called the apostolic succession. It will be noted that in this matter questions of Church unity fuse with questions of legitimate authority in the Church. If presbyters are like army officers, being invested with a duty and rights of leadership, then their title to office must be valid; they must have received their office from those who are already within the succession from the apostles.

The Church, we conclude, is in Clement's view not a purely spiritual affair without tangible historical embodiment. On the contrary, it is so fully historical that it takes shape, like other historical realities of communion or fellowship, as an 'institution' with officers and at least the embryo of a 'rule': Clement's notion of the Church is thus in harmony with that of the New Testament writers. Some modern scholars even date some of the New Testament documents after the year 100. In that case, an historian would place the Epistle of Clement within the New Testament age, since it seems to be agreed that it was written not later than 97. It is an invaluable link in our chain of evidences for the history of the Church. And we happen to know that late in the second century it was still regarded with veneration in the church of Corinth to which it was addressed.

2 Ignatius of Antioch

About a century ago the great English scholar, J. B. Lightfoot, following in the steps of an earlier Englishman and fellow Anglican, John Pearson, took in hand to establish the authenticity of the seven Epistles of Ignatius of Antioch. Lightfoot's findings are still questioned from time to time (they are disputed at this moment by at least two scholars, working – so far as I am aware – independently). The present essay is not the place to enter into this dispute. I understand that Lightfoot's thesis still commands the assent of the majority of scholars entitled to judge in this field. In what follows, I assume the genuineness of the Epistles, which in that case must date from about twenty years after the Epistle of Clement (accepting 96–97 as the date of the latter).

These Letters are written by the bishop of Antioch in Syria during his journey under arrest to Rome, where he was to suffer martyrdom as a Christian. We have seen that Clement is concerned for the unity and concord of the universal Church. Ignatius' central interest in these Letters is the internal unity of the local church. This unity comes to full expression, in his view, in the celebration of the Eucharist. The unity depends upon the local bishop, with the local presbyters surrounding him and in harmony with him, and with the assistance of the deacons. The Eucharist is to be celebrated by the bishop or by someone whom he delegates; it must not be celebrated by an unauthorized person.

Thus the Letters of Ignatius exhibit the Church, the koinonia, in its local manifestations as both eucharistic and institutional; a bishop is an office-holder in an institutional situation.

Ignatius has less to say about the unity of the universal Church. It is manifest, however, that the churches to and from which he writes are in close touch with one another. And although he comes from distant Antioch he takes it for granted that his advice to the local churches of Asia Minor will not cause offence. He writes also to the local church of Rome, asking the Christians there not to prevent his martyrdom, but also begging that church to take care of his own widowed church of Antioch. There is also a reference (*Ep. Smyrn.* 1:2) to the 'one body' of the Church, where Ignatius can hardly be thinking in terms merely of the local church:

> Christ through his resurrection has set up a standard for his saints and believers both among Jews and Gentiles, in one body of his Church.[3]

In the same letter to the church of Smyrna (8:2) we read:

> There where the bishop appears there should the collectivity (of the believers) be, just as where Jesus is, there is the catholic church.[4]

This is the first appearance in extant Christian literature of the word 'catholic'. In ordinary Greek usage this word signified 'general' as opposed to 'particular'. It is natural to suppose that this is the meaning underlying Ignatius' use of the word: the local church, unified in its bishop, is not entirely isolated; it takes its place in a wider whole in which Christ is the supreme unifying principle – the shared 'possession' of the believing koinonia. It is worth remarking that, in this first known Christian use of the word 'catholic', it refers not to doctrine but to the Christian Church. It is possible to argue that, when it was later applied to doctrine, it indicated doctrine that was guaranteed as true because it was the doctrine of the Catholic Church. It is not orthodoxy that makes a Christian or causes a Christian group to be Church, but belonging to the Church that ensures that one's beliefs are orthodox.

It is just possible that there is a third reference in Ignatius to the universal Church. There are passages in his letters where the word 'love' *(agape)* seems to mean not the abstract virtue of charity but its concrete realization as a local Christian church. Thus we read of 'the love of the Ephesians', 'the love of the brethren of Troy', 'the love of (the) Smyrnaeans and Ephesians'.[5] This use of the word *agape*, it has been suggested, gives the key to the description, in the Letter to the Romans, of the local church of that city as 'presiding over the *agape*'. There would be nothing surprising in the idea that the bishop of Rome presided over the *agape* of the local Roman church. But over what does the church of Rome herself preside? The suggestion is that this church presides over the *universal agape*, that is, the universal koinonia, the Catholic Church. It may be remarked, in passing, that *agape*, along with *eirene* or *pax*, is sometimes in later Christian documents used as a virtual synonym of 'communion' or koinonia.

When we compare Ignatius' Letters with the Epistle of Clement we note that Ignatius takes for granted, apparently as a universal Christian phenomenon, the leadership in each local church of a single bishop *(episkopos)* who is distinguished from the presbyters who form a sort of 'college' of which he is the head. In the Epistle of Clement the two words *episkopos* and *presbuteros* seem still (as, apparently, in New Testament passages) to refer to the same person. Does this difference of terminology between Clement and Ignatius show that the local ministry had, between 96 and the date of Ignatius' journey to Rome (perhaps about 116), taken a remarkable step forward from 'oligarchy' to 'monarchy'? Twenty years seems rather a short time for such a change to be effected, a change in no way foreshadowed in the Epistle of Clement, and for its effect to be taken utterly for granted by Ignatius. If we could accept an earlier date for the Epistle of Clement the difficulty would be eased. On the other hand, accepting the usual date proposed for that Epistle, it has been suggested that development had been more rapid in the East than in the West. But this implies that Ignatius was blissfully unaware that the West, to which he was actually on the way when he wrote, did not accept his 'monepiscopal' ecclesiology, although he himself takes it as something essential to the whole Christian picture. It seems to me just possible *(a)* that *terminology* in the West had not kept up with historical development, *(b)* that the 'bishop' or 'leading presbyter' of the church of Corinth was mixed up in the troubles there in some way that made it impolitic for Clement to refer to him and his special office explicitly.

The question remains, How did the Church in fact move from the ministerial arrangements evidenced in the New Testament to the 'threefold ministry' as evidenced by Ignatius and the subsequent history of the Church?

I have suggested, in the previous chapter, that the key figures were those representatives of apostles of whom Titus (in the Epistle to Titus) is an obvious example: Paul, as depicted in this Epistle, has authorized Titus to exercise a ministry similar to his own over a number of local churches. Since Titus was not an 'apostle' one might be tempted to describe him as a 'proto-bishop'; but this would overlook the fact that he ruled over a *number* of local churches, while a bishop ruled over only one. On the other hand, officials like Titus would be examples of men who were not apostles yet had a leadership status that was superior to the 'colleges' of local presbyters such as those mentioned as appointed by Paul in Asia Minor. As Titus and others like him grew old, they might well have transmitted their powers to *individuals* chosen from the presbyterates of their local churches, and these individuals would thus have been the first genuine 'bishops' – with powers of ministerial transmission derived from Titus and the others, just as Titus' powers were derived from the apostles and the powers of the apostles from Christ. What does require consideration is that, so far as we know, this transition from oligarchy to monarchy took place almost everywhere, and without provoking controversy or ill will. The result: bishops in their local churches, and the episcopal *ordo* as having authority over the universal Church, are the only claimants to fulfilling the principle of apostolic succession appealed to by Clement as unquestionable. The special case of the bishop of Rome and the connected issue of the 'Petrine primacy' may be left over for later consideration.[6]

3. Irenaeus

The Christian religion is not, basically, a religion finding its unity and true nature only in a series of true propositions. It is indeed a religion of 'word', no less a word than the Word of God incarnate. But 'incarnation' means that the divine revelation is not a statement but a person: Jesus Christ, born of Mary, crucified under Pontius Pilate, raised from the dead and glorified in heaven.

This Word is offered to man, and Christianity begins with the acceptance of the Word *as* divine Word. And this implies an act of faith, a cognitive act, a 'judgement'. The act of Christian faith is the act of (interiorly) saying 'Yes' to the content of the revelation. Inevitably, this faith is not only saying Yes to Jesus Christ, but saying (again interiorly, and not necessarily in human words) *that* Jesus Christ is such as the revelation discloses him as being. Paul, in Rom. 10:9, particularizes with special reference to the resurrection of Christ: 'If you ... believe in your heart that God raised (Christ) from the dead, you will be saved'. Faith 'in' inevitably involves faith 'that'.

We can call Jesus Christ and the truths relating to him ('we believe *that* ...') the 'content' of faith, as distinct from the act of faith; the act of faith involves assent to this content. If our hypothesis in this essay is correct, that Jesus is the fountainhead and shared 'possession' of the koinonia, to which koinonia the preservation and propagation of the revelation have been entrusted, then it can be inferred that the content of Christian faith, or 'the faith' as distinct from 'faith', belongs primarily to the koinonia, and only secondarily to the individual believer, who receives it from the koinonia. The faith is expressed in many ways in the life of the koinonia, and not least in its official common worship. In particular, it is expressed in human statements. I have already pointed out that Paul held that the word of God was conveyed to the Thessalonians in the human words with which he preached the gospel to them (1 Thess. 2:13). Modern scholarship has sought to make a list of faith-statements in the New Testament books that can be regarded as having being used, already in those primitive days, as both expressions and norms of what we today call 'orthodoxy', correct belief: 'Jesus is the Christ', 'Jesus is Lord', 'Jesus is the Son of God', and so on. Such formulas are, inevitably, not only expressions, but interpretations, of the revelation. And as soon as an interpretation is formulated in words, a continuing process is initiated – for every statement itself requires to be understood and therefore interpreted. A tension can arise between adherence to a traditional formula – perhaps little understood – and acceptance of a proffered interpretation of it, which may or may not be faithful to its genuine meaning. The struggle for orthodoxy against heresy, like the closely connected struggle between unity in the koinonia and schism, is an inescapable part of Christian history.

Already in the New Testament there is evidence of this struggle: Paul warning the Galatians against those who offer them a pseudo-gospel; Paul warning the Colossians against what looks like the influence of a sort of primitive Judaeo-Gnosticism; the author of 1 John denouncing the antichrists for their refusal to acknowledge in Jesus the actual incarnation of God's Word.

The trouble at Corinth leading to Clement's Epistle does not seem to have been doctrinal so much as 'political' – the sort of thing that would tend to schism rather than to heresy. But a recurrent theme in the Letters of Ignatius is the peril of what came to be known as docetism: the notion that Christ's humanity was something less than real.[7]

Before the end of the second century Gnosticism had become a serious problem for the Church. It is taken up by Irenaeus of Lyons in his great work *Against the Heresies.* He points out that the Gnostics have theories and doctrines which vary from sect to sect. These theories contradict the teaching of the Church. The question is: do they also contradict the truth of God as guaranteed through the processes of historical revelation? Yes, says Irenaeus, we can be sure that they do, and that precisely because of their discrepancy from the Church's teaching. For the truths of God, announced by the prophets of ancient Israel, were reaffirmed by Jesus Christ in person. By him they were entrusted to the apostles. Some of the apostolic teaching is enshrined in the four Gospels. Today their teaching is still propagated by the 'presbyters' (who include, or are identical with, the bishops). Hence, if you want to know the revealed doctrine, you have only to consult the bishops who, in every local church, are in legitimate succession from the apostles. These bishops have received (we must suppose, collectively) a 'sure grace-gift of truth'. If you look around the world you will see that there is unanimity of belief and doctrine in the local churches everywhere. In fact

The Church, planted throughout the world ... has received from the apostles and their disciples the faith in 'one God, the almighty Father ...' (he quotes what is in effect a Creed).[8]

Professing thus an identical faith everywhere, the Church has a single heart and soul, one voice, one mouth; the languages of the world are indeed multiple, but the (orthodox Christian) tradition is one. There is one sun for the entire universe. So too the preaching of the truth is the light that shines everywhere and enlightens all men who will know it.

> No longer must we receive the truth from others; that truth which it is easy to receive from the Church, since the apostles have stored up all truth in it, as though into a rich treasury. ...[9]

Irenaeus admits that some small point might lead to dispute among Christians. In that case, one should have recourse to the most ancient (local) churches, in which the apostles lived, and receive from them clear and certain truth about the questions at issue.[10]

In any case, schism is not the right way out of such doctrinal disputes.

> God will judge those who effect schisms, who are void of the love of God and look only to their own advantage and not to the unity of the Church; and who for slight and trifling causes cut and rend the glorious body of Christ and do their best to destroy it; who speak peace while they make war, straining out the gnat and swallowing the camel. For no reform that they can bring about is commensurate with the mischief of schism.[11]

In thus denouncing schism Irenaeus is at one with a long line of successors among the Fathers, and undoubtedly expresses the mind of the ancient Church. Nor is he alone when he speaks of schismatics 'cutting and rending' the Church. But if you do indeed cut something, it might be objected, then neither of the ensuing pieces by itself *is* the whole thing thus cut up. And this is in fact the contention of many modern 'ecumenists': they hold that it is flying in the face of facts to maintain that in a Christianity rent by schism the unity of the Church has not been lost. Such, however, is not the view of Irenaeus or of the ancient Church as a whole. In a curious symbolic treatment of Lot's wife, turned to a pillar of salt, Irenaeus writes:

> (Lot's) wife remained in Sodom, no longer corruptible flesh but

an ever-abiding statue of salt … thus showing that the Church also, the salt of the earth, is left in earth's confines, enduring a human lot. And, while often whole limbs are removed from her, she abides, a statue of salt, the firmament of faith, confirming and dispatching sons to their Father.[12]

In other words, the mutilation caused by schism does not in fact destroy the unity of the body from which the schismatics have separated themselves. Despite all such renderings – 'schism' means a 'cutting' – the Church remains one and united; and, so remaining, it is the pillar of right belief and the home of salvation. In the terms of the hypothesis of this essay, we shall say that the koinonia is a visible and enduring historical reality. Its visible unity is indeed integral to its nature and essential to its function. Whether it is a single man who leaves that visible unity or whether schism becomes the characteristic of whole groups of Christians – and even if a bishop or a group of bishops should remove whole sectors of Christianity from the unity of the koinonia – nevertheless the koinonia abides; schism is not 'in' but 'from' the Church, whose unity is no mere historical accident but something guaranteed by God and effectuated by the continuing protection and guidance of the Holy Spirit.

4. Cyprian

Irenaeus, though bishop of Lyons in Gaul, came from Asia Minor, where he had sat at the feet of Polycarp the martyr; and Polycarp, he tells us, had known John 'the disciple of the Lord'. This John, despite the questioning of some modern scholars, was probably – in Irenaeus' mind – the apostle and the author of the Gospel. The chronology is quite possible, if Polycarp died in 156 at the age of eighty-six. Irenaeus, then, might be described as a 'cradle Catholic' of Eastern provenance, and he wrote in Greek.

Cyprian comes from a quite different stable. He was an adult convert in Carthage, became bishop of his city very soon after his conversion, and died a martyr only a few years later. His outlook was fully Western, and he looked up to Tertullian as his 'master' – though he must have regretted Tertullian's lapse into Montanist schism. While Irenaeus was preoccupied with doctrine and heresy, Cyprian is more concerned about ecclesiology and schism. We have a large number of letters from his pen together with several small tracts, of which the most important for our present purpose is the one generally (today) entitled, *De Unitate Catholicae Ecclesiae*.

I have studied Cyprian's ecclesiology (apart from his witness to the Roman primacy) in three articles in *The Downside Review* (1952 and 1953).[13] I have there stated Cyprian's views on the Church, in writings other than the *De Unitate*, under the following headings:

(1) The title 'church *(ecclesia)*' is given by him to the universal Church.

(2) It is given also to any local Christian community duly constituted under a bishop who is in communion with the universal Church. When an episcopal see is vacant, the local church is maintained in ecclesial reality by the leadership of the remaining clergy, the *clericus ordo*.

(3) *Ecclesia* always means an actual association of human beings, both those in the state of probation and those baptized. (Cyprian does not talk about the Church triumphant or the Church in waiting as entities distinct from the Church on earth.) The local church is only a *church* if it is in communion with the other local churches of the universal *Ecclesia*, all built together into a unity of full mutual communion.[14]

(4) A consequence of the historical unity of the universal Church is that a Christian from one local church, with which he is in good standing, can receive Holy Communion in another place that he is visiting – provided that his own home church is within the universal Church.

(5) The Church is a historical reality in Cyprian's own world, an empirical datum from which he can argue; and so is its visible unity.

(6) The unity of the Church is not only unbroken; it is unbreakable. Christ founded only one Church. Schism is not 'in' the Church (the idea would be beyond Cyprian's conception and ruinous for his ecclesiology); it is 'from' the Church.

To these items taken from Cyprian's other writings we can add a few points that emerge from a reading of his *De Unitate*: (1) In this little book the term '*ecclesia* (church)' is applied almost exclusively to the universal Church. (2) The unbreakable unity of the Church (a visible entity) is here derived from the unity of the Holy Trinity itself. As in the other works of Cyprian, this unity is said to have been established when Christ founded the Church on Peter. This Petrine foundation is the *origo*, the source or fountainhead, of the Church's unity.

Cyprian was an author much appealed to in after-times in his native Africa. His rejection of the possibility of baptism outside the unity of the universal Church was convenient for the Donatists; but he was also greatly respected by Augustine (who, however, thought it necessary to differ from him on the subject of schismatical sacraments) and I think that, before Augustine, he had greatly influenced Optatus of Milevis in North Africa. I further suspect that his writings were treasured at Rome, and that his vision of Church unity as proceeding from the Petrine see as from a fountainhead was there re-read (e.g. by Innocent I in the early fifth century) as a vision of the Christian *faith* as similarly being diffused from Rome. Cyprian's influence on Eastern Christian thought is harder to determine. On the whole, my feeling is that the West took more theology from the East than the East took from the West.

In the painful circumstances of the Decian persecution Cyprian found himself and his church embroiled in controversies, largely connected with the thorny problem of the proper treatment of those who, in fear of government authority, had compromised their Christianity. His own position at Carthage was opposed by some of the local clergy. There were factions in Rome itself, leading to the Novatianist schism. There were troubles elsewhere. Against this background Cyprian's insistence on unity becomes understandable. But, as in the case of Clement on the legitimacy of presbyters, we can be confident that on the broad issue he was declaring, with Western clarity and decisiveness, the general conviction of the Church. He pushed his principle so far as to deny the possibility of even valid baptism, let alone a valid ordained ministry, outside the limits of the one visible and visibly united Church. At this point he encountered the intransigent opposition of bishop Stephen of Rome – an opposition that filled him with dismay, since it seemed to him that it threatened the very ecclesiology on which he depended. What would have happened in this dispute we shall never know. The persecutors, however, caught up with this great African ecclesiastic and he died within the communion of the universal Church and is venerated as a martyr. But the Western Church aligned itself with Stephen on the subject of schismatical baptism, and in due course extended the principle to the validity of schismatical ordinations (provided that the apostolic succession was maintained).

5. Letters of Communion

It would be tedious to pursue this review of ancient testimonies to the conviction that the Church is a 'visible' reality and that it cannot become *two* (or more) visible realities: that, in fact, schism is, when once it has taken firm and continuing shape, never 'in' but always 'from' the Church. The fact is not, I believe, seriously contested by those who have examined the evidence with careful honesty. It is not in dispute between scholars of different ecclesiastical allegiances. This conviction of the Church's visible unity was not confined to the Catholic Church of antiquity. It was maintained on the whole, so far as we can see, by those groups whom today we describe as schismatical. A schismatical 'Church' could legitimize itself in its own eyes only by claiming to be, not a separated part of a wider whole, but simply itself the universal Church; what historians now refer to as the ancient Catholic Church had to be denounced by these separated groups as itself a 'schism'. 'Branch theories' of the Church were not in favour in those days – though we know of one interesting Donatist theologian who argued that, whereas in Africa the Donatists were the true Catholics and those there whom we now regard as Catholics were schismatics, nevertheless outside the limits of Africa the true Church was the one we now refer to as the Catholic Church. So far as I know, this curious theory had a short life and no positive developments. For antiquity in general, visible unity was, to use a modern expression, of the *esse* of the Church. We may restate a quotation (given above) from Dr Wordsworth, and add to it thus: To this ancient Christianity 'we owe the fact that there is one Bible everywhere received in the Church, one Creed, one weekly holyday, one baptism and one eucharist, and *a conviction of the indivisible visible unity of the Church*'. On what principle do we accept from antiquity those items enumerated by Dr Wordsworth, if we wish to reject the item which I have added?

The question may naturally be asked: by what human mechanism was this principle of visible unity put into effect? We know that there was much intercourse between local churches in antiquity. We know of regional and, eventually, general councils of the Church. There is something to be said about an alleged Roman primacy. But at this point I wish to direct attention to a device studied by L. Hertling, S. J., in a paper entitled *Communio und Primat* and published in 1943.[15] It is the device of 'letters of communion'.

Hertling begins by referring to the notion of 'communion', and describes its meaning as follows. It is 'the bond of union between bishops and faithful, between bishops with one another, between faithful with one another; a bond effected and at the same time manifested by Eucharistic communion'.[16]

According to patristic Christianity, says Hertling, the Church is a single such communion. To create a new communion would be to found a new Church – which necessarily would not really be a Church at all, since there can be only one Church. The ancients had other words besides *communio* or *koinonia* to express this notion. Cyprian often speaks of *communicatio.* We find also *pax* (in Greek, *eirene*), Athanasius once couples communion and charity: *koinonia kai agape* – and so does bishop Julius of Rome in a letter to Athanasius. Communion is more, Hertling tells us, than doctrinal agreement: it is a being-together in a single actual historical fellowship or association.

I continue with Hertling's exposition. Communion, thus understood, is intimately bound up with the Eucharist. As between a resident bishop and a visiting bishop it would – or could – be expressed (for instance, when Polycarp of Smyrna visited Rome) by the resident yielding his place to the visitor for the celebration of the Eucharist. In later, Byzantine, times the mere physical fact of (even involuntary) reception of the Eucharist from the hands of a bishop was thought to create the bond of communion with him (and with his Church or sect, as the case might be). Reception of Holy Communion was thus a kind of consolidation of that membership of the Church which baptism effects.

What happened when a Christian, other than a bishop, travelled from his own locality to some place where he was unknown? Despite the poor and hazardous methods of travel there was, it would appear, much going about in the lands of the Roman Empire. It appears that such a traveller might arm himself with a letter of communion, a kind of ecclesiastical passport, issued by his own bishop.[17] Such letters were named 'canonical letters', 'symbols', or *tesserae* (labels, tickets or tags).

The evidence for such letters of communion is sporadic and one

can hardly say when a practice which must have begun informally
was developed into a system, or how complete the system was; nor
how long it effectively lasted. A synod of Antioch in the year 341
mentioned such letters. Later Augustine, in controversy with a
Donatist who claimed that he lived in communion with the whole
Catholic world, asked whether a letter of communion from this
man's bishop (a Donatist bishop, of course) would be accepted by
such apostolic churches as Corinth, Alexandria. ... The Donatist,
we are told, declined to make the experiment.

To the extent that this system was effectively operative, it would
seem that every important local church must have kept, under
continual revision, a list of bishops of other such churches with
whom they were 'in communion'. Less important churches would
be able to obtain information from the list of a neighbouring
important church. If a traveller arrived with a letter bearing the
name of a bishop not on your list, you would treat him as a
schismatic and refuse him the Eucharist.

A critical moment must have been the election of a new bishop
in a local church. He would need to get his name entered on the
lists of the other churches. The correspondence of and to Cyprian
which has been preserved shows the flurry of anxiety that arose
when there were two claimants to the See of Rome in 251; but one
admits that Rome was probably a special case.

It appears that the issue of letters of communion, at least from
Rome to distant places, was already in operation in the time of
Tertullian (about 200). Tertullian, emphasizing the apostolic
origins of the Catholic Church as against the claims of the
heretics, wrote:

> Thus these (local) churches, so numerous and so important, are
> that one original Church that comes from the apostles, and from
> this original Church they all derive. They are therefore all of
> them that original Church. And all are apostolic, since all
> together give proof of unity, since there is between them the
> communion of peace *(communicatio pacis)* and the shared name
> of brethren, and the *contesseratio* of hospitality.[18]

By 'contesseratio hospitalitatis' Tertullian may refer to the
practice of mutual sending and receiving of letters of communion,
which assured not only a welcome at the Eucharist but the
hospitality of the local church which one was visiting.

The evidence, scattered though it is, indicates the extent of the system in both East and West. Cyprian provides evidence that a schismatic might seek to obtain such a letter of communion surreptitiously, thus finding an open door to local churches within the Catholic communion.[19] Basil (fourth-century bishop of Caesarea in Asia Minor) points in a letter to the number of local churches which gave to him and received from him letters of communion. He implies that those who refuse to accept communion with himself thereby cut themselves off from the whole Church.

It is to be observed that in antiquity, when canon law was little developed, excommunication – the refusal of communion – could be the act of any bishop. But unless one who so acted could secure the agreement of the other bishops of the Church at large, this act, as Hertling observes, would recoil upon himself: he would have put *himself* outside the Catholic Church. Thus, in the baptismal controversy in the time of Cyprian, bishop Firmilian of Caesarea argued that Stephen, bishop of Rome, had, in disagreeing with Cyprian, separated himself from the communion of the Church (we only know this letter of Firmilian in a translation made of it by or for Cyprian, a somewhat suspect intermediary in the circumstances!). Probably Firmilian was being somewhat rhetorical in this outburst, but the letter shows how the ancient Church thought of the Church, its unity, and communion in the closest association. The letter also exposes the problem: how does one decide which of two groups of bishops, each united by communion among themselves, but each refusing communion to the whole of the other group, is the one which is in fact the Catholic Church and not the schismatical group? Problems arose, even in the third century, over penitential discipline and over rival claimants to the See of Rome. In the fourth century a variety of most difficult situations arose in the wake of the Council of Nicaea (325) and in face of the patronage extended to the Church by the Roman Emperors.

Hertling remarks that communion in the ancient Church was a sacramental reality: it found its focus in Eucharistic communion. But it was also a question of authority, inasmuch as admission to or exclusion from Holy Communion was determined by someone – the local bishop – having authority so to admit or exclude. On what did the bishop's authority depend? Doubtless it was necessary that he should have been duly ordained to his episcopal office. But was that enough? Apparently not. It was necessary also that he should be 'in communion with' the other bishops of the Catholic world. And who, in times of crisis, were these?

In the end, 'letters of communion' seem to have died away. Perhaps, Hertling suggests, it was from the lists of bishops it involved, retained in the files of the important local churches, that there developed the diptychs, lists of bishops acknowledged as being in communion with the celebrant, which were read out at Mass. To remove the name of a living bishop from the diptychs was equivalent to excommunicating him, or rather to declaring him excommunicate. By the time of Pope Hormisdas, these lists seem to have included the names of distinguished dead bishops, and one of the objections to Hormisdas' terms for ending the Acacian schism was that he required removal from the Easterns' diptychs of the names of dead bishops who had not been in communion with Rome but were revered and esteemed among the Easterns. Roman logic was in conflict with very genuine Eastern sentiment and sense of charity – since most of these bishops had, pretty certainly, no schismatical intent (they were under the control of an imperial system which did not clearly distinguish limits between civil and ecclesiastical authority in the way that we should do today).

6. Augustine

I conclude this chapter with a few words about Augustine, the African convert who became bishop of Hippo in North Africa and is the greatest name in Western theology before Thomas Aquinas. During many years of his life as a bishop, Augustine was a leader in the controversy with Donatism. The conflict dates from the period of the persecution under Diocletian when, it was alleged by the Donatists, a man selected to be bishop of Carthage was consecrated as bishop by a bishop who had been a *traditor,* one who 'handed over' sacred Christian books to the persecutors in order to escape persecution himself; the word *traditor* is the origin of our English word 'traitor'. In the Donatist view, a traitor was incapable of transmitting sacraments such as Holy Orders. They therefore had their own candidate consecrated for the See of Carthage and thus arose the classical schismatic confrontation of *altare contra altare.* The controversy became chronic, and over a wide area of the north of Africa Donatist and 'Catholic' bishops proliferated. Apart from deep differences of doctrine and practice (the Donatists refused to recognize the validity of baptism administered by 'Catholics'; the reverse was not the case), the basic difference, from the point of view of this essay, was that the Donatists were regarded as schismatics by the Catholic Church outside Africa, while the African 'Catholics' were recognized in the rest of the world as the true church in Africa – Augustine himself was among the bishops invited to the Council of Ephesus in 431, but he was in his last illness and unable to attend.

I have dealt at length with the whole matter in *The Idea of the Church*, chapter 7, and may here be brief. The question is: can Augustine be added to the list of the Fathers who held firmly to the conviction that the Church of Christ was to be identified with one single visible communion? The Anglican scholar, C. H. Turner, after mentioning Augustine, wrote:

> On the supreme duty of communion with the visible fellowship of the brethren in the one true fold of the Redeemer there was no shadow of wavering, however many the representatives, or however various the types and local expressions, of the Christian tradition.[20]

More recently, the late Professor Greenslade, also an Anglican, agrees that Augustine's recognition of (some) non-catholic Orders as valid was not 'intended to introduce any change in the doctrine of the Church'.[21]

Other writers have thought they could see some wavering in Augustine. Mr G. G. Willis argues that Augustine does not think of schism as 'automatically excluding a man from the Church, and leaving the Church as united as it was before: it is a true rending of the Body of Christ itself'.[22] In support, he quotes from Augustine, on the subject of the Donatists:

> They baptize outside the Church and – if it were possible – they rebaptize the Church. They offer sacrifice in dissension and schism ... The unity of Christ is rent, the inheritance of Christ is blasphemed ... We charge them with the madness of schism, the folly of rebaptizing, their wicked separation from the inheritance of Christ which is spread throughout all nations.[23]

Plainly, Willis rests his case on the words in this passage: 'The unity of Christ is rent'. If these words are taken at their face value (and in isolation from the rest of the quotation) they certainly prove Willis's point. But Augustine would have rejected this literal interpretation – probably with some violence. The fact is that the word 'schism' comes from a verbal root, to rend. On this etymological basis, then, a schism is a rent; and it would follow that those guilty of schism are men who *rend*. What do they rend? The answer could only be: 'the Church'.

The influence of this etymology is apparent in other authors besides Augustine. We have heard Irenaeus threatening with divine judgement those who 'for slight and trifling causes cut and rend the glorious body of Christ'.[24] But in fact Irenaeus did not hold that the result of schism was to leave the Church in two parts divided from each other. On the contrary, he says, 'while often whole limbs are removed from (the Church), she abides, ... the firmament of faith'.[25] Cyprian occasionally slips into a way of talking as if schism really did 'rend' the Church; but everyone admits that in fact Cyprian thought such a catastrophe impossible. If ever there was a firm champion of the indivisible visible unity of the Church as a single communion, it was Cyprian. Augustine himself elsewhere slips again into the same loose language, but at once corrects himself. Commenting on the Canticle of Canticles, he writes:

> It is to the catholic Church that the words are addressed: One is my dove ... Why have you torn the dove? Nay, you have torn your own entrails; for while you have been torn, the dove remains whole.[26]

Plainly, the explicit correction made in this last-quoted passage is to be applied to the passage appealed to by Willis. Indeed, the necessary corrections are already implicit in the passage to which Willis appeals. The Donatists are there described as being 'outside the Church'. Their followers are 'exiled from the peace of salvation'. They themselves are guilty of 'wicked separation from the inheritance of Christ which is spread through all nations' – sc. the universal Catholic communion. Elsewhere he maintains that 'Christian charity cannot be preserved except in the unity of the Church'. Donatists do not 'sing a new song unto the Lord', because they are separated from the communion of the Catholic Church.[27]

Greenslade, in turn, asserts that in Augustine's view 'many who appear to be outside the Church are really within it'. He here refers to a passage in Augustine's *De Baptismo*: 'In that ineffable foreknowledge of God many who appear to be outside are within, and many who appear to be inside are without'.[28] The question of course is *what* these two classes of people are 'within' and 'without'. Greenslade thinks that, in each case, it is the Church militant here on earth. This is not so. The fact is that Cyprian (from whom Augustine here dissents) had applied to the Church on earth a text which suggests that it possesses, in its members, a degree of holiness which obviously was not present in the Catholic communion; the passage could thus be used by the Donatists to discredit the Catholic Church in favour of their own body. Augustine, in reply, argues that the text cannot, without reservation, be applied to the Church militant; it refers rather to what he calls 'the fixed number of the saints, predestined before the foundation of the world'.[29] In other words, and using our own terminology, the Church triumphant will eventually be a communion of perfectly holy people; this is not true of the Church militant.

In the passage of the *De Baptismo* referred to above, Augustine points out that: (1) some members of the Church militant are already leading holy lives on earth (and in them the verse from the Canticle of Canticles already has a certain fulfilment); (2) some members of the Church militant are not yet converted (despite their membership) – hence the Church militant contains sinners as well as saints; (3) some persons eternally predestined to heaven are (not even in the Church militant yet, but) 'wallowing in heresies'[30] or in pagan superstitions. 'For in that ineffable foreknowledge of God many who appear to be outside are within, and many who appear to be inside are without' the 'enclosed garden' of the Canticle ('Thou art an enclosed garden ... a sealed spring, a well of living water, a park with fruit of the fruit trees' (Cant. 4:12f.)).[31]

What Augustine is saying is that not all of those who are members now of the Church militant will figure among the members of the Church triumphant; and some of those who are not yet members of the Church militant will nevertheless turn out to be members of the Church triumphant. He is *not* saying that bad Catholics are not really members of the Church militant, nor that some of those now wallowing in heresy *are* already members of the Church militant. He is specifically saying that Cyprian was mistaken in reading the Canticle text as applying, without qualification, to the Church militant. Greenslade is certainly wrong in contending that Augustine, by the phrase 'are really within', was attributing Church membership, already attained, to any 'heretics' – though of course he leaves it open that some who are at present heretics may later be reconciled to the Church. Greenslade seems to have overlooked the fact that, if Augustine was here asserting that you can be a member of the Church although you belong to a 'heretical' (or schismatical) communion, he was asserting *pari argumento* that some who wallow in pagan superstitions are already members of the Church. Neither the passage of the *De Baptismo* adduced by Greenslade nor that from *Ep.* xliii cited by Willis can be quoted as evidence that Augustine wavered in identifying the Church of Christ with the Catholic Communion.

There is one passage from the *Letters* that should be mentioned: 'Many when they are dying are separated from the Church who, while living, seem linked with the Church through the fellowship of the sacraments and Catholic unity'.[32] If the word 'seem' here is pressed, it might be inferred that sinners who are externally within the Catholic communion are not *really* united with the Church. The problem of members of the Church who are in a state of mortal sin is a difficult one linguistically. Modern Catholic usage would say that these persons are – despite their sinful state – *really* linked with the Church, i.e. are among her real members. Augustine is not so precise in his language. But I doubt whether one could seriously build up from this passage a plausible theory that Augustine rejected the universal – or almost universal – ancient conviction that the Church is an indivisible visible communion, to which one is admitted by baptism. Of the continuance and strength of that conviction he is in fact a powerful witness. We know what he would have said to anyone who sought to find authority in ancient tradition for maintaining a Christian communion outside 'the unity of Christ ... the inheritance of Christ which is spread throughout all nations';[33] for he has said it. The Donatist appeal to the authority of Cyprian, as justifying their theological grounds for opposing the Catholics in Africa, was countered by Augustine with words that express the mind not only of Cyprian himself but of the author of 1 John. 'How dare you make mention of the blessed Cyprian as though that great champion of Catholic unity and concord were a support of your separation. First be in the Church, which it is well known that Cyprian held to and preached, and then dare to name Cyprian as a supporter of your views' (*C. Cresc.* II, xxxi, 39).[34] 'First be in the Church.' Theology is a fascinating game and an important service to Christianity. But it is a service that can only be properly given within the visible unity of the koinonia.

Chapter VIII

Difficulties

The claim made in the preceding chapter is that the Christianity of the patristic age, including that of bodies which today we classify as 'schismatic', was profoundly and almost unanimously convinced that the Church is the legitimate and divinely willed outcome of the redemptive work of Christ, and that this Church in its historical existence is an indivisible visible unity of communion between all its parts and members. I am aware that some readers may suspect that this is a reading of Christian history that is biased because its author is a member of a body that perpetuates the same conviction and, on its basis, makes an intransigent claim for itself. I may therefore be allowed to quote from a writer, the late Dr Greenslade, who was a member of the Church of England (which makes no such claim for itself) and whose own ecclesiology was quite different from the ancient one. In the second edition of his important work, *Schism in the Early Church*, he wrote as follows:

> ... the Fathers, together with most early heretics and schismatics, were substantially agreed ... not simply that the Church ought to be one, but that it is one, and cannot but be one. This unity was predicated of the visible Church, and the visible Church was thought of organically as one structure, one communion. To their minds, divisions, breaches of communion, were not embraced and overshadowed by a spiritual and invisible unity, nor could a number of denominations aggregate into one Church. There was but one visible Church in one

communion; bodies separated from that communion were outside the Church. ... in such controversies as the Novatianist and Donatist, each side believed itself to be the true and only Church. Schism was not inside the Church, and transcended by a higher unity. ... Both for dogmatic theory and for spiritual life the crucial difference lay between those within and those without the Church.[1]

I may add: (a) that I know of no reputable historian of ancient Christianity who would dispute the truth of what Dr Greenslade here wrote; (b) that the agreement of which he wrote was not simply among the Fathers, as theoreticians. It was an agreement in belief and in practice of Christianity as a whole. I have sought to show in chapter 7 that it was expressed in the practice of 'letters of communion'. One could add that it was implicit in the behaviour of the four great General Councils (325–451). I am hardly exaggerating if I say that this conviction was held with a firmness, and was carried out in a practice, similar to the firmness and practice of early Christianity with regard to the authority of the canonical Scriptures.

The conviction in question persisted till the end of the patristic age and on through the Middle Ages, despite the tragedy of the estrangement of East and West and despite, in the West, the virtual chaos of the period of the antipopes, when bishops and Christian nations were at odds about who was the legitimate earthly head of the Church.

Substantially it is true that all modern questioning of the truth of this conviction dates from the sixteenth-century Reformation. When things began to settle down after the initial explosion of that vast upheaval, those who had seceded or been driven out of the Roman Catholic Church found themselves divided up into membership of a number of different bodies, none of which ventured to claim to be exclusively the one 'holy catholic Church' which they confessed in the Creed. It was inevitable that the ecclesiological question had to be opened up again by them, but now with an *a priori* abandonment of the age-old conviction that only one Christian communion is that 'catholic Church'. Solutions of the problem have varied from the notion that the Church is in essence an entirely invisible entity to the view, held by some Anglicans in the nineteenth century and later, that the Church is a visible entity, but divided into three 'branches': the Anglican

Church, the Orthodox Communion of the East, and the Roman Catholic Church. The one conviction that none of the heirs of the Reformation could entertain was that which had been almost unchallenged throughout antiquity and the Middle Ages. Meanwhile, both the Roman Catholic Church and the Eastern Orthodox Communion continued to proclaim that the Church is a single unique historical communion – although each of these great bodies claimed that it was itself that unique communion and denied the other's claim to be such.

The shift away from the ecclesiology of the unique visible communion was thus not generated internally within a continuing theological tradition but was precipitated from without as a result of the Reformation. A new impulse came with the birth of the modern ecumenical movement in the twentieth century. At first this movement was an affair of the Protestant and Anglican churches. As time went on, various autocephalous churches of the Orthodox Communion joined in and began to press the claims of the ecclesiology that the Reformation had discountenanced. Still more recently the Roman Catholic Church has officially approved, and become an official participant in, the ecumenical movement. For such and other reasons ecclesiology has assumed an important place in general Christian theology.

In *Schism in the Early Church*, first published in 1953, Greenslade combined with his historical study some reflections on Christian unity. I took notice of his views in *The Idea of the Church* (1962), and in the second edition of his book (1964) he in turn responded at some length and with characteristic courtesy. From his statements I here put together, though largely in my own words, what may be taken as a typical modern case against the continuing validity of the ancient view of the Church. The case is as follows:

(1) The ancient theory was not put into complete and rigorous practice. Quarrels occurred in antiquity between bishops which led to breaches of communion but not to permanent schisms. 'There were times when whole provinces and more were in what has been called mediate communion.'[2] During the troubles at Antioch towards the end of the great Arian crisis Alexandria was in communion both with Rome and with Antioch, but Antioch and Rome were not in direct communion with each other.

(2) The ancient view of the Church as a unique, indivisible, visible communion was expressed in its fullness by Cyprian, and

by him developed into the consequence that outside this communion there was no grace, no valid sacraments, no presence of
the Holy Spirit. Schismatical 'baptism', in particular, was (to use
modern terms) neither valid nor efficacious; it was a mere sham.
The same would have to be said of schismatical 'eucharists' and
schismatical 'ordinations'. Unless you were a Catholic, you were in
no better position than a pagan.

Greenslade considers Cyprian's position, taken in its entirety, as
untenable. It contradicts Christian experience, Christian thought,
and Christian charity. Augustine in fact explicitly rejected a
substantial part of the Cyprianic synthesis, for he admitted the
possibility of valid sacraments administered outside the Catholic
communion. But Augustine attempted to hold this relaxed view
about sacramental validity along with the Cyprianic and general
ancient view that the Church is a unique visible communion. Thus
Augustine held that there can be genuine sacraments outside the
Church. Should he not have taken the opposite course? Greenslade
argues that Cyprian was *right* in holding that where the Church is
absent there can be no valid sacraments; while Augustine was
right in holding that there can be valid sacraments outside the
Catholic communion. He himself draws the only possible inference: the Church is present wherever there are valid sacraments, and
these are found in more than one Christian communion; so the
Church is more than a unique visible communion. The Church is
present wherever the holy things that God has given us in Christ
are present, accepted, and turned to account. These holy things
include the sacraments but also the Bible, the Creeds, the gospel
or Good News, a ministry of word, sacrament and pastoral care. It
is not necessary for a Christian group to possess, recognize, and
utilize *all* these holy gifts of Christ, provided it has and cherishes a
certain number of them (Greenslade did not make clear where he
drew the line: e.g., if a human group acknowledged the authority
of the Bible but interpreted it in such a way as to deny to Jesus
any unique significance in the religious history of mankind, would
that group count for him as outside the pale?). In any case, where
a sufficient combination of these gifts or holy things are accepted,
there is 'the Church'. Once or twice Greenslade says: where you
find these holy things, there you have found 'churchness'.

(3) We thus reach an ecclesiology according to which the gifts
of Christ are *constitutive* of the Church; and the Church is present
in various degrees in various Christian groups – the degrees

varying with the number and importance of the gifts acknowledged and possessed by the several groups. Such an ecclesiology,
Greenslade maintained, is not an ecclesiology of an invisible
Church. The Church is necessarily 'incarnate' in history; this
'incarnation' is realized in varying degrees in different Christian
communions. And once we have realized that the Church is, even
imperfectly, 'incarnate' in more than one Christian communion,
we have to abandon the ancient view that the Church is a *unique*
visible communion. Schism, in the normal case, is not 'from' but
'in' the Church.

(4) Greenslade, in his second edition, pressed home his conten-
tions by an *argumentum ad hominem*, since he knew that the
author of *The Idea of the Church* was (as he remains) a Roman
Catholic and identifies the ancient Church with his own communion. It will be borne in mind, in connection with the following
quotation from Greenslade, that the Orthodox Communion, like
the Roman Catholic Church, claims to be *the* Church. Greenslade
writes that Butler

> appeals to history. So do I. Go back to the Orthodox Church,
> which for the most part he rather ingeniously uses as support for
> the principle that the visible Church is essentially one com-
> munion. But when did the Orthodox Church lose its continuity
> and go out of the Church? It is only if a papalist doctrine of
> authority and unity is true that it has ever done so; and then the
> argument has to be about papacy as such, and not about single
> societies. ... The Church ceased to be one communion, in the
> plain historical sense, long before the Reformation. For me it is
> impossible to locate either the Orthodox Church or the Roman
> Catholic Church *extra ecclesiam*.[3]

I shall return to these arguments, and to something that lies
perhaps behind them, later in this chapter. But before I do so I
wish to emphasize one great truth which I trust is accepted by
those fellow Christians who are not satisfied that the old
ecclesiology is tenable and who would agree with Greenslade's
objections to it.

A Christian is a man of faith. He does not rely simply on sense;
nor does he rely simply on sense data interpreted and judged by
the light of natural reason. He has a superior gift, a gift of grace,
whereby he lives on a level that neither sense nor reason nor both

in combination can reach by themselves. Faith, however, is not – as the schoolboy is alleged to have described it – the power to believe what you know is not true. The 'object' of faith, or *what* the Christian believes, is both true and real; it is not that he merely believes in this reality and in the truths that would follow if his belief were true. For a Christian knows (by faith) that what he believes by faith *is* true; reality corresponds with his faith. (It would seem to follow that you cannot *believe* by supernatural faith in an erroneous Christian doctrine.)

God, then, is real. His act of creation of the universe is a fact. The incarnation is a fact, and so is the redeeming death and resurrection of Christ. It really is true that, through the redemption, man, his history, and the created order in which he exists, are raised to a new and 'supernatural' level. And the Church and sacraments, taken together, constitute a 'means' whereby the fruits of the Paschal mystery are really applied to man, to men in history, and to the whole created universe. And it is a fact that the whole of creation and history, even though thus raised to a 'supernatural' level, is orientated to an accomplishment that we locate 'after' history (aware as we are that the concept is, on the surface, a non-sense): we 'await the life of the world to come'. As Dr Torrance expresses it:

(The correlation of faith with the objective reality of God's self-revelation ...) does not allow us to make 'faith' itself the ground of our 'belief' in the incarnation and/or the resurrection. The only proper ground of faith is the reality to which it is correlated as its objective pole.[4]

If the Church is intrinsic to the divine 'economy' or plan of total human and creational fulfilment, then the Church is a reality that is fully objective in the same way as the incarnation and the resurrection. And since the Church is our link with the Redeemer, it is of supreme importance for the individual to succeed in identifying the Church and in adhering to it in full historical 'belongingness'. The matters raised between the ancient (and to a large extent modern) ecclesiology and that propounded by Greenslade are therefore of the highest moment; and, since we all have various stakes in our own traditions, we are bound to try to eschew from their consideration our particular biases and the emotions that they enkindle.

When we speak of the redemption and what it entails as being 'objective' it is well to bear in mind that the word 'object' itself can mislead. It can mean something that is already present in our acquired knowledge, and present to the same extent as it is our 'object'; thus referring to something *in so far as* it is already understood by us. But the word has another meaning. When we make something 'an object of inquiry' we admit that we do not yet understand it. We may have some knowledge of it, but we look for more. It is less an object attained than an object that draws us on to search for it. We do not (perfectly) hold the thimble but we are hunting for it.

The mystery of our redemption, which includes the work of Christ and that of his Church – it is, as Augustine put it, the *totus Christus*, the 'whole Christ' who is both 'head' and 'members', both the historical Jesus and the historical Church – is an 'object', and therefore objective, in the second sense. It is greater than our present apprehension of it. It is a mystery that we for ever only partially grasp and indeed a mystery that is, as yet, only partially realized. Nevertheless, it is realized and we do grasp it – partially.

The Church lives its own mystery; and in its theology it continually explores it. New historical conditions open up new, hitherto latent and therefore unexplored, aspects of the mystery. Greenslade speaks of the early Church as 'becoming increasingly aware, through experience, of the theological problems raised by divisions among Christians, and anxiously wrestling with them'.[5] The modern ecumenical movement has again forced us to examine these problems. New questions require new answers. But we must be careful that our new answers do not contradict the achieved results of past theology, and above all that they do not abandon what is of the substance of Christian convictions that are not so much theology as the permanent infrastructure of all Christian theology.

(1) To revert to the points of the case against the inherited ecclesiology of the Church as a unique visible communion, with its corollary that only one Christian body can be identified *simpliciter* as the Church. Greenslade points out that communion within the Catholic Church was not at all times as complete as this ecclesiology might seem to require: 'There were times when whole provinces and more were in what has been called mediate communion'; two areas of the Church might be out of direct

communion with each other, while both were in communion with a third area of the same Church.

If Greenslade is here referring mainly to the troubles of the fourth century, it has to be borne in mind that during a crucial period of that century the Church was under unnatural and unprecedented pressure from the Emperor, himself a Christian. Terrible as persecution by a pagan state had been, these new problems were in some ways more insidious. Pagan persecution, as we see today in the 'Iron Curtain' countries, can have a stimulating effect and a uniting effect upon Christians. In Uganda, as I write these words, the Church is in splendid form. But the fourth-century Church was only gradually learning how to adjust itself to a civil government that was soi-disant Christian but had not yet learnt that the Church claims and requires a real autonomy. Anyone who reads Batiffol's account of this period in *La Paix Constantinienne* will find it difficult to derive, from the dislocations consequent upon the intervention of the state from outside, constructive insights and lessons in ecclesiology. And one can only add that 'mediate communion' is better than nothing!

(2) Cyprian's ecclesiology, in all its rigour, seems to Greenslade to be the only logical working-out of the doctrine that the Church is essentially a single visible communion and that all schism is 'from' (not 'in') the Church. But Cyprian's position is incompatible with Christian experience, Christian thought, and Christian charity. One may add that it is not the position of the Roman Catholic Church, which in practice has accepted Augustine's rejection of vital elements in the Cyprianic synthesis. It is difficult to speak with certainty about the position of the Eastern Orthodox Church on such matters as the 'validity' of sacraments administered outside the unique communion; but my impression is that in practice that Communion is closer to the modern Western position than to that of Cyprian. It is to be remarked that Augustine seems to have been moved to criticize Cyprian's position by the fact that the Church had *already* authoritatively repudiated it.

Cyprian, we have seen, accepted the doctrine of the indivisible visible unity of the Church as a unique communion and (logically, as he thought, and as Greenslade thought with him) inferred that all 'sacramental' ministrations outside that Church were – to use a modern term – 'invalid'.

Augustine, like Cyprian, accepted the almost universal conviction of antiquity that the Church is a unique communion. But he admitted – against Cyprian – that there could be 'valid' sacraments administered outside that Church.

Greenslade, who agrees with Augustine that Cyprian's synthesis must be rejected, holds that Augustine accepted in Cyprian's synthesis what he should have rejected, and rejected what he should have accepted. He should have accepted that, since sacraments are 'things of the Church', they can be found only within the Church. He should have rejected the view that the Church is a unique visible communion. Greenslade adds, to what I have called 'things of the Church', the Bible, the Creeds, the original Message of Good News (sc. the incarnate Word of God), and a ministry of word, sacrament and pastoral care. Each and all of these things or gifts must be seen, according to Greenslade, as – in varying measure, no doubt – constitutive of 'the Church'; and where they, or some of them, are present, there is 'churchness'.

One must surely agree with Greenslade that sacraments, and the other things that he enumerates, are 'things of the Church'. They are of course at a deeper level, one that Greenslade and I would both wish to emphasize, 'things of God'. But they are things of God given in and to and through the Church. He is also correct, I think, in holding that they are *constitutive* of the Church. The Church is not something that happens to be responsible for the sacraments; the Church *is* the Church because the sacraments – and the other holy things – make it such. I think we can go further with many modern theologians and say that the Church is sacramental through and through; and even that she herself is (after Christ, the 'sacrament of God') the sacrament of Christ.

Since sacraments are constitutive of the Church there is good reason to say that where valid sacraments are given and received there is 'churchness' – Greenslade's word, and a very useful one. This, incidentally, is the teaching of the Second Vatican Council, though it uses its own language to express it and nowhere, I think, avails itself of the word 'churchness'. Accepting that baptism can be validly given and received outside the communion of the Roman Catholic Church, the Council continues:

> Moreover some, even very many, of the most significant elements or endowments which together go to build up and give life to the Church herself can exist outside the visible boundaries of the Catholic church: the written word of God; the life

of grace; faith, hope and charity, along with other interior gifts of the Holy Spirit and visible elements.[6]

Thus the Roman Catholic Church grants that real sacraments (not least baptism and, as is clear from its subsequent observations about the Eastern Orthodox Communion, the Eucharist and Holy Orders) can exist outside its own boundaries. At the same time it maintains that these sacraments, and other items mentioned (the list is rather illustrative than exhaustive in intention) are among a group of 'elements or endowments' which together 'build up and give life to' the Church herself. This statement is almost exactly equivalent to Greenslade's view that the 'holy things', including sacraments, are constitutive of the Church. The Council adds that (not only do these things come from Christ, but that) they 'lead' to Christ and 'by right belong to the single Church of Christ'. And the 'separated' churches which have and use these things are thereby 'used' by the Holy Spirit as 'means of salvation which derive their efficacy from the very fullness of grace and truth entrusted to the Catholic Church'.[7]

The convergence between Greenslade and the Council is thus very striking. But it is not total. Adopting Greenslade's terminology, we can say that the Council, like him, accepts that, where these things exist – and they can exist outside the Catholic Church as well as inside – there is 'churchness'. The Council does not say, as Greenslade does, there is 'the Church'. And the Council adds that in the Roman Catholic Church these elements or endowments are all found together; that by right they all 'belong' to her, and that she is 'the all-embracing' *(generale)* 'means of salvation', through which 'the fullness of the means of salvation can be obtained'.[8]

The difference between Greenslade and the Council is not merely linguistic. The difference stems from the fact that the Council, in full consonance with a tradition which goes back, as we have seen, to a virtual consensus of belief and practice in antiquity, was determined to maintain that one of the 'gifts' of God to his Church (a gift not inherent indeed in what might be called the Church's mechanisms; a gift entirely dependent upon the continued, ever-renewed, assistance of the Holy Spirit; but yet a guaranteed gift that will never be revoked) is the gift of indivisible visible unity.

On the other hand the Council, wishing to do justice to the

existence of 'churchly' elements outside the visible limits of the Catholic Church, abstained at a crucial moment from saying bluntly: 'the Church of Christ *is* the Roman Catholic Church', and preferred to say: The Church of Christ 'subsists in the Catholic Church'.[9] The Council never said that the Church of Christ (as distinct from 'churchness') subsists anywhere else.[10]

(3) It may be asked: Does Vatican II register any advance upon the position of Augustine, who (as we have seen) was prepared to recognize the validity of sacraments conferred 'outside the Catholic Church'? The answer is: yes, there is indeed an advance and it is great and welcome; but it is not an advance which contradicts the central contention of Augustine and of antiquity in general.

The advance is, in technical terms, that while Augustine, despite his admission of valid schismatical sacraments among (some) schismatics, was very reluctant indeed to admit that these sacraments were not only 'valid' but also (ordinarily) efficacious – very reluctant to admit that a true supernatural life was nurtured by these sacraments among their recipients, the Council on the other hand is willing and eager to teach that the 'holy things' which originally and 'by right' belong to the Church can and do promote holiness in those who receive them 'outside the Church' – always, of course, provided that the recipient is in 'good faith' or, as Catholics put it, in 'a state of grace'. The proviso is of some importance. If Christ has endowed his Church with a guaranteed visible unity, and if an individual recognizes this fact and has succeeded in identifying the Roman Catholic Church as the body in which this 'gift' is preserved and continues to operate, then to refuse external allegiance to this Church is to refuse something that Christ has built into the very scheme of salvation. Such an individual is saying 'No' to Christ's offer and requirement. His will (it may be feared) is basically alienated from Christ and God, and God's sacraments are inhibited in their normal working in his case.[11]

Augustine, as I have said, was very reluctant to recognize 'good faith' among schismatics. He had a horror of schism (shared by the whole of antiquity; and we ought to share it too). It was to him an abominable sin. And the whole of antiquity was inclined to assume that if one committed an objectively immoral act one was subjectively guilty.[12] So, in general, Augustine, standing firmly on this 'objective' ground, teaches that even valid sacraments cannot promote the holiness of schismatics. 'First be in the Church'.

Nevertheless, Augustine was dimly aware that what is objectively a sinful act may be subjectively not sinful because it is performed in good faith. And he may have been aware that not all who live in schism, and are therefore – on his premises, though not of course necessarily on Greenslade's – in a 'state' of schism (which is, objectively, a sinful state), are as guilty as, on an exclusively objective view, they might seem to be. Thus, speaking of the Donatists (whom in the following quotation he reckons as not just schismatics but 'heretics'), he writes:

> But they are not to be reckoned among heretics who defend their opinion, false and perverse though it be, with no obstinate passion; especially if it is an opinion which they have not conceived with their own bold presumption but have inherited from parents who had been deceived and fallen into error; and if they seek the truth with anxious care, being ready to correct their views when they have found it.[13]

I have sometimes thought that Augustine stands on the dividing line between the ancient and the modern world. The ancients on the whole took a very objective view of guilt. Of what you had wittingly done you were presumed to be guilty. Only by slow degrees, and with the help of modern psychology, have we come fully to realize the meaning of our Lord's teaching: Judge not and you shall not be judged. But in the above passage Augustine comes out (or almost!) on the side of the gospel and our modern thinking against the prejudices of antiquity. It is true that he is speaking not of the creators of a schism but of its followers when it has become inveterate. Obviously, however, one can go further than he does in applying a perfectly general principle to which, in this passage, he has given his authority. Originators of schism may, for all we know, have acted in perfectly good faith. This does not make their schism objectively right, but it can alter, and profoundly, our attitude towards them. If Luther and Calvin were originators of schism, this does not mean that they were wicked men; nor of course, if they were not wicked men, are we bound to conclude that the schism they created is objectively a good thing. I infer that Vatican II, while it has enormously expanded the scope of the admission made by Augustine in the above quotation, has not, by so doing, contradicted the essence of his theological position.

Except, it might be objected, in one respect. You cannot conceive Augustine saying that the Donatist church had any significance in 'the mystery of salvation'. At the most, he would perhaps have said that it had the same significance as Antichrist. But Vatican II, speaking of Christian communions separated from the full visible unity of the Catholic Church, says that they 'have by no means been deprived of significance and importance in the mystery of salvation. For the Spirit of Christ has not refrained from using them as means of salvation.'[14]

This is indeed a momentous step taken by Vatican II. And it is important to remember that all such steps were watched with most careful eyes by the 'conservative' wing of the Council, to say nothing of the Pope, whose eventual responsibility it was to ratify, or deny ratification to, each of the Council's documents. Can this step really be reconciled with the ancient view of the Church as an indivisible visible communion? Is it not a deviation from the course that the Church has pursued for nearly two thousand years?

It appears to me to be a bold step, a perfectly orthodox step, in genuine development from, and not deviation from, traditional premises – and a most welcome step.

A stable human group may be regarded as having a quasi-personality. It is, for example, subject to the requirements of the moral law; and it can reach decisions which are not merely the decisions of its members but of itself as a collectivity. It can therefore be inferred that such a group can take immoral decisions. It can also be inferred that it can take decisions which are objectively immoral though subjectively not so because the group, as a group, is acting in good faith in taking these decisions. And such a group can inherit from its predecessors conditions of affairs that are objectively reprehensible (may even have been subjectively culpable at the time when the decisions were originally taken), and yet not be guilty (subjectively) in continuing such conditions of affairs. It is thus possible and should be easy, even for the most intransigent Catholic (as for the Catholic Church as a whole) to combine his objections to schism with a cordially fraternal acknowledgement that those who live in a particular 'state of schism' are in good faith, are in God's grace; and that what they do collectively as a group may have the blessing of God and bear fruit for their own salvation and that of others. After all, these non-Catholic churches are living by gospel principles (though perhaps overlooking some principles that belong to the gospel); and just as a man in good faith may be objectively in error and yet closely united by personal holiness to God, so too a group of Christians outside the Roman Catholic Church may, and precisely on Roman Catholic principles, be living and propagating holiness. But if that is what they are doing, then they themselves are playing a significant role in the divine work of redemption. To say this is by no means to admit that they are *objectively* right.

To sum up this part of our discussion, Vatican II in effect agrees with Greenslade that the operative presence of the 'holy things' bestows 'churchness'. It does not agree that it constitutes bodies which lack the 'holy thing' of the Church's visible unity, as (parts of, or branches of) the Church. The difference might seem to be very small, almost purely linguistic. But it is all the difference between the traditional ecclesiology and the ecclesiology espoused by Greenslade. I hardly need to add that Greenslade is here the spokesman of very many people in the non-Roman-Catholic churches, particularly such as are deeply committed to the quest of visible unity. I have tried to show that the traditional ecclesiology is still tenable and that it has shown itself capable of most desirable development. It will still remain to evaluate the two theories, the traditional one and that of which Greenslade was so distinguished an advocate.

(4) Greenslade presses me hard with what he considers to be an insurmountable obstacle to the acceptance of my thesis of indivisible visible unity: the existence of the Orthodox Communion over against the Roman Catholic Church today. He dismisses my argument at this point as 'rather ingenious' – a compliment which, I feel, is somewhat barbed. He asks: When did the Orthodox Communion 'go out of the Church'? And he thinks that I can escape the force of this question only by supposing the doctrine of the papal primacy. He holds, in view of the simultaneous existence of the Orthodox Communion and the Roman Catholic Church, that 'the Church ceased to be one communion, in the plain historical sense, long before the Reformation'. He refuses point-blank to 'locate either the Orthodox Church or the Roman Catholic Church *extra ecclesiam*'.[15]

The temptation at this juncture to make a merely debating

point is almost irresistible. I hope, however, that it is not captious to observe that Greenslade's strong language cannot really settle the issue before us. He is in fact saying: Forget about the Protestant Churches; the fact remains that the Roman Catholic Church and the Eastern Orthodox Church *are* both parts or manifestations of a Church which therefore no longer is a single communion. And to say this without rationally defending what you say is to substitute strong language for argument.

The 'ingenuity' to which I was alleged to have resorted in *The Idea of the Church* consisted in this: My main thesis was not that the Roman Catholic Church is, to the exclusion of all other bodies, the Church of Christ. My main purpose was not to *identify* the Church. It was, on the contrary, to offer a pointer to the sort of thing we must be looking for *if* we wish to identify the Church. I was asking not so much, 'Where and which is the Church?' but, 'What sort of a thing are we looking for, or should we be looking for, if we are seeking to discover the Church?' (Not: 'Where is the thimble?', but 'What sort of a thing is a thimble?') And one of my main arguments in support of my thesis was that, wherever and whichever the Church is today, the massive witness of ancient tradition and of most modern Christianity is that the Church is an indivisible visible communion. This, as we have seen, is certainly the witness of Christian antiquity, including in that term not only what we now look back upon as the ancient Catholic Church but – on the whole – those ancient bodies which we now refer to as schisms. In modern times it is not the opinion of the bodies whose separation dates from the Reformation. But Protestants together account for not much more than a quarter of modern Christianity. The rest of the Christian population is made up mainly of the Roman Catholics and the Eastern Orthodox; and these two great communions (together including almost three-quarters of living Christians) wholly agree with one another and with Christian antiquity that the Church is an indivisible visible communion. Now it is obvious that a Roman Catholic cannot use this agreement by itself to prove that *his* Church is that visible communion; nor can the Eastern Orthodox believer use the agreement by itself to prove that *his* communion is the true one. But both can, and do, unite to maintain: Whichever of our respective claims is true, nevertheless we are at one in rejecting the Protestant theory of a divided Church. In other words, I appealed to the witness of Eastern Orthodoxy, together with that of the

Roman Catholic Church, to support my main thesis: that the Church is a single visible communion. I think that the appeal was entirely valid intellectually. It is exactly parallel to the reference made by Greenslade and myself to the witness not only of the ancient Catholic Church but of the ancient schisms – each claiming to *be* the true Church (and thus contradicting each other on the *location* of the gift of unity) but all agreeing that the Church is and must be visibly one.

It remains of course to ask, if we accept the thesis of the Church as a visible unity, how a Roman Catholic can give a satisfactory rationale of the present position of the Orthodox Communion; and how an Orthodox Christian can give a satisfactory rationale of the present position of Roman Catholicism. I propose to leave this issue for subsequent consideration, only here making one remark: It is possible to argue, and has been argued from the Roman Catholic side, that 'schism' was never formally consummated between these two great communions.

Before proceeding to the major task of attempting to evaluate our two alternative ecclesiologies (one maintaining that the Church is an indivisible visible communion; the other agreeing that it ought to be a single visible communion but maintaining that it is not in fact indivisible and is actually at present divided) I venture to offer some reflections upon the quest, which can be pursued and is being pursued, by all the great churches for a reunion of Christians.

On what basis do we hope for such a reunion? There are, once again, two alternatives. One is (to put it crudely) the basis of compromise. It can be argued that what unites Christians is already far more important than the matters that still divide them. Protestant, Orthodox and Catholic all confess the reality of the one God self-revealed in the religion of the Old Testament People of God and, more sublimely and definitely, in Jesus Christ. All officially confess that Jesus Christ is the redeemer of mankind and indeed of the whole of creation. They also confess that he is the Word of God incarnate and – though some might sit loosely to the verbal formulations of Chalcedon – that he is simultaneously fully divine, the very Son of God, and fully human: 'consubstantial with us according to his manhood'. All proclaim that Jesus Christ, truly risen from the dead by his Father's power, has bestowed his Holy Spirit upon the Church to enlighten and enable it and to guide it on its pilgrim path while animating it in its mission to the world.

All proclaim that we are thus led on to confess that God is one God in three 'persons': the Father, the Son and the Holy Spirit. All teach that God is the creator of the universe and the lord of all history. All maintain that the Church is, in some sense, the gathering of those who by supernatural faith believe in this Christian revelation. And all agree that its mission is not only to proclaim the faith thus held but to apply its consequences for the betterment of the human condition here in history, while looking forward with ardent expectation and hope to Christ's final victory and to that 'eschatological future' in which he will hand over his kingdom to his heavenly Father, so that God may be 'all in all'. This hope they find embodied in the teaching of the New Testament books, indeed in the Bible as a whole. And they acknowledge the Bible as a norm for Christian faith and practice.

The depth and extent of this agreement among almost all the Christian bodies – I am speaking of the official stance of these bodies, not of the vagaries of individual adherents of them – appears in its full and massive significance when Christianity is compared with any or all of the alternative 'faiths', philosophies and agnosticisms current in the world outside Christianity. The more deeply a Christian reflects upon these things, the more he comes to realize the power and credibility of his religion; and the more he must lament that existing divisions between the Christian bodies diminish the impact of the gospel upon the world that we are sent to bring to Christ.

There is of course much more. Alongside all the sorrows, distortions and dangers of our modern world there are movements of the spirit that do honour to our common humanity. Not least is that movement of compassion that has grown out of the unlikely soil of a world-culture that in so many respects is full not only of misery but of heartlessness and cruelty. This impulse of compassion is something with which we Christians can at once feel at home and from which we can relearn lessons that are implicit in our own tradition. Our mission, recognized as such by all of us, is to preach compassion – we call it love – and more than that: to proclaim that the mystery behind and within all appearances is a mystery of infinite love – God *is* love. We can therefore tell the world, on the authority of God himself, that Reality is on the side of compassion, and that – despite, and indeed by means of, everything – compassion, love, will be victorious. We leave to our philosophers and theologians the theoretical task of dealing with the 'problem of evil', and we go out in faith and hope as well as charity to fight the universal human fight against evil in all its forms. Only by such co-operation with the compassion of our non-Christian fellow men, our brothers, can we make our own faith believable; just as it is our faith that makes compassion hopeful and persevering.

Compared with the things that unite us, it may be argued, those that divide us seem so petty and insignificant: questions about the validity of sacraments and of ministry, when it is obvious that both sacraments and ministry are fruitful without apparent reference to these questions; questions about the invocation of saints and abstruse dogmas about the mother of Jesus Christ; questions, today, not so much about a possible role of the bishop of Rome as leader of all Christians, but about his alleged universal jurisdiction by divine right and his alleged function of defining, under conditions laid down with much sophistication but still not easy to construe, points of doctrine which surely need no definition, now that we are already agreed on so much, and on such central and important issues of faith and practice.

The proposal, then, would be to set aside such 'secondary' matters and agree to unite on the basis of what we already hold in common. It should not be difficult to calculate the Highest Common Factor of our beliefs and on that foundation come together in the one visible communion which we all agree would realize the prayer and intention of Christ.[16]

The attraction of this suggestion is obvious. But it has one or two disadvantages. In the first place, it presupposes a determination of the line to be drawn between primary doctrines upon which agreement will be necessary, and secondary doctrines upon which we may agree to differ. Would it be easy to draw such a line?[17] Suppose, for example, a group of believers asked to enter into the wider unity, while rejecting the doctrine of the godhead of Jesus Christ, or the doctrine of the Trinity in Unity of God, or the normative role of the Scriptures. Perhaps it would be hard to find such a group – though I wonder whether the Society of Friends has *any* dogmas which it teaches as essential. Certainly there are theologians today, in various Christian bodies, who in effect refuse assent to one, or more, or all of the doctrines just specified. A proposal to unite on the sort of basis outlined above would at least involve an acceptance of the dogmatic principle; and the dogmatic principle itself is in question at the present day. A second disadvantage of our proposal is that inevitably it would mean that some members of the contracting groups would be in effect asked to regard as non-essential items of belief which they have hitherto held as of faith. Has anyone the right to make such a demand, even in the cause of Christian reunion? Nor is it sufficient to say that these people could be allowed to go on *believing* these 'non-essential' items, though they must not try to impose them on others. For there are many people who would find it difficult to believe as of faith matters which the Church (and we are thinking of Christians reunited into a single Church) did not itself so accept.[18]

There is a quite different suggestion for a basis of future reunion. Instead of the H.C.F. principle, we could adopt the principle of the Lowest Common Multiple. We could in effect say to one another: 'We have all grown up in separate traditions of Christianity: Protestant (in various forms), Eastern Orthodox, and Roman Catholic. We are very conscious that, through our mutual separateness, we have been deprived in our several traditions of riches that flourished in traditions from which we were separated. Let us seek reunion not by a process of discarding what divides us, but by one of seeking mutual enrichment in learning from one another. Let Catholics learn from Protestants what positive insight it was that led Luther or Calvin to brave the wrath of the bishop of Rome; and from the Eastern Orthodox what it means to see the work of Christ not merely as a remedy for human sin but as the crowning of the work of creation and the inauguration of the final goal of the creative act. Let Protestants explore the deep reasons for the Catholic and Orthodox conviction that the Church is by divine ordinance a single visible communion; and let Catholics and Orthodox understand the reasons why Protestants have difficulty with that notion.

This plea for mutual enrichment instead of mutual concession is bound to come up against a deep feeling within many people that an enriched Christianity must be a very complicated affair, whereas the gospel, they think, was a simple one. At an extreme point this desire for simplicity will lead to some such proposition as that Christianity is the religion of mutual human love; and there are very many good people quite outside the visible limits of Christianity who would agree that to love one's neighbour is a desirable maxim. It is more likely that the advocates of simple Christianity would add a clause to the maxim and say: Love God by loving your neighbour – which introduces a metaphysical dimension to the maxim and raises a multitude of entailed questions.

Perhaps it is relevant to remark that this notion that Christianity is essentially a simple, not to say a simplistic, thing is itself an interpretation, and a disputable one. Certainly the Christianity of the New Testament writers was not simple in that sense. And if it is sought to take refuge from Paul, the author of the Epistle to the Hebrews, and the Johannine theology, and to fall back on the Jesus of the Gospels, it is inevitable that one will get caught up in modern gospel scholarship and criticism, and it is quite uncertain whether Jesus proclaimed a merely 'simple' message. It can be argued that, on the contrary, he was engaged on an enormous task of resuming the Old Covenant in a new and higher synthesis that was anything but reducible to a bare and easily understood single proposition.

The case for thinking that Christianity has within it a potentiality that will unfold itself in a majestic and continuing development, analogous (though only analogous) to the development of some great tree from a tiny seed, need not be expounded here. It has been put magisterially by Newman in his *Essay on the Development of Christian Doctrine* – and, more succinctly, in his earlier sermon, 'The Theory of Developments in Religious Doctrine' (1843). From the latter, I may be allowed to quote a short passage in which Newman relates the faith of the Mother of Jesus ('Blessed is she that believed') to her reflections upon the content of her faith ('Mary kept all these things, and pondered them in her heart'):

Thus St. Mary is our pattern of Faith, both in the reception and in the study of Divine Truth. She does not think it enough to accept, she dwells upon it; not enough to possess, she uses it; not enough to assent, she developes it; not enough to submit the Reason, she reasons upon it; not indeed reasoning first, and believing afterwards, with Zacharias, yet first believing without reasoning, next from love and reverence, reasoning after believing. And thus she symbolizes to us, not only the faith of the unlearned, but of the doctors of the Church also, who have to investigate, and weigh, and define, as well as to profess the Gospel.[19]

Newman points out that this unending process of interpreting the faith leads to the accumulation of a tradition. We may add that, in our quest of Christian unity, we, who are as much the creature of our own age as the Fathers, the Schoolmen and the Reformers were of theirs, cannot afford to bypass this tradition, to which of course we are adding our own small contribution, not least by the dialogue in progress today between the churches.

For our present purposes it will be enough to take the great alternative put before us by Greenslade and those who think with him. Is the Church, by divine institution, a reality partially realized in each of our communions but in none so uniquely realized as to constitute that communion as the body in which alone the Church of Christ 'subsists'; or is the Church, again by divine guarantee and the perpetual assistance of the Holy Spirit, an indivisible visible communion? It is likely that, to develop an adequate answer to that question, we shall have to consider what so far this essay has scarcely touched upon: the alleged Petrine primacy and its alleged realization in the primacy of the bishop of Rome. And whichever answer commends itself to us as a result of our comparison of the two positions, we should try to see how the position adopted can reply to the objections of those who support the other position, and how the preferred position can incorporate the values that give power to the rejected position.[20]

Chapter IX

The Church in Context

Faith, Christians agree, is a grace that enables us to apprehend and acknowledge realities, or a dimension of reality, hidden from the 'natural man'. Speaking of the self-revealing Act of God which we call the incarnation of the Word and the resurrection of Christ, Dr Torrance says:

> '... what is particularly staggering is the fact that [this Act] gives Jesus Christ a place of cosmic significance, making him, man of earth as he the incarnate Son of God is, the point of supreme focus for the whole universe of space and time, by reference to which all its meaning and destiny are finally to be discerned.'[1]

They are to be discerned by reference to the Act of God which is Christ, because in that reference they are discoverable as true, as real. 'Blessed are your eyes, for they see'; and what they see is not an hallucination but a reality.

This Act of God has an historical location, 'under Pontius Pilate'. It is an act of giving. It conveys a gift that is to be made known by communication. And when it is thus known, it calls for a radical revision of our understanding of the created order. To quote Torrance again:

> [Through this divine Act, as known,] the natural order is open to control and explication from a higher and wider level of reality, in a way similar to that in which the various levels with which

we operate in any rigorous science are each open to the meta-level above it.[2] [And again, speaking of the incarnation and the resurrection in the plural, they] are acts of God who is the creative Source of all order in space and time, ... essentially ordering events within the natural order, restoring and creating order where it is damaged or lacking, and it is in terms of that *giving of order* that they constitute the relevant boundary conditions within the natural order where it is open to the transcendent and creative reality of God.[3]

A word about levels of reality. If we accept that the 'laws' of chemistry are neither sheer illusion nor the mere statement of a number of coincidental phenomena in the physical order (which is reductionism); that the laws of biology are neither sheer illusion nor the mere statement of a number of coincidental phenomena in the chemical order but genuinely objective as 'laws'; and if we similarly take the laws of psychology as objective and not mere 'biology in disguise'; if finally we admit, as we must, that each of these sciences is dealing with the same empirical universe and that its objects of interest are interlocked with those of the other sciences, then we believe in orders or 'levels' of reality. But if we are Christians we can go a stage further: we believe that the divine Act in Christ is no less objective than the levels of physics, chemistry, biology and psychology. We believe that it is the focal point of a level of reality higher than all the others in this ascending scale of reality. And we believe that this higher level is, nevertheless, rooted, made concrete and indeed historical, in that whole created order which provides the several sciences with their data.

This higher level or extra dimension of reality was brought into historical reality in the redemptive and elevating Act of God which we call the redemption. Was it a new dimension? Or should we rather say that it is a dimension that was hidden from our apprehension until we became aware of that divine Act through the witness of the apostles, and thereafter of the Church – their witness to the resurrection and consequently to the incarnation of the Word?

There is an ancient dispute among theologians about the incarnation: would it have occurred if man had not fallen into sin – or, at least, if no creature, human, angelic or intelligent-extraterrestrial, had ever sinned or would ever have sinned? One powerful tradition affirms that the incarnation is only to be understood as the divine answer to sin; it is essentially redemptive or reparative. But another tradition has argued that the incarnation is part of God's primordial plan, a plan that has never had to suffer essential modification. Thus, on the former hypothesis, it would seem that, but for sin, creation would never have received an actual elevation to the incarnational level; while, on the alternative view, sin is not a condition *sine qua non* of the incarnation, but at most a complicating factor.

I confess that I find this dispute somewhat unreal; perhaps because all questions of the type: 'What would have happened if an event X had not occurred (but it has)?' are unreal. It seems to suppose that sin 'entered in' as a potential threat to a divine plan or purpose; and that God adjusted his procedures to this unwelcome disorder. It seems to think of God as of a master chessplayer whose opponent has made a move against which the master had not made provision, for he had not foreseen it before it occurred; a move, however, which his mastery enables him triumphantly to exploit in order to achieve a more splendid victory than he had at first envisaged. 'O happy fault', says the Paschal *Exsultet*, of Adam's fall. And a lovely old English poem says:

> Adam lay y-bounden,
>   Bounden in a bond;
> Four thousand winter
>   Thought he not too long;
> And all was for an apple,
>   An apple that he took,
> As clerkes finden written
>   In theire book.
> Ne had the apple taken been,
>   The apple taken been,
> Ne hadde our Lady
>   A been heaven's queen.
> Blessed be the time
>   That apple taken was!
> Therefore we may singen
>   'Deo Gracias!'

God, however, does not plan in time but in eternity. The only universe, so far as we know, that he actually plans[4] is that in which we exist, a universe containing sin but containing also the Divine Act which simultaneously repairs evil and raises the universe to a level which is strictly supernatural. We are not confronted with a universe that bears the mark of an obsolete divine plan that has somehow gone awry and of a marvellous reparation of that disorder. We live in, we are part of, a single universe whose fallenness and redemption are, together (and neither without the other), eternally known to God and, in their conjunction (but only in their conjunction), willed by God with an eternal will. Because we are finite and temporal, we find it convenient to distinguish within God's will a positive and a permissive will, the former effecting whatever is good and the latter not preventing whatever is evil. But God's will in itself is utterly simple and un-distinct. His plan, too, is simple, completely unified, infallible.

A plan or purpose is to be understood in its completion; and so are all the details and processes involved in the plan. The physical level of reality is to be understood as 'in potency' to the chemical; the chemical level as in potency to the biological; and so on. It is reasonable, then, to seek the meaning and reason of the whole 'natural' created universe in the divine Act, the Word incarnate, crucified and risen, and in the consequent mission of the Holy Spirit.

On this view we find ourselves impelled to seek understanding in what Aristotle called 'final causes', that is to say controlling purposes. As the foundations of a building, and the work which went into them, are to be explained by the style and nature of the completed building, so the most comprehensive explanation of any reality is the end for which it exists; and the only satisfying explanation of any process of growth is not the seed from which it sprang but the fruit in which it culminates.[5] The goal and meaning of the whole process of creation is therefore to be found in the glorified *totus Christus* (Augustine's term for Christ the Head in conjunction with the members of his body the Church) or the ultimate and all-inclusive 'kingdom' of Christ which, according to Paul, Jesus will, 'in the end', 'hand over to his Father, so that God may be all in all'. This *eschaton* (last thing), this post-historical term and fruit and goal, is the 'cause of causes', or the explanation explaining every subsidiary explanation, of the whole synthesis of creation and supernatural elevation. To it everything in creation is orientated. From our point of view, since we think in time, this whole universe can be seen as one vast, comprehensive movement or process or growth. And since growth and upward striving, in our experience, involve labour and suffering, Paul can write: 'We know that the whole creation has been groaning in travail together until now; and not only the creation, but we ourselves, who have the first fruits of the Spirit, groan inwardly as we wait for adoption as sons, the redemption of our bodies' (Rom. 8:22f.). Grace, according to Aquinas, is the perfection of nature; but we have to bear in mind that it is a gratuitous perfection. Without grace nature cannot be perfected; but nature cannot demand perfection as of right. It has no claim in justice for God's perfecting act, but it can look with confidence to his mercy. And the gospel is that mercy brought into divine Act and so proclaimed.

Aristotle observes that in a process of ordered movement the goal or term of the movement is immanent in each and all of its stages: if I have decided to walk to the Post Office to buy some stamps, then this goal of my walking is immanent in every step I take; if my purpose ceased, so too would my progress. Growth is, in Aristotelian terms, a 'movement'. The oak tree is immanent in the seed and the seedling. We may therefore ask whether the Word incarnate and risen is 'immanent', in some sense, in the whole of creation from its beginning to its end – immanent not, indeed, as an intrinsic exigency of the creature but as a divine orientation, like the direction given to an arrow's flight by the bowman. We need not be deterred from considering this possibility by the fact that the incarnation occurred at a late date.[6]

It has been the Church's doctrine that the redemption was the redemption of the whole of mankind. This is what gives the Church its 'catholic' character and universal mission. The New Testament states that God 'wills all men to be saved'. And Acts puts on the lips of Peter the affirmation that there is 'no other name by which a man may be saved' except the name of Jesus. Is this purpose of universal salvation confined to those who have lived after the historical accomplishment of the redemptive Act?

The Church was never content to write off the holy people of the Old Covenant as outside the sphere of salvation, that salvation which the Church could find only in Jesus Christ. There may be a mythological element, but there is profound significance, in the statement in St Matthew's Gospel that, after the crucifixion, 'saints' of the Old Covenant were seen alive in Jerusalem. This passage has not only to be demythologized but, I take it, harmonized with the Church's ordinary teaching that the time of our human probation, the time in which it is open to us to accept redemption, ends with our mortal life. Does it not follow that, somehow or other, God's redeeming grace, his incarnate Word, was within the range of people who died centuries before that Word was born of Mary?

It is not sufficient to say that the not-yet-incarnate Word, or rather the Word of God considered in abstraction from his historical incarnation, was able to effect this contact because he is God and therefore transcends the temporal order and its temporality. For we are redeemed not by the Word in abstraction from the incarnation but by Jesus Christ the incarnate Word. Inasmuch as the redemptive and 'elevating' Act of God transforms the whole created order (of which it is, in history, the anticipated term and goal), and thus raises it to a level of which by itself it is incapable but to which it is destined, we seem to need to link Jesus of Nazareth, the historically incarnate Word, with the totality of the created order from its beginning to its final consummation.

This we may be encouraged to do by reference to two scriptural passages. In the Epistle to the Colossians (1:15ff.) the author speaks of the Son of God, and must – in my view – be thinking of the Son of God as incarnate.[7] Now, in the Epistle to the Philippians (2:9–11) Paul had already said: 'God has highly exalted (Jesus Christ) and bestowed on him the name which is above every name, that at the name of Jesus every knee should bow, in heaven and on earth and under the earth, and every tongue confess that Jesus Christ is LORD, to the glory of God the Father'. In other words, the crucified, risen and exalted Christ is the due object of the universal adoration of all creation. And in our passage from Colossians we are told that 'In him all things were created, in heaven and on earth, visible and invisible, whether thrones or dominations or principalities or authorities – all things were created through him and for him. He is before all things and in him all things hold together'. Thus the incarnate Word is not only the object of the adoration of all creation, its term and goal, but the agent of creation and its sustaining and unifying principle. Not dissimilarly, in the first chapter of the Fourth Gospel, we are told that 'all things were made' through the Word, and 'without him was not anything made that was made'. In considering this Johannine statement we have to bear in mind the sound theological principle that the creative effects of God (his works *ad extra*) are the common work of the Godhead, not in any instance the particular work of One of the three divine Hypostases. How is it, then, that the fourth evangelist feels himself able to assign creation in some special way – or so it would seem – to the Word? Is it because he envisages the Word precisely as the Word incarnate? Is there any sense in saying that all things were made through the *incarnate* Word?

One can hardly avoid the reflection that, so long as Jesus, the incarnate Word, is considered without reference to his resurrection, he remains within the horizons of a historical existence that in no sense preceded his conception in the womb of his mother. Hence we can cordially agree with Dr Torrance that the resurrection of Christ is the real focus of the whole divine Act; its focus and its accomplishment. For in his risen and glorified humanity Jesus both subsumes his historical life, up to and including his dying on the cross, and also transcends (as we are destined in our future resurrection to transcend) the historical and temporal order. As Fr Peter Chirico expresses the matter,

> By the resurrection, Christ is constituted as the supreme and all-encompassing object of faith. When the Christian expresses belief in the resurrection of Christ, he is accepting the risen condition of Christ as the central reality of faith; and implicitly he is saying yes to all that is implied in that primary acceptance. ... Because in [the risen Christ] all the capacities of humanity are realized, he is capable of expressing his unique divine sonship to every aspect of creation. He sums up, interrelates, and unifies all of creation in himself. In and through his humanity which recapitulates all, he images forth the divine personality he is. In him every aspect of creation becomes the vehicle of divine revelation.[8]

I would add that every aspect of creation must, in my view, include the temporal aspects of creation that, historically, preceded the incarnation in time. And I emphasize that in the glorified Christ every such aspect of creation becomes the vehicle of divine revelation – obviously of *the* divine revelation that is the incarnate Word, whose revealing presence is always personal and always active.

The eighteenth-century Jesuit, Jean Pierre de Caussade writes:

All creatures are living in the hand of God; the senses perceive only the action of the creature, but faith sees the action of God in everything – faith believes that Jesus Christ is alive in everything and operates throughout the whole course of the centuries; faith believes that the briefest moment and the tiniest atom contain a portion of Christ's hidden life and his mysterious action. The action of creatures is a veil concealing the profound mysteries of the divine action. ... All that occurs within us, around us and by our means covers and hides his divine action.[9]

The question of course at once arises: since redemption is not really given (though it may be really offered) until it is actually received, and since the reception of redemption is by an act of faith and therefore an act of cognition, how can Christ incarnate be an object of cognition to men before the historical event of the incarnation?

Once again we have to revert to the distinction between two meanings of the word 'object'. The distinction is thus stated by Lonergan.[10] I paraphrase, with quotations:

Etymologically, the word 'object' connotes something sensible (i.e. apprehensible by the senses), something localized, 'locally related presumably to a spectator or sensitive subject'.[11] This is the meaning of the word supposed by Kant. 'Accordingly, our cognitional activity is', on this view, 'restricted to a world ... of sensible phenomena'.[12] In much modern philosophical discourse the word 'object' has this restricted meaning, and logical statements and arguments, if they are to be meaningful, must (it is agreed) be restricted to what can be verified or falsified by sensible 'objects'. It is obvious that the incarnate Word was not an 'object' of cognition, in this meaning of the word 'object', before Christ's historical conception.

There is, however, says Lonergan, another meaning of the word 'object'. By 'objects' we may mean 'what are intended in questioning and what become better known as our answers to questions become fuller and more accurate'.[13] All intellectual inquiry pursues some as-yet-not-adequately-known object, but with the help of some clue or clues. The clues may be very ordinary or, on the other hand, so scientifically constructed as to guide the inquirer, if he remains faithful to the intrinsic exigencies of intellectual inquiry, with surety to his goal. In this second sense, then, an object is not a presentation to sense (even to some interior sense) but a goal of the desire to know. And, precisely as such an object, it is 'immanent' or, in the case of mathematics we might rather say implicit, in the whole process of inquiry relevant to it; and it becomes explicit when the inquiry is successfully concluded. In this meaning of the word 'object' the incarnate Word can be an object of the human mind before the historical date at which it occurred, and also the object of minds that have never been evangelized in the Christian era.

The Christian tradition has not entirely neglected this theme of a gospel before the gospel. We can perhaps say that this notion lay behind the constant, and at times oddly applied, determination of New Testament and other ancient Christian writers to present Christianity as the fulfilment of Old Testament prophecy. For to say that Christianity fulfils what was best in the Old Covenant is tantamount to saying that the Old Covenant was, to some extent at least, an anticipation of the gospel: the New Testament, said Augustine, lies hidden in the Old, and the Old Testament finds its explication in the New. St Paul even goes so far, if he was not merely seeking what today we call an 'accommodated' interpretation of an Old Testament passage, as to identify the rock that flowed with water in the desert with Christ. 'Our fathers ... were baptized by Moses in the cloud and in the sea, and all ate the same supernatural food and all drank the same supernatural drink. For they drank from the supernatural rock which followed them, and the rock was Christ' (1 Cor. 10:1ff.). It is significant that the primitive Church identified Christ the Lord with the Old Testament Yahweh. There is a strand of source utilized in the Old Testament which is somewhat free with the divine name Yahweh, and, using that name, is prepared to portray God in a vividly anthropomorphic way. It is as though, at the heart of that extraordinary, developing tradition, the religion of Israel, there was a sense of a need for 'God in human terms'. But there is also a tendency in the Old Testament to shrink from such anthropomorphisms, to recoil from this dangerous familiarity. In some passages we find that not God immediately but the 'angel of the Lord' is presented as the heavenly interlocutor with men. If man in the actual order of creation and history (which has never been a merely natural order, since it has always been involved in God's supernatural redemptive and elevating 'plan') has always been not only a rational animal but a religious animal, the twin and complementary poles of man's notion of God as *mysterium tremendum et fascinans* have rarely been exploited, before the coming of Christ, with greater poignancy and sublimity than in the Old Testament tradition. God is the supreme object of awe, and there is thus an instinct to increase the distance between him and us: to consign him to an exclusive transcendence which, while seeming to increase our reverence, would in practice leave us free to manage without him. But he is also the supremely attractive Object, so that like Moses we draw near to the burning bush and presume to inquire his 'name'. There is evidence that primitive Judaeo-Christian theology gave to Christ the title of 'the Name', sc. the name of God.

There is at least one New Testament passage which utilizes a pagan dedication as an anticipation of the gospel: 'Whom therefore you ignorantly worship, him I declare to you'. Early Christian writers saw in elements of Greek pagan philosophy a 'preparation for the gospel', and they attributed this preparation to that Word of God which in due course was incarnate as Jesus, and which they identified with the word or *logos* of which the philosophers spoke.

Man is not only a sensing, a feeling, an instinctive animal. He is an intellectual animal; he has an unrestricted desire to know. This desire is not simply for the satisfaction that comes from knowing, though knowledge – so far as it goes – does satisfy us. The desire is, at its heart, not for satisfaction but for the knowledge itself. And it is an unrestricted desire. Present it with a boundary; say to it, 'Thus far shalt thou go and no further', and even if it is resigned it remains unsatisfied. The dissatisfaction is an indication that the desire itself really is unrestricted. Plainly, nothing could satisfy this desire except the knowledge of the infinite, the unrestricted.

The infinite, however, is God; not an abstract theory, nor an impersonal object, but One who is personal or rather super-personal. And so we find that man is not only an intellectual animal but, as already said, a religious animal. God made us for himself, says Augustine, and our heart is restless till it comes to rest in him. That is why the gospel can be heard by those not hitherto Christianized.

God, however, even more than any finite person, can only really be known as what he is to the extent that he discloses himself. And the infinite yearning of the human intellect and heart can only be actuated to the extent that God himself awakens the desire.

God discloses himself in and as the incarnate Word and 'there is no other name given whereby a man may be saved'. If, then, the whole of human history is pervaded by the religious factor; if man is and always has been man in quest of God; and if this quest, being a quest for God as he is in himself in his 'super-personality', is a quest that only God can satisfy and only God can stir into action; then – unless we are prepared to dismiss all such religion as empty of real meaning – we are driven to say not only that the incarnate Word is the objective of all religion, but that this incarnate Word is present, immanent or really implicit, in all genuine religion to the extent that it is genuine. It is genuine not to the extent that its religious imaginations and doctrines are correct, but to the extent that it itself is honest and sincere. And it is not too much to say that the incarnate Word is present and active in the whole created order, since everything in that order has its focus and its goal first in the intellectual creature and then, supremely, in the Man who is God.

A twentieth-century Jesuit, in close harmony with the passage of de Caussade quoted above, writes as follows (and it will be observed that he writes not only of the uninformed, the misinformed, and the misunderstanding, but of sinners):

Lord, tell me your relation to those who seek; what you do for those who do not find or who mislead themselves, and for all those who have voluntarily forsaken the light. I should like to be able to see everything from your point of view and adopt your judgements as my own; I want to avoid bitter severity and soft complacency. ... All these people have a supernatural vocation; that means that all of them, from their birth onwards, are uniquely destined for everlasting union with you. This 'call' is not inactive within them; it is 'your word' which will 'not return void'. Hence you are urging all these wanderers, these indifferent people, these guilty men, towards light and peace. You are at work in them, like a labourer underground, an unseen labourer whose work is scarcely audible but who gets on with it down there unceasingly. ... You are the redeemer of those without the faith, father of the poor, friend of sinners. ... So I must think of these wanderers as of a great people *en route* to destinies unknown to them, to a goal which you know ... For so long this humanity, to which I belong and which is dearer to me than I am to myself, has been dreaming, from the depths of its wretchedness, of the unique hope. ... These people have been in quest of you ... and that shows that your grace was co-operating with their effort and you were closer to them than they thought: 'Among you stands one whom you do not know.' ... You have arranged 'dispensations' of salvation, progressive manifestations of the total truth which you at last gave us when you came among us. I don't think I am being disrespectful to the light when I seek its first reflections in the night. Life has such deep origins; and man gets his experience by slow degrees. Ever since the fall he has been groping and calling for you, like a child stricken with sudden blindness who cries out for some compassion which he cannot know. ... Wherever someone is making efforts he deserves our infinite esteem; every visage turned towards the light has an invisible halo above it.'[14]

Considerations like these should, in the first place, affect our attitude towards the 'other religions' and our practice of the 'wider ecumenism' that brings Christians into dialogue with the other world-faiths. This dialogue should not be pursued simply on the basis that man, throughout the ages and in every culture, has been searching for God. What we have to affirm is that God, everywhere and at all times, has been searching for man, for ever 'beats at our own clay-shuttered doors'.[15] In Mary of Nazareth he at last found someone who, instead of seeking to diminish his word, his appeal of love, to the narrow limits of her own presuppositions, offered herself without any reserve or limit to his invitation: 'Be it done to me according to thy word'. It is the Word, thus, in consequence, incarnate, who has been the hidden inspiration of all the religions. Unless we maintain the uniqueness of that historical incarnation we have lost the foundation of our ecumenical effort on this wider field. People sometimes speak of the 'cosmic Christ' as though this notion were the invention of a modern and adventurous theology. Our quotations from Pierre Charles and from the earlier Jean Pierre de Caussade show that it has a good traditional pedigree.

Nevertheless, if we admit that Christ's presence and operation are universal, we shall not infer from the *a priori* arguments and the empirical evidence that we are presented, in the non-Christian religions, with 'churchness', still less with 'the Church'. Christ, we are bound to conclude, is active outside his Church as well as within it.[16]

Against this background of a whole humanity redeemed and encountering the appeal of the divine Word in all its experience, we can now turn back to Greenslade's theory of the Church. He does not, if I am correct in my understanding of his argument, set out to prove the 'churchness' of separated Christian communions by appealing to the fruits of grace in behaviour that commends itself to the Christian conscience. His contention, rather, is (as we have seen) that Christ gives himself in various gifts that spring directly from the gospel; that these gifts, in full combination of them all, would constitute a fully united visible Church; and that, wherever they are given and received in some substantial, even though partial, combination and richness, they at least constitute 'churchness'. 'Churchness' is thus a quality that he feels able to predicate of a number of Christian bodies. These bodies, however, are at present separate communions. He concludes that no one body at the present time can claim to be *the* Church, since outside any one body there are other bodies, each of which shows at least some measure of 'churchness'.

The theory of gospel gifts and resultant 'churchness' enables us to mark off Christians and their communions from the rest of mankind and successfully preserves the uniqueness of the historical gospel and of Christianity, while in no way retreating from the 'universalism' outlined above.

The distinction seems to be a valid and valuable one. I fully accept it: Christians are distinct from those who are not Christians; distinct not only sociologically but religiously. There is no arrogance in maintaining this distinction, for Christianity is a pure unmerited gift of God's grace. It was the gospel, the good news, explicitly accepted as such, that marked off the primitive Christians alike from the Jews who had not accepted the gospel and from the pagans or Gentiles. And as we have seen, the Christians were not just a sociological group but a new theological reality. They are those who have received the gospel and, along with the gospel, certain rites and 'gifts', and a mission to propagate the faith that has been entrusted to them.

But just as Augustine found it necessary to accept Cyprian's main thesis (the indivisible visible unity of the Church as a single communion) but to reject the corollary (that there was nothing truly Christian outside that one communion), so one can properly accept, and with gratitude, Greenslade's thesis that these gifts, wherever they are received and acted upon, constitute 'churchness', yet reject his further argument that where there is 'churchness' there of necessity is 'the Church'; at least if that corollary is pushed to the point of denying that any one Christian communion at the present day can be that unique communion in which the gift of visible unity is preserved by the action of the Holy Spirit. Greenslade's insistence on this final alleged consequence of his thesis goes beyond the logic of the case.

I suggest that there is an important parallel between the existence of the grace of Christ 'outside' Christianity and the existence of 'churchness' outside the unique visible communion. The grace of the incarnate Word, I have been arguing, is operative throughout history. It is operative everywhere. Wherever a Socrates is faithful unto death to principles and values that he has conscientiously accepted; wherever a modern scientist refuses to 'cook' his results in the interest of a (probably true and important) hypothesis; wherever an enemy of society spares a victim out of genuine compassion, we may reasonably hope that Christ's grace is not only being offered but is being accepted. But we do not feel obliged to infer from this that there is nothing unique about the gospel or about the Christianity that derives from its proclamation.[17]

Similarly, we can agree that that specifically Christian quality, 'churchness', is found outside the one visible communion, without feeling obliged to deny (as Greenslade denies) that there is one Christian communion that uniquely has a 'gift' or 'holy thing' which the others do not have, namely visible unity.

A preliminary conclusion thus seems to be fully assured: none of the considerations adduced by Greenslade makes it necessary to abandon the traditional doctrine that the Church is, by divine guarantee and the Holy Spirit's abiding help, a permanent unity in the historical order, an indivisible visible communion. Augustine was right to move beyond the rigid and exclusive ecclesiology of Cyprian; and Greenslade was right to insist that where Augustine could recognize valid sacraments, there we can recognize genuine 'churchness'. But Augustine was also right to locate his development of sacramental theology *within* the ambit of the traditional principle of the Church as a single communion. Augustine's developments with regard to sacraments were in fact an exploitation of latent possibilities in positions already held in theory and practice by the Church before his time: e.g. the conviction that catechumens who died before baptism and unbaptized martyrs for the faith could be saved. We too can therefore claim justification for pushing matters somewhat further than Augustine was willing to do, in order to find room for our modern, much deeper, appreciation of both the universality of the redemption and the existence of 'good faith', coupled though it be with intellectual error or simple ignorance.

Augustine had a horror of the sin of schism. In this he was right. The sin of schism shuts one out from the koinonia which is the 'incarnation' of charity. The sinful schismatic goes out, like Judas, into 'the night'. But common sense rejects the notion that the majority of modern non-Catholic Christians, or their churches for that matter, are *subjectively* guilty of this terrible sin. The opposite may rather be held to be true of a Christianity that is deeply moved in our time by the quest of visible unity. And Augustine went a long way towards this developed position when he distinguished between the original Donatists and their descendants who had grown up, in all good faith, in the form of Christianity which they had learned from their parents and were not deliberately shutting their eyes against the divine light. We today shall only be taking Augustine's insight to its logical term if we agree that Luther, Calvin, Wesley and other originators of schism may have acted not only under extreme provocation but in entire good faith. A Christian is called upon to be firm about the claims of truth but to be non-judgemental in his attitude towards those he considers to be in error. After all, if Catholics think that 'schismatics' are in error, the compliment is inevitably returned by the non-Catholic communions and their members; otherwise they would not delay to join the Catholic Church.

It may be asked, But are you not trying to salvage the ancient doctrine of the indivisible visible unity of the Church at the expense of the equally ancient principle: outside the Church there is no salvation? For certainly a modern Catholic, with his ecumenical attitude towards other Christians and their churches, does not believe that these 'separated brethren' are outside the scope of salvation.

Such a question provokes a reply at two different levels. First, if it may seem a peculiarly 'Catholic' notion that there is no salvation outside the Church, it is surely a general Christian principle that there is no salvation apart from faith in Christ ('there is no other name ...'). But is any of us really prepared to consign to hell not only all the pagans of pre-Christian times but all who, since the incarnation, have not been evangelized or who, having heard the gospel message, have (apparently in all good faith: think of Gandhi) not accepted its message as true? Aquinas himself contemplated the possibility that an unevangelized person might be offered by God a private revelation that would stand as valid substitute for the Church's public proclamation of Christ. I have offered, earlier in this chapter, a more sophisticated version of Aquinas' suggestion. I submit that we all have to find some way of reconciling the principle that apart from the gospel Christ there is no salvation and the principle that God wills all men to be saved. That being so, have we any reason to refuse *a priori* to contemplate a sophisticated exegesis of the principle: outside the *Church* there is no salvation?

After all, our exegesis of 'there is no other name than Christ's' has already committed us to such sophistication, since apart from Christ there is no Church.

Greenslade's theology of the 'holy gifts' which (together) constitute the Church and which (in various incomplete combinations) establish 'churchness' can be helpful here. As the grace of Christ is operative outside the area of mankind that has been effectively evangelized, so (we can say) the Church is operative outside her own God-given visible limits through these 'churchly' gifts.

In fact, we shall have to go further. We have to find an interpretation of 'outside the Church there is no salvation' which will be compatible with affirming as possible the salvation not only of separated Christians but of those who are in no sense Christians and have no element of 'churchness'.

We have, then, to consider once again the place that the Church occupies in God's redemptive plan – that is to say, in the whole 'economy' of creation supernaturalized. The Church – or, to revert to the more pregnant language of an earlier chapter, the koinonia – is not an extrinsic addition to the mystery of Christ the head of creation and the focus of God's redemptive purposes. On the contrary, the Church is integral to God's plan and purpose. I have already argued that the revelatory and redemptive Act of God, which is the Word incarnate, his 'Paschal mystery' of death and resurrection, and the consequent outpouring of the Holy Spirit, is only fully 'given' to the extent that it is actually 'received' in faith. This reception in faith is the act of the koinonia and its constitutive factor: the Church is 'the gathering of the believers', *societas fidelium.* Strictly speaking, there are not two mysteries, the mystery of Jesus and the mystery of the Church. There is one mystery, what Augustine called the *totus Christus*, Christ in both Head and members. It is this *totus Christus* that is the actualization of God's one plan for the created universe; and this means that the *totus Christus*, Jesus Christ in the Church and the Church in Jesus Christ, is the hidden (but now partially revealed) inwardness of the whole of history and of the whole created order. 'Outside' – or, as we should more naturally say, 'apart from' – the *totus Christus* there is indeed no salvation. But, to revert to considerations set out earlier in this chapter, only those are, in this sense, 'apart from' it who deliberately sin against the light they have been given in their own conscience – sin to the extent and depth of making a fundamental option that is inconsistent with God's call to their conscience.

It will be observed that I have (ingeniously, as Greenslade might say) proposed to substitute 'apart from' for 'outside'. I think that this substitution is justified. We inherit 'extra ecclesiam nulla salus' (there is no salvation outside the Church) from Christian antiquity. But the ancient Church did not press this principle to such an extreme as to exclude from salvation everyone who had not found his way into the visible Church by sacramental baptism: as we have seen, the ancients acknowledged that one who died as a catechumen (and therefore unbaptized) could attain to heaven. The same principle was applied to unbaptized martyrs. The Fathers would have said, as even Cyprian at one moment said of some schismatics, that the heart of such persons was in the Church, although they were in the material sense sacramentally 'outside'. The principle 'extra ecclesiam nulla salus' has, nevertheless, an important pastoral aspect: it is a warning that the Church's claim is grave and serious and that it is flouted at one's own peril.

Once again we are constrained to make a distinction between the two meanings of the word 'object'; and to remind ourselves that the 'final cause' is the 'causa causarum'.

We are accustomed to viewing the Church as primarily a sociological phenomenon, a concentration of power in a collectivity, a human grouping that affects its surroundings by efficient causality. We think of the Church, in other words, as we think of a great nation, as an object directly subjected to our senses. Clearly, there is truth in this way of thinking of the

Church; and it is because there is truth in it that we can talk about the Church as visible and speak of its visible unity. But by an object we can also mean that which, though hidden or partially hidden from view at present, or not yet identified by us as the object for which we are looking, is nevertheless the objective of our quest. If, then, the Church is integral to the goal for which creation and redemption have been ordained; and if the man of good will is orientated, however little he may be conscious of the fact, towards this goal of existence; then the Church is in real fact involved in what he is looking for, and is exerting its attraction on him to the full extent of his good will.[18]

The Church, on the other hand, in pursuance of her divine commission, is for ever seeking to communicate her gospel and herself to every man. Thus, behind the appearance even of mutual hostility and despite serious mutual misunderstanding, human good will and the reality of the Church are on converging courses. Each is in fact crying out for the other. They tend to meet.

Obviously, subjective good will is of itself no guarantee of the truth of an individual's formulations of his goals and principles, and these formulations will be, and are, very diverse. History presents us with a variety not only of mutually contradictory philosophies but of mutually incompatible religions. We need not, however, ordinarily doubt the good faith of mistaken philosophers or that of followers of religious error. In a simpler age than our own it seemed possible, even necessary, to suppose that error was an indication of bad faith. Not only heresy was condemned, but heretics. We have made the vital distinction between erroneous good faith and deliberate sin against known truth. By making this distinction, it cannot be doubted, we have achieved a level of truth not often attained, in this matter, by our predecessors.

It remains for us to recall, what earlier generations perceived so clearly, that truth itself is not plural: that, if logical positivism is true, then Hegelian metaphysics is non-sense; and that if Christianity is true, then Islam, so far as it positively rejects or contradicts the gospel, is false. And within the limits of historical Christianity itself, we have to be honest enough to affirm that, if the Nicene Creed is true, then Arianism is false; and if Catholicism is true, then forms of Christianity that contradict this truth are false. And we have to bear in mind that, if religion can in one sense be viewed as the human search for God and if this search has at its heart a need or hope or trust that God will meet, or indeed will have anticipated, our search by a self-disclosure, then it may be expected that there will be a religion in which God has thus disclosed himself; one in which, when it is viewed more profoundly, it will be seen that the human search is a response to that disclosure already made; a search that gets its ultimate direction not from our questing but from God's move towards us: Behold, I stand at the door and knock; if any man will open unto me ...

What is true of individuals is true, in due measure, also of religious groupings and religious traditions. They are severally incorporations of man's sincere search for God. As such they merit respect and are to be studied with a docility which seeks to discern whatever light has been thrown upon the ultimate mystery in the results of their endeavours. Still, after all such efforts to understand, a Christian will rightly say – and Christianity itself will rightly say – that the other religions, to the extent that they propound doctrines inconsistent with the Christian gospel, are false. This is not arrogance. It is simply the combination of faith in the gospel with a commonsense acceptance of the philosophic principle of non-contradiction: A proposition and its contradictory cannot simultaneously be true.

Something similar has to be said about the varieties of Christianity itself, to the extent that their differences amount to mutual contradictions. The area of agreement between the Christian churches is of course enormously larger and deeper than that between, for instance, Christianity and even its closest alternative, Judaism. Nevertheless, so long as these churches remain deliberately separate from one another, this can be a justifiable stance only if they either are teaching incompatible doctrines or are not all agreed about the extent of the doctrines of faith.

It follows that we all have to fall back upon the implications of the notion of good will or good faith – or what in classical moral theology is called 'invincible ignorance'.[19] But the commitment of all of us to the truth of the gospel means that we cannot rest content with our separateness and are therefore bound to take seriously the 'dialogue' of ecumenical theology. What can give us hope is that we are today, as rarely before, alive to this duty. Moreover, we should bear in mind that no form of Christianity is a completely closed system. The truth that is Jesus Christ is as inexhaustible as his godhead. We all have much to learn, and the more we learn the closer we shall grow to one another. Whatever our ecclesiology, we all deplore 'schism', the scandal of our divisions. A great Catholic ecumenist, Fr Yves Congar, has pointed out that the sinfulness of schism is already purged away when any of us, or any Christian group, has determined, in penitence and hope, to make every sacrifice for the achievement of visible unity.

Chapter X

The Alternative

In the preceding chapter an attempt has been made to show how the positive Christian values of other churches can be recognized and acknowledged by a Church which maintains that among God's gifts in Jesus Christ is the gift or 'charism' of the indivisible visible unity of the koinonia. Such recognition must of course lead to a full and persevering commitment to the ecumenical movement.

The Orthodox Church is a strong adherent today of* the principle of the indivisible visible unity of the Church. In a recent study, *Ecclesiological Problems*, the Archbishop of Thyateira and Great Britain criticizes a dissident group for its 'self-isolation and departure from the Body of the Holy Eastern Orthodox Church' and speaks of the group's 'schismatic schemes and plans'.[1] The group in question bears some resemblance to the Lefebvrist group in the Catholic Church and, like it, is strong in its criticism of the official stances of the body from which it is dissociating itself. It is interesting to note parts of Archbishop Athenagoras' rejoinder: 'How can one forgive [them] for their protestations at the ecumenical outlook' (of a document emanating from the Orthodox side)? 'We would inform them that Christian doctrine can no longer be antagonistic ... What have the cruel and polemical confrontations of Christians produced in the past? – nothing but shame, dissatisfaction and confusion in the hearts and minds of *antagonistic* Christians ... Unless this tactic ceases Christians will fight each other for ever'. The Archbishop himself has suggested that the Church 'has a door and no walls'. The door is baptism.

The Archbishop might repeat P. Evdokimov's statement that, while one can indicate where the Church is (sc. in and as the Eastern Orthodox Church), it is not possible to say where it is not. 'At what point from the Centre, that is, Christ Himself, can we encage or limit the activity of the Holy Spirit? ... If Christ is with those "two or three" who pray and together invoke His Name, then who will prevent His Presence with others who believe in Him, who are baptised and who invoke His Name? ...'[2] (In the example of ancient Israel, divided into 'two quarrelling groups', sc. the Northern and Southern Kingdoms, God) 'inspired prophets in both groups. So, what was the limit of the walls then? ... The grace of the Holy Spirit is limitless and the purpose of God's labours for the salvation of man and [the] whole of creation is invincible. We may also appreciate that the walls of the Church are continually and invisibly moving. No one knows, nor will ever measure, the distance of the walls from their Centre.'[3] The Archbishop counters the dissident group's appeal, in its rejection of ecumenism, to the Sacred Canons, by himself pointing to the change of presuppositions induced by the very fact that Christians are now seeking unity. Nevertheless, he retains the sense and importance of actual visible unity, as appears when he condemns the group's members as being 'self-anathematised because they are not in eucharistic communion with any of the Orthodox Churches'. He adds, in words reminiscent of the ancient practice of 'letters of communion': 'With which of the Orthodox Churches have they exchanged canonical letters?'[4]

The purpose of the present chapter is to examine some of the consequences entailed, in principle, by acceptance of the view of the Church advocated by Dr Greenslade and espoused by the churches (other than the Roman Catholic and Orthodox) whose separate existence dates from the sixteenth-century Reformation. It is characteristic of these churches that, while recognizing that visible unity is a good thing, a desirable aim, and indeed something that flows as an obligatory consequence from the gospel, they do not see this unity as guaranteed and maintained through the continuing action of the Holy Spirit. Visible unity, it is not unfair to say, is for these churches not of the *esse* of the Church in her earthly pilgrimage, though certainly of her *bene esse*.

We may begin with some reflections upon the sacrament of baptism. Partly through the influence of the late Cardinal Bea, the first president of the Rome Secretariat for Christian Unity, baptism has come to hold a central place in most ecumenical thinking. Cardinal Bea pointed out that by this sacrament (which Catholics believe can be administered by anybody, though it should normally be administered by an ordained minister) human beings are incorporated into Christ; which can only mean, on Christian principles, that they become members of the Church. Thus all baptized persons start with one enormous thing in common. They are already 'brethren'; but, because of our unhappy ecclesiastical divisions, groups of them are separated from one another. The problem of ecumenism, it is therefore suggested, is to bring all the baptized into one visible unity.

There is an obvious difficulty about this neat scheme of thought: not all believers in Christ are, or intend to be, baptized – they don't see it as necessary. This is true, I think, of some members of the Salvation Army and of the Friends (or, as they are often called, Quakers). But surely the great dividing line is between all those who believe in Christ and the rest of mankind who do not explicitly so believe. And surely there would be something wrong about an ecumenical movement which regarded the Salvation Army and the Quakers as outside its scope. St Paul said that we are justified 'by faith'; but you can have faith in Christ without being baptized. Yet nearly all Christian groups do administer baptism – though some others besides the Quakers and the Salvation Army seem to think of it as optional.

Why do most of us think baptism so important that only 'invincible ignorance' can excuse people for not being baptized? Is it because the Bible attaches great importance to baptism? Or is it that there is some evidence that Jesus Christ himself instituted Christian baptism? Even so, why was baptism instituted by him – or, if you like, by the primitive Church? Why this external rite, comprising the use of water and a form of words, when what surely matters is the interior reality of faith?

There is at least one reason which makes sense. If it is integral to Christianity that the believer should become part of the koinonia, and if the koinonia is not merely a union of spirits but a historical community, then an outward sign, or what we may call an external initiation ceremony, makes sense. Some sort of external sign is pretty well universal when we join a community – unless it's our family or some quasi-natural group that we enter without deliberation either on the group's part or our own.

Baptism, then, can be understood as the initiation ceremony not just to Christianity – as we have seen, not all Christians are baptized – but into the koinonia. This is presumably why baptism is unrepeatable: membership of the koinonia is not a terminable contract but the establishment of a permanent relationship. This sharply divides baptism from the merely interior, only personally expressed, act of faith in Christ. For the faith can be rejected by the individual believer by a contrary interior act which must automatically exclude him from 'justification'. But no act of the individual can alter the fact that he has been sacramentally baptized; and the tradition of the Church is that no act of the Church will rescind his baptism. It is further the case that in Catholic theology the unbaptized are incapable of receiving the other sacraments of the Church; for these are intended for the Church's members.

In 1975 the Faith and Order Commission of the World Council of Churches issued a paper, *One Baptism one Eucharist and a mutually Recognized Ministry*. The World Council of Churches claims no doctrinal authority. But this paper is the work of a body of theologians of 'widely different traditions', and it embodies their unanimous findings. 'Almost all the different confessional traditions are included in the membership' of the Faith and Order Commission, under whose auspices the paper is published.[5] The following are extracts from this paper:

> The sacraments ... are Christ's gift to his Church. ... Our baptism unites us with Christ who took upon himself our sins and those of the whole world that they might be forgiven and blotted out, and opens to us newness of life. ... In baptism ... we are baptized by one Spirit into one body ... which is the Church. ... The necessity of faith for the reception of the salvation embodied and set forth in baptism is acknowledged by all churches. ... Through their one baptism, Christians are brought into union with Christ and with each other and into the life of the Church Universal as well as the community of the local church. ... The churches are in agreement that the usual minister of baptism is an ordained minister, though there are cases where baptized believers may baptize. ... All churches are convinced that in the life of any one individual baptism is a unique and unrepeatable act.[6]

The paper further reminds us that 'in the early centuries, baptism was normally performed by immersion', whereas today most Christian churches ordinarily baptize by pouring a little water (with the appropriate verbal formula) on the candidate.

This account of baptism plainly represents a rich and important theological consensus. There is reasonable probability that it would broadly win general acceptance from the churches (including the Roman Catholic Church) to which the theologians responsible for the account belong.

The experience of the Roman Catholic Church, however – I cannot speak here for the other churches – has been that even so rich a statement does not settle all questions that arise for baptism, considered not just as a theological concept but as a practical element in lived Christianity. For example: the statement notes that 'there are cases where baptized believers' who are not themselves ordained ministers may baptize. The Catholic position is that even an unbaptized person can validly baptize, provided that in so doing he intends 'to do what the Church does' when baptism is administered by an ordained minister. Secondly, the simple-looking clause 'intend to do what the Church does' has behind it a considerable discussion. For example, can a Christian group, or an individual, validly baptize if its (or his) belief about baptism is at deep variance with that of the Church? Can a Unitarian baptize validly? Can an atheist baptize validly? Considerable theological acumen has had to be expended on such questions; and the decision upon them has had to come from ecclesiastical authority, not merely from the opinions of a majority of theologians.[7]

Moreover, a profound theological disagreement is concealed within the words of the statement. There are Christians, and Christian churches, which hold that baptism is not valid if the recipient is incapable at the time of making an act of personal faith. This contradicts the practice of the great traditional churches where baptism is administered to babies. Anyone can see that this divergence involves theological issues of the greatest moment – especially in view of the agreement that baptism (when valid) is unrepeatable. Is there any way in which such a disagreement can be resolved? Is there any conceivable way, except by the intervention of an authority which commands assent not because of the theological acumen which it possesses by itself, but because of its official status? And if it were suggested that such authority is not needed because the consensus of the faithful is of itself sufficient for the determination of such issues, then the urgent question arises: What constitutes a consensus and who are 'the faithful' for this purpose? Certainly at present one can hardly talk of a consensus of *churches* on the subject of infant baptism – unless one is prepared to exclude from the ecumenical dialogue some groups that are fully at present within it.

When we mention the consensus, we are back on familiar territory. The statement on baptism expresses a consensus among theologians which is impressive, and – within limits suggested above – this theological consensus adequately represents a consensus of churches and, by implication, of Christians. But by what right do we accept a consensus on baptism while rejecting – if we propose to reject – the consensus on the indivisible visible unity of the Church? In particular, if we are prepared to say that the disagreement of the churches that reject infant baptism does not destroy the consensus on the subject of infant baptism, by what right can it be said that the rejection of the principle of indivisible visible unity by the Churches of the Reformation damages the consensus that otherwise obtains and that was practically universal for fifteen hundred years?

It would be wearisome to consider each of the other sacraments in the way in which, very briefly, I have tried to examine the implications of an agreed statement on baptism. But perhaps it is worth while to mention one Christian ordinance which most Christian Churches regard as a sacrament, though – at least linguistically – there is not agreement on this point in the Protestant tradition: I mean, ordination.

The statement on baptism refers to its administration by 'ordained ministers'. It is well known that the phrase covers a profound disagreement, again particularly between the Protestant tradition and the rest of Christendom. The ancient tradition, still operative in the Roman Catholic and the Orthodox Churches, maintains that ordination must be conferred within a 'succession' which, in fact, is preserved in the historical episcopate and is transmitted through ordination conferred by men who are themselves in this episcopal succession. Implicit in the idea of an ordained ministry is that, like baptism, it confers status not only in the particular Church or local church, where and for which it is conferred, but in the universal Church. I have heard a Baptist minister stoutly maintaining that his ordination gave him such status in the universal Church; and I gather that Baptist ordination is not only within the local Baptist community (each of these communities considering itself a 'Church'), but also (in some cases) *by* the local community without any indispensable co-operation of ministers already ordained. Can it be left to particular groups to decide such momentous questions as the 'validity' of ordinations that claim universal status? And is this an issue that can happily be left for decision by some Great Church of the future when the ecumenical movement shall have reached its goal? By what authority would such a Great Church reach its decision?

As we have seen, one reply to the question of authority has been a (partly tacit) appeal to consensus. A difficulty about this is that consensus is never literal unanimity; so that someone has to decide what, for practical purposes, shall be deemed a consensus. Another reply will doubtless be: not consensus, but the authority of inspired Scripture.

I will not here enlarge on the old and trite (but true) argument that Scripture by itself has been shown by Christian history not to produce the sort of agreement which, by implication, the ecumenical movement is seeking. Scripture needs, for its practical utility, a decision on what in Scripture is of permanent validity and what is to be read as an expression of validity in contingent circumstances and terms, thus requiring re-expression when the circumstances change. In other words, what is the 'canon within the canon'? More broadly, Scripture requires interpretation, exegesis or a hermeneutical action on the part of somebody. Who is to perform this exegetical function?[8] Is it to be left to theologians and scholars, thus giving us a Church of 'the scribes'? Or to officially recognized holy people, giving us a Church of the 'Pharisees'?[9] There is very strong reason to hold that the true 'exegete' is, in the long run, the Church – and this view takes us away from *scriptura sola* (the Bible alone) to Scripture and tradition.

More urgent is the question: How do we know that Scripture is inspired, and inspired in order to provide a basis for doctrine and indeed a source of doctrine? And how do we know that precisely the books contained within the covers of a modern Bible – and they alone – are to be deemed thus inspired? – this is the question of the constitution of the 'canon' of Scripture. In fact, we are indebted both for the belief that Scripture is inspired and for the determination of the canon of Scripture to the tradition of that Church which has, with virtually equal insistence, claimed that the visible unity of the Church is, by divine guarantee and assistance, indivisible.

The truth is, of course, that even members of those churches whose official standpoint is that Scripture is the sole authority for Christian belief and consequent practice are indebted, more perhaps than they are aware, to tradition – the tradition of Christianity as a whole and the particular tradition of their own communion. The Creeds deeply colour the belief of us all – or almost all! They represent a condensation of the faith, or an abridgement of it, which we owe to our forefathers and which we accept. We may say that we accept it because it is faithful to Scripture; but in fact and in large measure we believe it to be faithful to Scripture, because we have inherited it. And every 'confessional' Church is deeply indebted to the constitutive documents drawn up by earlier generations as an explication of the faith 'once delivered to the saints'. On the whole it is not true that an individual becomes a Lutheran because he is satisfied by the Lutheran confession and therefore joins the Lutheran Church, or that an individual in the Reformed tradition is personally satisfied that his own church's confession, and precisely where it differs from the Lutheran, is correct, and just for that reason gives his allegiance to his own church. The reverse is normally true: a Lutheran believes in Lutheranism because he is a Lutheran; he is not a Lutheran because he has come to believe in Lutheranism. The same is true, *verbis mutatis*, of a Reformed believer. It may be added that the same is true of a Roman Catholic or an Orthodox believer; but, in their cases, the Church to which they belong and which determines their beliefs claims to be *the* Church of Christ and to have his authority for the interpretation of the gospel.

We can generalize the argument. Dr Greenslade, as we have seen (and he speaks for a widely spread Christian conviction), speaks of the 'holy things' which, in his ecclesiology (and mine), are 'constitutive of "churchness" '. He mentions 'the Gospel, the basic tenets of the Christian Faith, the Bible, the sacraments of Baptism and Holy Communion, a ministry of Word and Sacrament and pastoral care'.[10] If we revise this list in the light of the Faith and Order paper on Baptism, Eucharist and a recognized Ministry, we can rewrite his reference to ministry as 'an ordained ministry'. We owe our knowledge of every one of these 'holy things' to tradition. And it is to tradition that we owe our positive evaluation of these things, our recognition of them as gifts of God to his Church, our conviction that these, and whatever other gifts fall into the same category, are 'constitutive' of 'churchness'. And I suggest that we can add, without doing violence to Greenslade's thought, that such gifts, in full combination and interaction, would be constitutive of the one visible united Church of the future which is the goal of the ecumenical movement.

The fact, however, is that precisely that tradition which has transmitted to us these holy things and has guaranteed to us their value and function is the tradition which transmits the conviction of the indivisibility of the visible Church as a single communion. If we should feel bound to reject this traditional conviction, by what arguments do we defend our retention of the other 'holy things'? I press this question on my friends in the ecumenical movement – both my non-Catholic friends and my many Catholic friends or fellow workers who, it seems to me, have in recent years been less than explicit about indivisible visible unity as a guaranteed gift of God.

There is, of course, a possible escape from this problem. It consists in arguing that *none* of these 'holy things' is a gift of God in such sense that it is indispensable. In other words, essential Christianity is neither a sacramental nor a doctrinal religion, not a religion of Scripture, not a religion embodied in a historical community, not institutional. Each and all of these characteristics of the Christian Churches as they have existed and do exist in history are therefore contingent, dispensable, not essentially bound up with the Good News taught by Jesus and completed in his resurrection and the (alleged) mission of the Holy Spirit.

For my immediate purposes, I venture to call such a view of Christianity pure liberalism. It is a view that is capable of exercising a great appeal upon at least two groups of people: intellectuals, and some pragmatic laymen with a healthy distrust of the clergy and a sense that, to use a famous phrase, 'history is bunk'. Among these latter at the present day we must no doubt include a good many young people, often actuated by high idealism, who are repelled by the complications and apparent irrelevance of so much that is presented to them on the authority of tradition.

We must take the measure of liberalism. It is not a question of identifying ministerial efficacy with ministerial validity. It is not a question of the services or disservices rendered to traditional

Christianity by the Reformation or the estrangement of Western and Eastern communions. It is not a question of justifying occasional departures, in critical situations, from traditional practice or requirement. It is not a question of saying: Jesus is God, or: Jesus is the universal Redeemer, 'and nothing else matters'. It is a question of relativizing the whole Christian thing as it has been known in history from the very beginning, indeed from the days of John the Baptist. It is to reject or to treat as dispensable the central claim of all: that 'there is no other name by which we can be saved' except the name of Jesus. Lest it be thought that I am exaggerating the drift of liberalism, I would point to Professor John Hick's paper, 'Jesus and the World Religions', in the symposium, *The Myth of God Incarnate*. Professor Hick there proposes the following way of dealing with the Christian affirmation that Jesus is the incarnate Word of God: 'That Jesus was God the Son incarnate is not literally true, since it has no literal meaning, but it is an application to Jesus of a mythical concept'.[11] Later, he writes: 'Christianity will – we may hope – outgrow its theological fundamentalism, its literal interpretation of the idea of incarnation'.[12] The same scholar suggests that we should not see in Jesus the universal Redeemer: 'He was a saviour to many, and continues to be so today'.[13] 'To many': the hidden implication is that for others (and presumably with equal validity) the saviour might be the Buddha, or some other notable religious figure (St Francis of Assisi?). The Epilogue to *The Myth of God Incarnate* is contributed by Dr Dennis Nineham. It sets out the melancholy dilemma of the liberal who would wish to preserve some even tenuous link with Christianity. Nineham remarks that writers like Professor Hick offer us, instead of the incarnate Word, a Jesus who is a man totally dedicated to God and therefore our model (and our inspiration?). He proceeds: 'So long as the doctrine of the incarnation was taken as a statement of an objective metaphysical fact', as in the Christian Creeds, '[namely] that Jesus was literally divine, then the unique perfection of his humanity was a legitimate deduction from the fact of its hypostatic conjunction with divinity'. But if we reject the doctrine of his divinity, on what do we base a belief in the perfection of his humanity and his historical human life? He asks, very pertinently: 'Is it ... possible to validate claims of [this] kind', e.g. the moral perfection of Jesus, 'on the basis of historical evidence? To prove an historical negative, such as the sinlessness of Jesus, is notoriously difficult to the point of impossibility.'[14] He then points out that, if the claim is given a different basis, or a somewhat different meaning, we can no doubt say that Jesus – whether or not he be considered divine – is capable of making an impact on people that can change their lives. But – in case this should be taken as meaning the same as any sort of uniqueness in Jesus – he reminds us that a similar impact could be made by a saint such as St Francis of Assisi or a living Christian like Mother Teresa of Calcutta. One might have expected that, after thus explaining that no attempt at a historical reconstruction of Jesus will succeed in assuring us of his uniqueness as that uniqueness is assured by the Christian doctrine of the incarnate Word, Dr Nineham would dissociate himself from the other writers of *The Myth of God Incarnate* and revert to orthodoxy. But that he does not do. Rather, he asks whether it is 'necessary to "believe in Jesus" in any sense beyond that which sees him as the main figure through whom God launched men into a relationship with himself so full and rich that, under various understandings and formulations of it, it has been, and continues to be, the salvation of a large proportion of the human race'.[15] And he steadily withstands the temptation to infer that Jesus was in any sense empirically unique.

Such is liberalism, liberalism taken to its logical conclusion. I am fully aware that, at least in this pure but logical form, it would be repudiated not only by distinguished scholars and thinkers like Greenslade, but by the main Christian Churches officially linked with the ecumenical movement in the World Council of Churches. Obviously, too, it would be rejected by the Roman Catholic Church.

Where have Dr Hick, Dr Nineham and their friends gone wrong, since the Churches are agreed that they have gone wrong? It is surely in the end because they have rejected the authority of the Christian tradition and have substituted for it the (highly precarious and ever changing) authority, not of historical method as such, but of historical scholarship as it is actually used by men who – many of them – have a prejudice against metaphysics, the miraculous, and the strictly supernatural. But I am not here engaged in a refutation of pure liberalism, I simply point to it as the probable effect of indocility to Christian tradition. Yet can we be docile to the tradition and yet choose to reject from it that very

powerful and all-influencing element that consists in the principle
that the koinonia is an indivisible visible unity?

Pure liberalism spells revolution:

> The Revelations of Devout and Learn'd
> Who rose before us, and as Prophets burn'd,
>   Are all but Stories, which awoke from Sleep
> They told their comrades, and to Sleep return'd. ...

> Would but some wingèd Angel ere too late
> Arrest the yet unfolded Roll of Fate,
>   And make the stern Recorder otherwise
> Enregister, or quite obliterate!

> Ah, Love! could you and I with Him conspire
> To grasp this sorry Scheme of Things entire,
>   Would not we shatter it to bits – and then
> Re-mould it nearer to the Heart's Desire![16]

Who is there who has never felt any sympathy with this
revolutionary impulse? Who has not felt the burden of the past?
Who has not felt that thrill of youth and challenge of which
another poet spoke, as he recalled his own reaction to the French
Revolution, when it was bliss to be alive, but to be young was very
heaven?

The enthusiasm of the young, or the young of heart, is not to be
despised. But for those who care about the future unity of
Christians in a visible Church there are other considerations to be
borne in mind. I venture here, then, to turn to a witness from a
quite different field of interest: Sir Karl Popper, addressing the
annual conference of the Rationalist Press Association in 1948.
His subject is tradition, and he proposes some ideas 'which may be
useful' for the construction of a theory of tradition.

He describes a possible rationalist attitude: 'I am not
interested', a rationalist might say, 'in tradition. I want to judge
everything on its own merits; I want to find out its merits and
demerits, and I want to do this quite independently of any
tradition'. This sounds very like the position of the 'pure liberal' in
theology, and Sir Karl at once, somewhat drily, comments that
'the rationalist', or as we might say the liberal, 'who says such

things is himself very much bound by a rationalist tradition which traditionally says them'.[17]

After mentioning that, in coming to England from Vienna, where he had grown up, he found that the 'atmosphere' here was very different from that of Vienna, and commenting that atmosphere presumably has something to do with tradition, he observes that some important traditions are both local and very precious. Even the scientific tradition is very difficult to transplant, e.g. from England to New Zealand. He is not in favour of an uncritical acceptance of tradition, but advocates 'a *critical* attitude, which may result either in acceptance or rejection'. But he does not think that we could ever free ourselves entirely from the bonds of tradition: 'The so-called freeing is really only a change from one tradition to another. But we can free ourselves from the *taboos* of a tradition; and we can do that not only by rejecting it, but also by *critically* accepting it'.[18]

Popper illustrates his views on tradition by a study of the emergence of 'a rational philosophy' in ancient Greece. He points out that the philosophers were not the first to seek reasons for events; the myth-makers had done that before them (to say that 'Poseidon is angry' is to proffer an explanation of a storm at sea). What the philosophers did was to *question* the traditional myths – and to substitute new myths for the old ones. But besides substituting new myths they 'invented a *new tradition* – the tradition of adopting a critical attitude towards the myths, the tradition of discussing them; ... My thesis is that what we call "science" is differentiated from the older myths not by being something distinct from a myth, but by being accompanied by a second-order tradition – that of critically discussing the myth.'[19] And he thinks that a young scientist should be advised thus:

> Try to learn what people are discussing nowadays in science. Find out where difficulties arise, and take an interest in disagreements.

In other words, he says, you should

> pick up, and try to continue, a line of inquiry which has the whole background of the earlier development of science behind it; you fall in with the tradition of science. It is a very simple and a decisive point, ... that we cannot start afresh; that we

must make use of what people before us have done in science. If we start afresh, then, when we die, we shall be about as far as Adam and Eve were when they died (or, if you prefer, as far as Neanderthal man). In science we want to make progress, and this means that we must stand on the shoulders of our predecessors. We must carry on a certain tradition.[20]

Turning to the question of a sociological theory of tradition, Sir Karl points out that people are anxious and even terrified when the social situation is one in which they cannot predict what will happen. Order can help to give them a 'clear idea' of what to expect in their social environment, but institutions and traditions are also very important. 'There is a need for tradition in social life. ... Just as the invention of myths or theories in the field of natural science has a function – that of helping us to bring order into the events of nature – so has the creation of traditions in the field of society'. And he argues that the existence of traditions gives us something that we can criticize and change.

Too many social reformers have an idea that they would like to clean the canvas, as Plato called it, of the social world, wiping off everything and starting from scratch with a brand-new rational world. This idea is nonsense and impossible to realize. ... There is no reason to suppose that a blue-printed world will be any better than the world in which we live.[21]

It is indeed obvious that what will follow a complete break with all tradition will be the creation of a new tradition, which will soon need to be tinkered with and adjusted as it reveals its defects. But if the need of 'little changes and adjustments' will always be with us, 'it is very much more sensible and reasonable to start with what happens to exist at the moment, because of these things which exist we at least know where the shoe pinches. ... The blue-prints have no meaning in an empty social world, in a social vacuum. They have no meaning except in a setting of traditions and institutions – such as myths, poetry, and values – which all emerge from the social world in which we live. ... we should always remain conscious of the fact that all social criticism, and all social betterment, must refer to a framework of social traditions, of which some are criticized with the help of others, ...

A tradition is, as it were, capable of extending something of the personal attitude of its founder far beyond his personal life.'[22]

Thus Karl Popper defends tradition alike in the sphere of scientific inquiry and in that of social relations. Since Christianity is concerned both with truth and with relations between men and God and men and men, it does not seem entirely out of place to apply his arguments and his conclusions to the question of tradition *versus* revolution in theology and doctrine; the more so since Christianity, with its foundation in the historical incarnation, is irrevocably committed to a past event made known to us through tradition. Could we retain our hold on the event if we decided to discard tradition?

It will not have escaped notice, however, that Popper advocates not any sort of tradition but a tradition that accepts and, we may say, incorporates criticism within it. The myth must be subject to discussion, to the scrutiny of intellect; and the process of discussion will lead to a development of the myth. Similar, I think, is the message of Professor John Macquarrie in his recent book on Unity and Diversity. He there speaks of Catholicism as the champion of continuity (which we may compare with Popper's 'tradition') and of the Protestant principle as the principle of criticism. It is clearly his view that the Christian Church should contain both these principles. If reliance on tradition can become traditionalism and dogmatism, and if 'protest' can become sheerly negative, nevertheless the two, when held in combination, can work in healthy tension and produce a synthesis which is acceptable.

Criticism is the work of theology. For theology is reflection upon revelation and consequently upon doctrine. It is the application of intelligence to religion. We are all, in our measure, theologians; each of us has to follow the example of the Mother of Jesus who, as Newman pointed out in his Anglican sermon on the Development of Doctrine, was not only the blessed one who believed, but one who 'pondered all these things'. And because theology is a mode of behaviour intrinsic to mature Christianity, it is natural that there should be a class of people to whom the term 'theologians' is ascribed in a special sense. Bernard Lonergan, who thinks of himself as a rather conservative Catholic, faces the issue of the tension between theology and tradition, or rather theology and the guardians of tradition:

... it may be thought that one endangers the authority of church officials if one acknowledges that theologians have a contribution of their own to make, that they possess a certain autonomy, that they have at their disposal a strictly theological criterion, and that they have grave responsibilities that will all the more effectively be fulfilled by adopting some method and working gradually towards improving it. But I think the authority of church officials has nothing to lose and much to gain from the proposal. There is no loss in acknowledging the plain historical fact that theology has a contribution to make. There is much to be gained by recognizing autonomy and pointing out that it implies responsibility. For responsibility leads to method, and method if effective makes police work superfluous. Church officials have the duty to protect the religion on which theologians reflect, but it is up to the theologians themselves to carry the burden of making theological doctrine as much a matter of consensus as any other long-standing academic discipline.[23]

It may be possible to say something more concrete about the critical role of theology in a form of Christianity which holds to the principle of the indivisible visible unity of the Church when we have devoted some attention to a question long left over, namely the apparent difficulty in the fact that already two different Christian communions, the Roman Catholic and the Eastern Orthodox, claim to be possessed of this gift of unity. For the moment, and in concluding this chapter, I wish to reaffirm my conviction that to reject this principle is to embark on a Christian revolution, and to illustrate the point by considering some consequences of adopting the alternative principle, that the Church, though visible, is at present divided, along with the aspiration to achieve, by God's grace, victory over these divisions by the establishment of a Great Church of the future.

I have already argued that the 'holy things' which Greenslade enumerates as constitutive of 'churchness' are bequeathed (and one may add, interpreted) for us by tradition; and that it can hardly be reasonable to abandon the tradition of indivisible unity without casting doubt upon these other holy things. How, in face of modern biblical scholarship, can one affirm with certainty a high doctrine either of baptism or of the eucharist, except by appealing to the judgement of the Church already formulated in tradition? And how would one propose to deal, in some future ecumenical agreement leading to visible unity, with Christian bodies who reject the sacramental system altogether? How can one preserve doctrine at all without the help of tradition – remembering that Scripture itself is, originally, a traditional element, and that our common belief in its canonical limits and its inspired authority are themselves debts owed to tradition?

A second question to which there is no easy answer is: How can the Roman Catholic Church and the Orthodox Communion be persuaded, within the foreseeable future, to abandon their conviction that the Church is indivisibly visibly one? There may be those who optimistically think that, at least in the Roman Catholic Church, a process has already set in which will lead to this abandonment. I trust I shall not be thought to be making an unfair point if I cast doubt on this expectation. There are, I agree, Catholic scholars and theologians who appear to accept the idea that the Catholic Church has been mistaken in teaching that it has, as such and in distinction from the other Christian Churches, a divine mission to the whole of mankind and a divine guarantee which is not shared by the other churches. It was to be expected that, in the relaxed climate of the years since the Second Vatican Council, such an idea should be mooted. An orthodox Catholic will of course be certain that it is a mistaken one. But even those who do not share the orthodox Catholic belief in the uniqueness of the Catholic Church will realize that the private opinions of some theologians are not necessarily an indication of the mind, present or future, of the Church to which they belong. I am confident that there is no wavering on this matter in the college of bishops as a whole or in the mind of the present Pope. Theologians occupy an intermediate place between the official teaching body of the Church and the mass of the faithful spread over all the continents of the world. And the faithful, now and for the decades, indeed centuries, to come, stand and will stand on the whole with the bishops rather than with these theologians.

Certainly, Catholic theology is engaged at present in a tremendous reconsideration of the theological tradition. But Lonergan's words are deserving of attention in this connection:

> The breakdown of classical culture and, at last in our day, the manifest comprehensiveness and exclusiveness of modern culture confront Catholic philosophy and Catholic theology with

the gravest problems, impose upon them mountainous tasks, invite them to Herculean labors. ... Classical culture cannot be jettisoned without being replaced; and what replaces it, cannot but run counter to classical expectations. There is bound to be formed a solid right that is determined to live in a world that no longer exists. There is bound to be formed a scattered left, captivated by now this, now that new development, exploring now this and now that new possibility. But what will count is a perhaps not numerous center, big enough to be at home in both the old and the new, painstaking enough to work out one by one the transitions to be made, strong enough to refuse half-measures and insist on complete solutions even though it has to wait.[24]

There is a hidden strength in Catholicism, much more profound and, in the long run, much more decisive for the future than the froth of discussion and controversy that so often fills our journals and attracts the attention of the great public. It is not precisely allegiance to particular dogmatic formulas. It is not a personality cult of the Pope. It is a reliance on the 'mind' of the Catholic Church as the ultimate criterion and an unhesitating rallying to that mind in face of the seductions of other intellectual positions and passing fashions. The ecumenical movement needs to recognize the reality of this hidden strength and not allow itself to be deluded by false hopes.

Obviously I cannot speak with the same assurance of the stance of the Eastern Orthodox Communion. But there is no secret about its profound devotion to the principle of tradition, a principle that is directly contradicted by the suggestion that the Church's visible unity is something that can come and go with the vagaries of historical controversy and theological innovation.

Does this mean that in effect the ecumenical movement will have to leave the Catholic Church and the Orthodox East on one side and concentrate its efforts on seeking to end the divisions among Protestants and those between Anglicanism and the Protestant churches? I am sure that this is not so, and I am sure that such a restriction would be a betrayal of great hopes legitimately born in the last few years. We must not lose heart because the way forward is not easy to discern; and there is one consideration that appears to me to be worth reflection.

I wrote earlier of an open-endedness in all the modern versions of Christianity. This open-endedness takes different forms. I am satisfied that in the great traditional Churches of East and West it does not and will not amount to an ability to discard the principle of the uniqueness of a single Christian *koinonia* guaranteed by God and sustained and assisted by the Holy Spirit. Before the end of this essay, I hope to consider what sort of flexibility is consistent with this principle. But open-endedness in other Churches, those at least whose roots are in some sense in the Protestant Reformation, is a different matter.

A Christian Church that in no sense claims to be *the* Church *tout court* is in a peculiar position. It can adhere without any reserve to the Scriptures and to the Creeds of antiquity. It can accept the formulations of the ancient Councils in matters of faith. But when it comes to its own particular confessional formulas, the position is somewhat different. The authority of a confession of faith is, in the long run, the authority of the body that propounds it. And none of these post-Reformation bodies claims, by itself, to embody the authority of the whole Church. And there is a feeling among some of those who have given deep thought to ecumenical aspirations that, beyond the authority of these particular confessional statements, there is the possibility of revision and adjustment when the Great Church of the future is able to meet in general council to sort out the differences that have emerged between the Churches in the course of four centuries. This frame of mind would be illustrated by those who, faced for instance with the Catholic teaching on the immaculate conception of the Mother of Jesus, might say that they can themselves respect this as a pious opinion but cannot see that it has, at present, the status of an article of faith. Presumably, they would agree that if the Great Church of the future endorsed this belief, its status would attain a level that called for the assent of faith. A Church that does not claim to be the whole Church, and in particular a Church that declines to claim 'infallibility' for its own confessional formulas, is a Church that is open to the future in a way that neither the Catholic Church nor the Eastern Orthodox Communion can be.

Thus one is brought to a final question to those who maintain that visible unity, though desirable, is not of the essence of the Church. On what basis will the Great Church of the future establish its unity? What could be its own sense of identity, what its interior principle of cohesion, what its message to the world, unless it took its stand on an agreed interpretation of the faith?

This interpretation might, one concedes, on the view of Church unity that they advocate, include some, while rejecting other, of the traditional tenets of Christianity. But however the Creed of the future Church is drawn up, the question of its authority will need to be answered. To appeal to the authority of Scripture in a fundamentalist way is not sufficient; and we have seen that fundamentalism is incapable of showing its own self-evidence. On the other hand, to appeal to Scripture alone, while accepting principles of exegesis that are not fundamentalist, will always, judging by our past experience, lead to a continuing diversity of interpretations. The Church of the future would find itself bound to accept one out of a diversity of interpretations; so again, the question arises: what would be the authority for such a choice? It is hard to conceive of any other authority except that which would derive from a consensus. And everything suggests that that consensus would be not more than a 'moral unanimity', or the agreement of a majority against a minority of continuing dissidents. Neither experience nor faith encourages us to think that literal unanimity will ever be attained in this life. Yet, if in the end we shall be constrained to accept a majority view, how can we escape the conclusion that, already today before the goal of the ecumenical movement has been attained, the criterion is the agreement of the majority? And that agreement is already definite on one point: the rejection of the suggestion that visible unity is not of the essence of the Church. The witness of Christian history is here confirmed by the witness of the Catholic and the Orthodox Churches, together accounting for perhaps more than two-thirds of Christian believers.

Chapter XI

East and West

It is easy, too easy, for us in the West, and more particularly for those of the English-speaking West, to regard the Reformation and its consequences as the gravest issue for resolution with a view to the reunion of Christian Churches. From the point of view adopted in these pages, however, the 'estrangement' (to use Fr Congar's word) between East and West is graver still. The Catholic Church of antiquity was a Church embracing both halves of the Roman Empire. The gradual retreat of that Empire within Eastern limits and its practical supersession in the West by new civil governments, and especially by the so-called Holy Roman Empire of Charlemagne and his successors, were paralleled by a growing mutual incomprehension between those parts of the Church which looked naturally to Rome as their centre and those Eastern parts where the Patriarch of Constantinople was in constant touch with the Byzantine Emperor. The ultimate consequence of this estrangement is the existence today of two Christian Communions, the Roman Catholic and the Orthodox, each claiming to be in some sense *the* Church, and together accounting for something like two-thirds to three-quarters of the (nominal) Christians of the world. We have seen how this 'schism' provides its own ammunition to the Protestant contention that visible unity is not, as was held in antiquity, of the essence of the Church but rather an ideal to be aimed at with a view to a more effective witness to the gospel of Christ. A few words about the story of the estrangement may not be out of place, though I make no pretence to be an authority in this field and, in any case, within the limits of this essay, a full treatment of it is out of the question.

Fr Louis Bouyer has pointed out that the official conversion of the Roman Empire to Christianity was a sudden affair, unprepared in the previous history of Church and State.[1] In the decade previous to the year 313, the Church had been reeling under the blows of the persecution initiated by the Emperor Diocletian. Suddenly, overnight you might say, Constantine declared himself in word and act the patron of the Christian Church. His predecessors, however, had held the title of 'Summus Pontifex', supreme priest or highest religious authority, in an Empire that considered itself co-extensive with the civilized world (the *oikoumene*, or inhabited earth). The title survived Constantine's assumption of the role of protector of the Church. More importantly, the notion that the State had some ultimate authority in religious matters survived too. Meanwhile, the Church herself encountered the serious doctrinal and disciplinary issues raised by the Arian controversy. Although the Council of Nicaea, which gave official sanction to the word *homousios* in the Creed and condemned Arius, was overwhelmingly Eastern in its personnel (the bishop of Rome was represented at it by a legate, as became customary in ecumenical councils), dissatisfaction with the word 'consubstantial' was soon to show itself among the Eastern bishops. Just at this time, the centre of civil power was being moved from Rome to Constantinople, and before long the bishop of that city, 'New Rome' as it liked to call itself, was the prelate whose ecclesiastical functions brought him into the closest contact with the civil government.

Doctrinal problems which were of profound religious significance were less immediately important to the civil government than the peace of the Church. And when prelates seemed to be locked in insoluble disputes about highly abstract doctrinal theories and language, the temptation to force conformity upon them from without could hardly be resisted. But the See of Rome, now at a relatively safe distance from the seat of Empire, was not content to leave the future of the faith to be determined by the civil power.

As early as 343, the Council of Sardica, intending originally to be an ecumenical council, and loyal both to Nicene orthodoxy and to the primacy of the bishop of Rome, was boycotted by the majority of the Eastern bishops, who held a rival council of their own and found their support in the imperial authority. The eventual estrangement was already foreshadowed in these events.

In the centuries that followed, the East and the West developed two different tendencies with regard to the civil power. The Eastern attitude has been caricatured by the West as 'Caesaro-papism', or the according to the Emperor of quasi-papal power over and in the Church. The attitude of the West may equally be caricatured as 'Papo-caesarism': the arrogation to the papacy of political powers which are no part of Christ's mandate to his Church's hierarchy.

These diverse orientations in the area of the Church's relations with 'the world' (considered, at least in the East, as a world converted to Christ and become a Christian replica of the Old Testament People of God) went hand in hand with growing cultural alienation, with a difficulty of intercourse due to the dominance of the Latin language in the West and the Greek language in the East, and with different ecclesiological emphases. The West, more and more as time went on, saw ecclesiology summed up in the papal primacy. From as early as the fifth century, in fact, Rome was propagating the idea that (a) the power of the apostles had been given *in toto* first to Peter, and then by him communicated to the rest of the Twelve; (b) this same indebtedness to a single human source remained as a principle of the Church, so that all episcopal authority was a derivation from that of the Pope. The East, far more sensitive to the sacramental (as opposed to the jurisdictional) nature of episcopal authority, tended to see the apex of ecclesiastical government in the 'pentarchy' of the five great patriarchates – of which, it was acknowledged, the patriarch of the West, namely the bishop of Rome, was the chief. Direct papal intervention in the affairs of Eastern Christendom was steadily resented. Such interventions, indeed, were often of a nature (and based upon a theory) which the Second Vatican Council would hardly approve.

In the event, of course, the 'split' between East and West was, in theory at least, based on matters more strictly religious. The West, already before 1054, had inserted unilaterally into the Creed the phrase concerning the Holy Spirit's 'procession': 'and from the Son'. Subsequently, in general councils not recognized by the East as ecumenical, it introduced new dogmatic formulations, and particularly the First Vatican Council's dogmatic definition of the papal primacy and the Pope's 'infallible' teaching function.

The Pope, for his part, defined the immaculate conception and the assumption of the Blessed Virgin Mary (to whom the East has a most touching, tender and deeply evangelical devotion as 'the one who gave birth to God').

Thus, while the Reformation in the West was a sudden explosion within the Church and can be dated, in substance, to a few decades, the estrangement of East and West was a centuries-long process, less like a matrimonial divorce than the slow alienation of two sisters who live in different places, who understand each other very little, and whose mutual correspondence becomes rarer and rarer. It is ironical that the event in 1054, which has come to be regarded as the consummation of the schism, was, on the Roman side, the act of a papal representative who, in excommunicating the Patriarch of Constantinople, was exceeding his mandate; moreover, it may be reasonably held that his powers, whatever they were, had automatically lapsed through the previous demise of the Pope in question. Moreover, the excommunication envisaged directly only the Patriarch, not the Eastern Churches as a whole; and the retaliatory excommunication issued by the Patriarch struck only at the papal legates, not at the Pope.

Seen by the historian, the events of 1054 look more like one further stage in the long process of alienation between East and West. The separation even then was neither complete nor final. There was a long history of intercommunion in areas where one or other of the hierarchies was not available. There was even, at the Council of Florence (1439), a paper reconciliation at a Council of East and West regarded by the Roman Catholic Church ever since as an ecumenical council. But the acts of the Council were repudiated by the Eastern Churches on the return of their signatories, and shortly afterwards the fall of Constantinople to the Turks ended the political background against which so many ecclesiastical quarrels and negotiations had taken place.

The general picture of relations between East and West since Constantine I is such that Bouyer has even mooted the idea that the schism has never been formal and that the Eastern Orthodox Church and the Roman Catholic Church are still one Communion. In that case, the argument against our view of the koinonia as essentially a single visible communion, could no longer rely on the 'schism' between East and West.[2]

Attractive as such a theory must be to theologians, the ordinary man is bound to feel that it is contradicted by the facts of the case. For practical purposes, he must think, I am offered two bodies, each of which, to the at least virtual exclusion of the other, claims to be the koinonia. How can one choose between them? Or is one bound to admit that the koinonia is not, essentially, a single visible communion?

I have given reasons for holding that to surrender the idea of the koinonia as essentially a single communion of believers would be a choice of revolution in preference to development. I propose in the following pages to argue that the decision between non-Roman Orthodoxy and Roman Catholicism can be made by seeking an answer to the question: Is the Petrine office, of which some modern New Testament scholars speak as of a biblical datum, and which antiquity saw as vested in the 'See of Peter' or the church of the city of Rome, an element in the concrete historical fact of the koinonia such that, apart from it, the koinonia does not exist?

The last ecumenical council to be recognized as such by East and West alike is the second ecumenical council of Nicaea, held in 787 – two and a half centuries before the disaster of 1054. One of the tasks undertaken by this council was to determine the official attitude to an Iconoclastic council, claiming itself ecumenical, which had been held in Constantinople thirty-four years earlier (753). The second council of Nicaea repudiated this claim officially and solemnly.[3] Reasons for so doing were put before the council by John the Deacon and the text of his presentation received the unanimous approval of the members of the council. John the Deacon, in his statement, enumerates certain conditions which must be fulfilled if a council is to enjoy authority as an ecumenical council in the line of such councils that opens with the first of Nicaea (325, four hundred and fifty years before this second of Nicaea). The relevant passage of John the Deacon begins as follows:

How can (a council claim to be) great and ecumenical which was neither received nor agreed by the presidents of the other churches (i.e. the bishops of local churches not represented in the actual council), but was rather condemned by them with anathema? (The council under consideration) did not have as co-operator the then Pope of the church of the Romans and the church leaders who collaborated with him, neither through his legates nor through an encyclical letter, as is (canonically) required for councils. Nor did it have the consent (to its findings) of the East, Alexandria, Antioch and the Holy City or of the prelates and chief persons associated with them. ...[4]

When John the Deacon laid these and other objections against the status claimed for the previous Iconoclastic Council, he must have known that he was articulating the received opinions of his time. The unanimity with which his speech was received is highly significant. And it must not be overlooked that the second council of Nicaea took place in an age when the East and West were slowly drifting away from each other. Nevertheless, the East in this episode acknowledges that Rome has a special, and indeed the leading, place in the structures of the universal Church.[5] So far as I am aware, the Eastern Orthodox Church has never limited its acceptance of the second council of Nicaea as ecumenical by expressing reservations about its welcome to the views expounded by John the Deacon.

Not that relations were always, or even often, easy. There is an instance at the time of the second ecumenical council of Constantinople (mid-sixth century) when the Emperor, angered by the Pope's alleged obstructionism, demanded that the Pope be deposed by the Council – explaining, however, that this would not be an attack on the Holy See but only on its incumbent!

Earlier in that century, and with the help and the pressure of the Emperor, the thirty years' breach between East and West known to historians as the Acacian schism was terminated by the acceptance in the East of the Formula of Pope Hormisdas. In accepting this formula the Patriarch of Constantinople led the way for the Eastern bishops. His signature was subsequently followed by those of other Eastern bishops as they came into communion with Rome (the proceedings were not conciliar). I quote from the Formula (preserved for us in several slightly differing forms) as subscribed by the Patriarch in his reply to Hormisdas:

This I say. The principle of salvation is to keep the rule of right faith and in no way to deviate from the tradition of the Fathers. And because we cannot ignore the statement of our Lord Jesus Christ when he said, Thou art Peter and upon this rock I will build my Church. Facts confirm the saying; for in the apostolic see [sc. the See of Rome] the catholic religion is ever kept undefiled. Not wishing to fall away from this hope and faith and in all things following the constitutions of the Fathers, we anathematize all heresies ... Hence, as we said before, following in all things the apostolic see we preach all that has been decreed by it, and therefore I hope that I shall be thought worthy to be in one communion with you, which the apostolic see proclaims, in which (see? or communion?) is the complete and perfect solidity of the Christian religion, promising that in the future all those removed from the communion of the catholic church, that is (all those) not agreeing in all things with the apostolic see, are not to have their names recited in the holy mysteries (sc. included in the diptychs of the Eucharist).[6]

The Acacian schism had been caused by imperial efforts to conciliate the local churches which had rejected the Formula of Chalcedon. A new document of reconciliation was proposed and was accepted by the Eastern bishops. It did not contradict Chalcedon, but neither did it reaffirm the Formula. Rome withdrew its communion from the East, and the Acacian schism lasted for thirty years. We may therefore go back to the Council of Chalcedon itself (451).

The Pope at that time was Leo the Great, of whom it has been said that he advocated a doctrine of the papal primacy that was as complete (though it was less theologically nuanced) as that of the First Vatican Council fourteen hundred years later. However disinclined the Eastern clergy were to take careful note of Western theology, the Fathers of Chalcedon (predominantly Easterns) could hardly have failed to notice the primatial 'claims' underlying Leo's doctrinal letter (the *Tomus*) on christology, which letter they accepted with enthusiasm. The Easterns, however, had an axe of their own to grind at Chalcedon: it was desired, and a canon was passed to the effect, that the See of Constantinople should be regarded as next in honour after that of Rome, and should be given a wider jurisdiction in the East. This celebrated 28th canon displeased Leo (who had not been personally present at the council) and he delayed his official response to the Council's Acts. It is interesting to note that the Emperor himself urged Leo not to prolong his delay, since the whole effect of the council rested upon his ratification of it. Leo granted this ratification – except to the 28th canon. This episode of the ratification seems to illustrate the principle laid down by John the Deacon at the second council of

Nicaea: that the Acts of an ecumenical council needed, for their validity as such, the approval of Rome. Later, Anatolius, the then Patriarch of Constantinople, wrote to Leo to excuse himself in regard to the 28th canon, and observed that all the Acts of the council were provisional, in the sense that they depended on Leo's confirmation for their validity.

The christological doctrine defined by the council of Chalcedon in effect balanced the work of the council of Ephesus twenty years earlier. The council of Ephesus is celebrated for its condemnation of Nestorius and its canonization of the title 'she who gave birth to God' as appropriate for the Blessed Virgin. The papal legates arrived late at the council, and before their arrival the Fathers passed sentence on Nestorius, being, as they said, 'necessarily impelled thereto by the canons, and the letters of our holy father and colleague, Celestine, bishop of the Roman Church'.

From 431 to 787, then, the witness of the East to the Roman primacy is impressive. The events to which I have referred relate to ecumenical councils or to the crucial conditions for the termination of a lengthy schism. It is worth while to add to these witnesses some words from two Greek historians who wrote in the fifth century, though they were in what follows referring to a letter of Julius, the bishop of Rome at the time of the council of Sardica and of the earlier troubles of Athanasius. The historian Socrates, commenting on a letter of Julius in defence of Athanasius, says that Julius reproved the Easterns for their behaviour towards the bishop of Alexandria 'since the ecclesiastical canon orders that the churches shall not make canons against the judgement of the bishop of Rome'.[7] The other historian, Sozomen, is dependent on Socrates when he, in turn, writes: '(Julius blamed them) saying that it was a sacerdotal law that what was done against the will of the Roman bishop was null and void.'[8] As a matter of fact, we happen to know what Julius actually wrote. He was protesting against what he deemed the irregularity of condemnations, by a council of Tyre, of Athanasius and some other bishops. He says: 'The trial ought to have conformed to the Church's rule. All of us ought to have been written to ... Especially, why were we not written to about the Alexandrian Church? Are you unaware that such was the custom, that first we should be written to, and so justice should be defined from here?'[9] It may be that Socrates (and Sozomen) read more into this letter than it actually contains. But their words are at least confirmatory evidence of what was seen as canonical propriety in the century in which they were writing. The Roman primacy was then taken for granted; and the witnesses for this adduced above – apart, of course, from Leo and Hormisdas – are largely Eastern.

Going back to the fourth century, we find three important testimonies to the function of the church and/or See of Rome as the centre of the koinonia's unity. They are Western testimonies, although Jerome's was written from Antioch.

In 381 a Council of Aquileia, in which St Ambrose took part, reminded the Emperor that it was from Rome that the 'rights of communion' emanated. This must mean that, to be correctly Catholic, individuals and local churches had to be in communion with the local church of Rome (and its bishop). Ambrose, incidentally, stands out among the Western Fathers as a communicator to the West of Eastern Christian thought.

About the same date, Jerome wrote from Antioch to the bishop of Rome for guidance. As a sad result of the 'Arian' controversies and of the interventions of the Empire in ecclesiastical affairs, there were at that time three rival Christian communities in Antioch. To which was Jerome to associate himself?

Making none my leader save Christ, I am united in communion to your Beatitude, that is to say to the See of Peter: on that rock I know the Church to have been built. He who eats the Paschal Lamb outside this abode is profane. If a man is not in Noah's ark he will be submerged by the flood.[10]

Thus, for Jerome, both ecclesiastical communion and doctrinal orthodoxy[11] depend on Rome.

Also about the same time Optatus of Milevis was arguing in Africa against the Donatists:

You cannot pretend to be unaware that in the city of Rome the episcopal chair was bestowed upon Peter first, on which chair sat Peter the head of all the apostles ... in which single chair unity was to be preserved by all (or, was preserved by all), lest the other apostles should maintain each his several chair; so that he who established another chair over against the unique chair would be a schismatic and a sinner.

This 'unique chair', Optatus says, was one of the 'endowments' of the Church (we may compare Greenslade's 'gifts'):

> The unique chair, the first of the endowments, was first occupied by Peter, to whom succeeded Linus ... (and at length) Siricius, who is our colleague today; with whom the whole world agrees with us in a single fellowship of communion by the intercourse of official letters.[12]

We have moved, in this chapter, from the language of Roman 'primacy' to that of Rome as 'centre of communion'. If we take *koinonia* as our model for understanding the Church, the two notions are closely linked. At the level of a local church, to refuse 'communion' to an individual – involving his exclusion from the reception of 'Holy Communion' – is equivalent to denying him the status of a member of that church. It is therefore an act of authority. The bishop who so acts is implicitly claiming authority in the local church; he is acting as its local 'primate'. In effect – though the term is uncomfortable – he is exercising 'jurisdiction'.[13] If the bishop of Rome is the arbiter of the communion of the universal Church, then his 'primacy' is indisputable – if only because he who disputes it is liable to find himself banished from the koinonia.

We may therefore now return to a question left unanswered when we were examining 'letters of communion' in Chapter 8. Granted that to be 'in communion' was in antiquity the criterion – for individuals as for local churches – of being *en règle* with the Church universal, how did you decide between two *groups* of local churches, in each of which there was communion between its constituents, but which were as groups out of communion with each other? Already in the fourth century the reaction against the Council of Nicaea and, coupled with that reaction, the interventions of the secular power in ecclesiastical affairs, had led (after the Council of Sardica in 343) to something very like this situation. A century and a half later the Acacian schism divided the East from the West for thirty years.

We have heard clear answers to our question from the fourth and later centuries; from Optatus, from the Council of Aquileia (including Ambrose), from Jerome, from the Formula of Hormisdas as endorsed by the Patriarch of Alexandria and the Eastern episcopate: to be in communion with the bishop of Rome (or, as the linguistic usage then put it, with the 'Apostolic See') was to be in the koinonia; to be out of communion with Rome was to be outside the koinonia. Can we get any indications from evidence before 300? I think one can say at once, and as a preliminary, (*a*) that there is no evidence from the first three centuries *against* the opinion that from the earliest sub-apostolic times it was recognized that communion with Rome was essential; (*b*) that it is hard to see how affairs could be conducted without such a principle being adhered to at least in practice. But is there any positive evidence?

In the fourth century we have heard Jerome describe communion with the bishop of Rome as communion with the See (or chair) of Peter. The same doctrine is propounded by Optatus: the See or chair of Peter is the first of the Church's 'endowments' and is occupied by the bishop of Rome. Can we trace this usage back into the third century?

Before Constantine gave the Church the right to exist Christians were living in a cultural 'ghetto'. Our sources of evidence for this period are not as good as we could wish. We have, however, the works and letters of Cyprian of Carthage, to whom we have already devoted some attention. He uses the term 'See of Peter (*cathedra Petri*)'. What does he mean by it?

Batiffol devotes an Excursus in his *Le Catholicisme de Saint Augustin* [14] to the term 'cathedra Petri' in Augustine's controversy with the Donatists. He points out that in a letter of the year 400 Augustine prefers, to a Donatist claim of local legitimacy, to appeal to the reckoning from Peter himself, to whom, as figuring the whole Church, Christ said: On this rock I will build my Church, etc.; Augustine then proceeds to give the list of the bishops of Rome up to Anastasius. This makes it almost certain that the reference to the *sedes Petri*, in Augustine's *Psalmus contra Donatistas* of 393, is similarly a reference to the See of Rome. In this 'psalm' Augustine invites the Donatists to be (re-)engrafted into the Vine, sc. the Church, and with that in view to 'reckon the bishops in succession from the very seat of Peter'.[15] Elsewhere he speaks of the Roman Church 'in which there has always prospered (*viguit*) the primacy (*principatus*) of the apostolic See'.[16] Batiffol is probably right in inferring that Augustine held that to be sure of one's Catholicism it was useful – to say the least – to know that one was in communion with the bishop of Rome. But the argument tends to disappear from the later stages of his controversy with the Donatists, and he is not so categorical about it as had been Optatus (from whom, Batiffol thinks, he derived it).

Batiffol is similarly unwilling to derive an argument, for Rome's position as the centre of the Church's communion, from Cyprian's use of the term 'cathedra Petri'. But here I think a strong counter-case can be built up.

It is true that Cyprian regards the unity of the Church as established when Christ founded his Church on Peter, and that this 'Petrine principle', so to call it, is realized, so far as a local church is concerned, in the local bishop. But the actual term 'cathedra Petri' occurs in Cyprian's writings in two passages where it must mean the See of Rome (I think we can regard it as now pretty certain that the so-called 'Primacy Text' in the *De Unitate Ecclesiae* comes from the hand of Cyprian himself).

The Primacy Text is as follows:

(Christ says to Peter, Feed my sheep). On him alone Christ builds his Church and to him he entrusts his sheep to be fed. And although all the apostles received equal power, nevertheless he established one chair (*cathedra*) and arranged the origins and nature (*rationem*) of unity by his own authority.

I agree that the others were what Peter was, but a primacy (*primatus*) is given to Peter and one chair is shown forth. And all are shepherds, but one flock is shown to be fed by all the apostles with single-minded agreement. How can a man who does not keep this unity of Peter (or, of the Church) believe that he yet keeps the faith? How can a man who deserts the chair of Peter on whom the Church has been founded trust that he is yet in the Church?[17]

It should be noted (though it has been disputed) that the unity here in question is not that of a local church but of the universal koinonia. The *cathedra Petri* must be supposed to be located in some single See. Once again we ask: which See?

We know from a letter of St Firmilian of Cappadocia, written a few years after the (probable) date of the Primacy Text, that the bishop of Rome at that time boasted that he sat on the *cathedra Petri*. It seems probable that this was already an habitual claim of the bishops of Rome; and that Cyprian must have known, when he wrote the Primacy Text, how the phrase would be understood.

The clearest evidence, however, comes from a letter of Cyprian himself to Rome. Some African schismatics had sent representatives to Rome, apparently to secure the bishop of Rome's recognition of their own group as being the true local church of Carthage. Cyprian is very indignant indeed:

> They dare to take ship and carry a letter, from schismatical people who are *profani* [sc. outside the 'temple' of the true Church of God] to the *cathedra Petri* and to the original (*principalem*) church whence the unity of the bishops took (or, took and still takes) its rise, and to give no thought to the fact that these are the Romans whose faith was praised by the apostle's proclamation [Rom. 1:8], to whom false faith can have no access.[18]

This passage should settle the question that Cyprian meant, by the *cathedra Petri*, the See of Rome.[19] We must reasonably conclude that, in the Primacy Text, a breach with Rome is regarded as tantamount to a breach with the Catholic Church; the church and see of Rome are the centre of communion, the incorporation of the unity of the universal Church to which Cyprian attaches such supreme importance.

In the light of these witnesses to the position accorded to Rome, particularly after 313, the alleged behaviour of bishop Victor of Rome in the Quartodeciman troubles, some fifty or more years before Cyprian's writings, takes on its full significance.[20] Eusebius tells us that because the bishops in Asia (that is to say, Roman Asia) refused to abandon their custom of observing Easter annually on a day which differed from that assigned by the rest of the universal church, Victor, the head of the church of the Romans, 'attempts to cut off, as though heterodox, the dioceses of all Asia, together with the adjacent churches, from the common unity; and he makes proclamation by letter, announcing that all the brethren there are excommunicated'.[21] This action, Eusebius adds, did not please all the bishops (sc. in the rest of the world); and he mentions Irenaeus of Lyons particularly as urging Victor to have more concern for neighbourly charity and unity.

To assess this episode at its proper value it must be borne in mind that, as indicated earlier in this essay, any bishop (in the days when canon law was still unborn or in its infancy) could deny his own communion (and that of his local church) to any other bishop – at the risk, of course, of finding that he had alienated himself from the rest of the Catholic world. One of the principles for which Rome was fighting in the chaotic years of the fourth century was that a bishop who thought himself unjustly treated by his neighbours should have the power of appealing to Rome. But Victor's action, as described by Eusebius, was of a very different and more momentous character: he not only announced that he had broken communion with the churches of Asia and their friends; he 'attempted to cut them off from the *common unity*', in other words to exclude them, by his own act, from the universal koinonia. It is as if the Archbishop of Canterbury had not merely let it be known that he personally was not in communion with the American dissidents, but had proclaimed that these dissidents were excommunicated from the whole Anglican communion. The fact that this intention of Victor's provoked protest from bishops who agreed with him on the actual issue of the date of Easter is irrelevant. Indeed, it is remarkable that they are not alleged to have disputed his power to pass such a sentence of general excommunication, but only to have criticized his (proposed) use of that power as being, not illegal, but contrary to charity. Any loyal Catholic today might say as much about some exercise of papal power.

The point that seems to be worth making is that Victor's proposed sentence of excommunication would have harmonized exactly with the thesis that the ultimate criterion of communion within the universal Church was, in the early centuries, communion with the local church of Rome.

We have no evidence of the origin of this criterion in the history of the post-apostolic Church. But this may be the point at which to draw attention to the so-called Petrine texts in the New Testament, and particularly to Matthew 16:17–19 and John 21:15–19. The latter passage is from the so-called 'appendix' to the Fourth Gospel and, in a literary sense, is indeed additional to the scheme of the Gospel, which finds its culmination in 20:31. It will be remembered that it is widely held by modern scholars that the Fourth Gospel reached its present form at a late date, more or less about the year 100. The Matthaean passage, on the other hand, is regarded by many as the insertion into its present context of a narrative relating to some alleged appearance of the risen Jesus. I am unrepentant in holding that the Matthaean passage is original in its present context. It is not seriously denied that it is a rendering into Greek of an Aramaic text; it must therefore be supposed to have originated within the sphere of influence of Palestinian Christianity, and I see no good reason for doubting, unless on *a priori* grounds, that it goes back to the lifetime and lips of Jesus of Nazareth.

If, however, the passage is a relatively late construction, we are justified in asking what was the motive for its creation and for its use by the author of the first Gospel. That Gospel, it is agreed, has a strong ecclesiastical theme. Clearly, the author is here affirming a divine guarantee for a primacy of Peter over the whole Church. But supposing that, by the date of the composition of the Gospel, Peter was already dead (he was martyred in Rome before the fall of Jerusalem in 70), why did the author preserve this passage? Was it not to provide the foundation for a Petrine primacy that was (a) over the universal Church and (b) still in existence – somewhere – though Peter himself was dead?

The same line of argument can be applied to the Johannine passage, where Peter is given the role of divinely appointed shepherd of the flock of Christ (i.e. the koinonia). For the author of the Fourth Gospel, Jesus was the original Shepherd of that flock. But Jesus was to die, to rise again, and to ascend to heaven. Meanwhile the flock, the historical reality that found the roots of its existence in the historical Jesus and the inspiration of its life in the Holy Spirit sent at his request by his heavenly Father, would live on in the world and continue to proclaim the revealed word of God. Who would be its centre and focus, as Jesus had been hitherto? The answer of the New Testament documents is that Peter performed this office. The Fourth Gospel in its last chapter portrays the risen Jesus Christ as giving the requisite commission to Peter. But why was this appendix added, or rather this passage included in it, if at the time of composition Peter had long been dead? (Indeed, one can infer from John 21:19 that his martyrdom had taken place.) If the flock needed a representative of Jesus to lead and unify it in the generation immediately succeeding his death and resurrection, would it need it less after Peter's death? Would there not be a cruel irony in emphasizing the Petrine office, as the appendix seems to do, if the office died with its first incumbent? It would be consonant with John's allusive style to suppose that he is reminding his readers that the office is still alive, and still vital to the life of the koinonia.[22]

Earlier in this chapter I asked: How is an individual to choose between the rival claims, as it would seem, of Eastern Orthodoxy and the Roman Catholic Church to be the one visible koinonia of Jesus Christ? If that question were unanswered, a hitherto uncommitted individual, convinced that the koinonia is a single historical communion, would find himself in an inhibiting situation. Others, considering his predicament, might feel inclined to raise again the question whether the 'communion' model has been rightly understood; and whether, if it has, it can be made a guide for practical decision.

The evidence adduced in this chapter may go some way to recommend the view that Eastern Orthodoxy, a Church celebrated for its devotion to tradition, has in recent centuries allowed one element of the tradition to drop somewhat into the background. History allows no doubt that – to look back no further than the fourth century – the See of Rome was, from the time of the later decades of that century onwards, making no secret of its primatial claims. They come to the fore impressively not only in the ecclesiology of Leo the Great but in the events and aftermath of the Council of Chalcedon. One of the canons passed by this council remained inoperative because Leo refused to ratify it. The rest of its findings were held in suspense until he had given his confirmation, and the world waited anxiously for his review of its decisions. The Roman claims continued to be asserted thereafter for half a millennium till 1054, and of course have remained in vigour till the present day. Although, as that half-millennium wore on, the East became more and more intent on living its own life and tended to pay little attention to Rome, it is extraordinary that the essence of the Roman claim encountered practically no protest from the official Eastern Church – though the East steadily resisted Rome's tendency to use the primacy as an excuse for interventions in the East which, to put it mildly, paid scant respect to the principles of subsidiarity and the divine rights of local bishops.

It is not as though the East was allowed to remain unaware of the Roman claims. As we have seen, these claims were clearly stated in the Formula of Hormisdas, which the East, through its individual bishops, accepted as a formula for terminating the Acacian schism. And finally, the second ecumenical council of Nicaea's members concurred – unanimously, we are told – in the statement by John the Deacon of the conditions requisite for conciliar ecumenicity, the first of which was acceptance of a council's decisions by the Church of Rome. I understand that it is still the view in Eastern Orthodoxy that the Patriarch of Rome is the first of the five traditional patriarchs. Is it possible that Orthodoxy's admirable avoidance of any claim to have held an ecumenical council since 1054 is an indication that the tradition of the Roman primacy, however diminished over the years in the consciousness of the East, is still not entirely without practical influence in that Communion?

History moves on. Much has happened since John XXIII inaugurated the Second Vatican Council in 1962. One of the most moving occasions during that council was the simultaneous abolition, at Rome and at Constantinople, of the excommunications of 1054. Doubtless this abolition had more symbolic than legal content. But if the Church is not so much a legal structure as it is a communion of charity, the symbolism was of high significance; and it had practical results. Preparations are going forward for dialogue between official groups of theologians from the Eastern Orthodox Church and the Roman Catholic Church respectively with a view to resolving, with God's help, the remaining doctrinal and theological obstacles to the resumption of full communion between them. Meanwhile, in a message to the Pope formally delivered on 14 December 1975, the Patriarch of Constantinople, referring to the 'Pentarchy' of the five great patriarchates of antiquity (Rome, Constantinople, Alexandria, Antioch, Jerusalem), expressed himself as follows:

It is in the Word of God that our Holy Church of Christ in Constantinople embraces the Bishop of Rome and the Holy Church of Rome, in an act which is like a perfume of praise rising towards God from the pentarchy of the One, Holy, Catholic and Apostolic Church, in which the Bishop of Rome is designated to preside in love and honour; it (the Church of Constantinople) embraces him (the bishop of Rome), rendering him all the honour that is due to him through this designation. Expressing ourself, after consulting our Holy Synod, in this way, our most holy Apostolic, Patriarchal and Ecumenical See is convinced that it expresses the thought of the early Church.

[After referring to his decision to establish an inter-Orthodox theological Commission to prepare for the dialogue with Rome, the Patriarch concluded:] Communicating this happy news to Your Holiness, the first in rank and in honour of the whole

Body of the Lord (sc. the Church), we embrace you with a holy kiss. ...[23]

To this moving communication, delivered in an official ceremony by the Metropolitan Meliton, the Pope replied in an address; after which he approached the Metropolitan and, going on his knees, kissed his feet – another 'symbol', no doubt, but one which signified that Christian unity is much more than a legal agreement; it is a unity in love, service and humility. The Pope, in the 'Great Church' of the future, will be called to be not the dictator of a world-wide quasi-political organization, but *servus servorum Dei*, the humblest of God's servants.

To serve God is to serve the koinonia. It is to promote the God-given unity of the koinonia in self-forgetting charity. For the heart of the koinonia, the heart of the Church, is not power but love. The unity that love engenders, and in which love has its perfect work, is a unity that seems to require a visible focus within the Church as a visible historical entity. Tradition has guided us to see that focus in the local church of Rome and the See of its bishop. It seems more helpful, and more profoundly true, to regard him as the centre of charity than as the chief officer of an institution. Without such a centre, could the koinonia in the end survive?

Chapter XII

In Conclusion

This essay has taken its starting-point for granted. That starting-point is common to all Christians. Others can accept it as a hypothesis 'for the sake of the argument'. It is simply the assumption that the basic Christian affirmation is true.

I

Christianity claims to be no mere human invention. It is not a new and interesting way of viewing a reality that would have been fundamentally the same if Jesus of Nazareth had never existed. Of course, every human life, and in particular every human life of genius, impinging on the world in which it exists, leaves the world in some way different from what it was. Our world is changed from what it would have been, because Socrates lived and Plato was his disciple; because Archimedes once leapt from the bath crying 'Eureka'; because someone created the Egyptian sphinx, and Shakespeare wrote *Hamlet*. But Christianity makes a difference that is uniquely unique, because it originates in a divine Act that radically changes the whole universe. To safeguard the double uniqueness of this historical occurrence which is so peculiarly original that it can be compared only with the creation of the universe, Christianity found itself driven inexorably to affirm that Jesus the son of Mary of Nazareth, while undoubtedly a man like the rest of us, 'consubstantial' with us in his humanity, is consubstantial also with the God whom Jesus worshipped and whom we worship too.

Christianity is an objective reality. It is the historical point and the consequent process in which God's purpose in creation is definitely inaugurated and disclosed, no longer merely anticipated and foreshadowed. Not only is the Christian believer a new creation. The whole universe is re-created in and through this divine Act: 'Behold, I make all things new'.

The historical inauguration of this higher order of creation is the Word of God, incarnate as Jesus of Nazareth. Like the rest of us, Jesus lived and grew and died in history. What the incarnation is and means reaches its culmination in his actual resurrection from the dead. Christianity does not spring just from a faith in the resurrection of Christ; it springs from that resurrection itself.

The incarnation is not an isolated event without consequences. It is an inauguration. It inaugurates a process and is orientated towards a goal. That process I have tried to understand as embodied in the koinonia, the fellowship of those who, because they had come to believe in the divine Act, were able to become its representatives and its heralds. First in the original disciples, grouped around the Twelve and Simon bar-Jonah their leader, the koinonia began to radiate, to transcend its own limits in a 'mission' of evangelization.

For, just as Jesus Christ transcends himself in the koinonia, so the koinonia transcends itself in its Spirit-inspired mission. The koinonia is so intrinsic to the purpose of God inaugurated in the divine Act that we can truly say that the incarnation, the resurrection of Christ, the outpouring of the Holy Spirit, and the koinonia constitute a single mystery of divine love, wisdom and power. Christ becomes fully himself – within the historical order – in the koinonia. The 'whole Christ' – *totus Christus*, as Augustine put it – is Jesus Christ the head of the body, *and* the koinonia in which believers are fellow members with him.

The goal and end of the historical process inaugurated in Jesus Christ will coincide with the end of human history: that final transcendence in which Christ, active throughout the process through his Holy Spirit, will 'hand over' his kingdom to his heavenly Father so that God may be 'all in all'.

Meanwhile, and with a view to that final goal, the koinonia has the task of communicating the one mystery of redeeming divine love. It is to be communicated to all mankind. To the extent that the communication receives a positive response, new believers are added to the koinonia and towards them the communication takes on a new shape: it is no longer only evangelization but also education, nurture and sustenance.

Thus, while Jesus Christ is both Message and Messenger, for as Word he speaks and as God he is spoken, the koinonia, or, as we call it, the Church, is messenger, communicator of the Word, and only self-communicating in the Word. Nevertheless, the Church has an indispensable role to play. For the Word, the Message, has to be communicated historically in times and places to which Jesus in his historical life had no access. As we saw in our opening chapter, we know virtually nothing of Jesus, historically, apart from what the Church tells us – directly or indirectly (through the lips of others who have heard of him from the Church). The New Testament itself is a collection of Christian writings, preserved for us by the Church.

It is through the 'words' of the Church – meaning by 'words' not only verbal utterances and writings but cultic acts and Christian behaviour in general – that the Word is communicated, not by direct reproduction, as though that were possible or could be helpful apart from the historical context in which Jesus himself lived. In order to be communicated in varying human situations, the Word has to be understood, and in order to be understood it has to be interpreted. If I am explaining the meaning of a Greek poem to someone who is ignorant of Greek, I have to understand it myself by interpreting its meaning in the context of my own prior grasp of meanings, and then to find ways of expressing this meaning in a language that my pupil can understand and interpret to himself.

The proverb is well known: *traductor traditor*; whoever undertakes to translate something betrays its meaning in the process. Had the Church been left to its own unaided powers to carry out its task of communicating the Word, the latter would have run the risk of uncontrollable distortion, diminution or inflation, in the course of centuries and in an incalculable variety of different human contingencies.

Therefore, our tradition tells us, Christ not only commissioned his followers to communicate the message, but poured out upon them the divine Spirit to enable them with supernatural powers and guarantees. He will bring to your memory, says the Johannine Jesus, all that I have said to you; he will lead you into all the truth. In its proclamation, and so in its understanding and interpretation, of the gospel the Church is therefore 'infallible': it will not go astray and it will not lead astray. We need not quarrel about the *word* 'infallibility'. We know – it is part of our faith – that the Word of God, spoken at a particular time and in a particular place, was spoken for all humanity everywhere and for all time. We know, therefore, that, by God's grace and not through any merely human ingenuity or contrivance, that Word will for ever be available through the teaching of the Church. The truth, the gospel, carries with it this guarantee.

Such infallibility, it has been thought by some, belongs indeed to the inspired books of the canonical Bible, and this scriptural infallibility is enough. That is not so. The Bible also has to be interpreted and understood; and if this task is left either to the individual believer or to the scriptural scholars and theologians, there is by now sufficient evidence that the Word will be lost behind the variety of inconsistent versions of it. Only within the koinonia can this variety be contained without fatal results. And in the end it will be the koinonia that endorses or rejects the exegesis of scholars.

In order that the Word, entrusted to the koinonia, may be preserved in its integrity and universally proclaimed, the unity of the koinonia in history is necessary. Augustine once remarked that heresy is schism become inveterate. If the life-blood of the whole Church fails to circulate everywhere, the instruments of the Word which the new 'churches' purport to be will speak with inconsistent voices. It is then 'anybody's guess' which is the right version of the gospel; and the probability must be reckoned with that none is correct – that in fact the Word is no longer being communicated. And this is an impossible conclusion, because it would mean that the indefectible purposes of God in the incarnation and the constitution of the koinonia had been frustrated.

The koinonia is therefore for ever historically one human fellowship. This a Christian can know, even if he has not yet succeeded in identifying for himself which of the various claimants is that divinely guaranteed koinonia, that 'one holy catholic and apostolic Church' for which he is seeking. The Church – however it is to be identified – is, he will come to realize, the single visible divinely guaranteed exponent of the revelation, communicator of the message, of the Act of God.

II

Christianity is meant for everyone, and so the Church is meant for everyone; it is 'catholic', universal of right, even when it is not yet universal in fact. And since it is meant for everyone, and can only be accepted by an act of personal faith, it is apprehensible by each mature human being – at least, its credibility and its claim on his acceptance must be so apprehensible.

Man of course is collectivity as well as individual person. And the Christian life is a common life, a life in the fellowship, the koinonia. But it is inexorably true that human life, Christian life, is lived by each in the incommunicable uniqueness of his own personal experience – and can be lived nowhere else. There is a perfectly correct way of speaking of 'the mind of the Church', as there is a correct way of speaking of British policy. But in the end the mind of the Church exists only in the several minds of concrete individuals. And when we look forward to the conversion of some great continent we mean, fundamentally, the conversion of the individuals who constitute its population. If Christianity is a fact with a meaning, we have to admit that meanings exist in individual persons. To assent to the claims of a collective group, be it Catholic Church or communist party, is an act of profound personal responsibility – no one can do it by proxy, and each has to answer for it before God.

Christianity is intended for everyone. Everyone is capable, when he reaches a certain degree of maturity, of reflecting upon religion. Everyone, therefore, is at least an amateur theologian. But not everyone is a professional theologian. Professional theologians have a tremendous service to perform for the Church and the world. But it is not their task to turn us all into professional theologians.

Ordinary human beings, ordinary Christians, actual or potential – what are they? They are housewives and workers, doctors, lawyers, artists, politicians; tinker, tailor, soldier, sailor, as we used to say. By and large they are busy people, too busy to have a second profession as professional theologians; and not all have the intellectual capacity to become such. They have neither the will nor the capacity nor the time nor the call to enter into the controversies of the theological schools – or even of the ecclesiastical denominations.

Yet the gospel is meant for each and all of them, and there must be some way in which, from whatever human situation they begin, they can become capable, once the gospel is proclaimed in their hearing, to recognize it for what it is: the truth of God without which man's life is meaningless. And since assent to the gospel carries with it the obligation to belong to the Christian fellowship; since, further, there are many concrete embodiments of Christian fellowship – at one time Catholic or semi-Arian, at another Chalcedonian or anti-Chalcedonian; Catholic or Eastern Orthodox; or Catholic, Protestant, Anglican or Eastern Orthodox – it is only possible to fulfil this obligation in the concrete by joining one or another of the contemporary alternatives. Some readers may remember C. S. Lewis's remarkable book, *Mere Christianity*,[1] and his defence of that concept and of his treatment of Christian apologetics under that heading. Lewis conceded that it is only possible to be a Christian by adhering to one or other of existing Christian Churches. But, he said or implied, the choice of a particular Church is consequent upon a recognition of the basic Christian claim. He had, he hoped, brought his readers into an ante-room though not into the inner sanctum. The ante-room was surrounded by doors, each purporting to afford access to that sanctum, and on each door was the name of one of the Christian denominations. It was for the reader to decide through which door to enter. One or other of the doors was the right door.

How can the ordinary man discover the right door? We may imagine that outside each door there is available a prospectus of the qualities of the particular denomination whose door it is. With such experience, reflection and judgement as he is capable of, he sees that each has its apparent merits and demerits. Is there any criterion that goes to the root of the question and will enable him to make correctly a decision of immense importance – for surely it is true that a Christian must also be a churchman, and surely it is true that the claims of the several Churches, to the extent that they contradict each other, cannot all be true?

About half a century ago, in the course of my exciting but also painful journey from one Church to another, I spent a good deal of time on what, to the average layman, would appear to be the abstruse minutiae of Christian history. But I also received a piece of hard-headed advice which served me well, and which I consider permanently valid. It was all very well to weigh up the probabilities about whether the Council of Sardica (of which most laymen have never heard) had bestowed, or only recognized, a Roman primacy; or whether the Council of Chalcedon had seriously recognized that primacy or only made polite noises in order to keep Leo the Great happy. But, said my adviser – I am not quoting his words but reporting my memory of their drift – it is surely probable that, if God has provided for mankind a true and universal religion, it will be fairly recognizable in its universal claims and presence. As a sore thumb stands out, so surely the true religion will stand out, for the responsible and prayerful inquirer who is not a professional theologian or a professional scholar, as unique and uniquely credible.

The potential Christians of whom I am thinking will have their own lines of reasoning, and they will not be too much upset if logicians find it difficult to classify their reasoning processes. They are likely, I suggest, to think that it is, at the very least, probable that the Christian body which has the divine mandate and guarantee to proclaim and sustain God's message to mankind will be aware of that commission and will be vocal in publishing its awareness. They are not likely to think that a body that makes no such claim, a body, for instance, that points away from itself either to a recognizable Church authority which existed in the past but unfortunately does not exist today, or to a Great Church of the future which may or may not one day exist, but is not likely to exist before our contemporary inquirers are dead – that such a body is, unbeknown to itself and despite its own disclaimers, the one mouthpiece of a divine revelation intended for all mankind and in every age. And if they overhear theologians and scholars murmuring that it is not permissible to bypass the controversies of experts, they will comfort themselves with the thought that Jesus of Nazareth does not seem to have had too great a reverence for the traditions of the scribes.

Prayer and reflection may go a little further. Of course there are several Christian bodies today, as there were in the fourth or fifth centuries, each actually making the claim to be the unique Church of Christ – a claim which the mainstream Protestant bodies and the Anglican Communion do not make. There are the Exclusive Brethren, the Copts and Armenians, the Eastern Orthodox Communion, and the Roman Catholic Church, to name but a few. One could spend a lifetime examining the history, credentials and specific doctrines of these various bodies. But Christianity is for life, not just for enjoyment after death. A selection has to be made. I think most inquirers, if they are sufficiently detached and have some little common sense, will conclude that in the end the option is between the Eastern Orthodox and the Roman Catholic Church. I have tried in preceding pages to suggest that, when the issue is thus narrowed down, there is a way of reaching a conclusion.

III

In writing these pages, I am acutely aware that I shall seem to be rejecting the whole drift and meaning of that ecumenical movement which the Second Vatican Council declared to be a movement under the impulse of the Holy Spirit. I may claim to have had some connection with ecumenical endeavours for over thirty years, and in recent years I have been officially involved in the movement. Perhaps, then, I may be allowed to make a few comments.

I am quite sure that the movement has God's blessing on it. I am sure that it has already done an enormous work for Christ. I am sure that we must persevere with it. But I am sure that in pursuing what is called the ecumenical dialogue we have severally to be quite honest in admitting our fundamental convictions, while at the same time being willing and anxious to be treated with equal frankness by those with whom we are in discussion.

This is not the place to catalogue the good that has already been done by the movement. I find it convenient to view it at three different, though connected, levels. There are the relations between Church leaders throughout the world; and here the improvement has been enormous and obvious. One might say that we have moved from a period when a rather stiff private courtesy was combined with public recriminations to a period of great public courtesy combined with warm personal friendship. And this not only at levels below the top. Englishmen will particularly have noticed the series of personal meetings and joint consequent statements between successive Popes and Archbishops of Canterbury. More important still have been the change in private and public attitudes as between Popes and Patriarchs of Constantinople.

Secondly, there has been theological dialogue. Perhaps the most important aspect of this – apart from the mutual respect and friendship of the participants – has been the willingness to postpone discussions of the theological and linguistic dissensions that were partly causes and partly consequences of our divisions, and to look again at fundamentals with the help of concepts and terms that, because they are new and shared, are free from the *damnosa hereditas* of past controversies. Speaking again as a British Roman Catholic, I may be permitted to refer in particular to the three Statements of the Anglican/Roman Catholic International Commission.[2] In this field we have been immensely helped by a general trend away from philosophical scholasticism to the historical and meta-historical perspective.

Thirdly, there has been a tremendous growth of friendship and even co-operation at the level of ordinary Christians – I mean those who neither carry the responsibilities of official leadership nor claim theological expertise. Despite tragic areas of the world where the old hostilities and mutual suspicions seem still to be dominant, the general picture at this level is – considering the weight of a long past – immensely comforting.

After the first session of the Second Vatican Council, and about the time of John XXIII's death, I heard the late Arnold Toynbee, whose historical vision was world-wide and unbounded by historical restriction, saying that he thought that with the general acceptance by Christians of the principles and practice of ecumenism the world was entering a new epoch. Religion had in the past been a divisive factor, productive of intolerance and hostility. It was now becoming a uniting factor, inspired by and tending towards mutual love. Such a judgement by the propounder of the theory of challenge and response deserves to be pondered.

Why, then, it may be asked, do I publish this essay which may seem to many to be an act of treachery to the ecumenical movement and its principles? I have at least three pleas in defence or at least in mitigation.

There is, first, the question of integrity. The object of the ecumenical movement is Christian unity. Its method is, in general, what we have come to call dialogue. A first principle of dialogue is to find some common ground from which discussion may take its start. One of the joys of engaging in dialogue between Christian Churches and their respective members is the discovery of the enormous range and importance of what we already share in common. After all, we may have known, in an abstract kind of way, that our fellow Christians, in the midst of a not yet Christian world, really do believe like us in one living God and in the reality of the incarnation of his consubstantial Word. It is another thing, and a deeply moving thing, to experience this community of faith in actual talk, work and prayer shared between us. The same is true of reverence for the Bible, of shared Creeds, or of devotional practices and, not least, of a common moral outlook – despite differences in matters of comparative detail or of some intellectual complexity. In this first stage of dialogue, differences are left in the shadow, and quite properly so. If two Englishmen meet in a foreign country they are likely, at first, to take more seriously their British identity than the local differences arising from the fact that one is a Cornishman and the other's home is in Yorkshire. And it is what already unites us that seems to hold out the best hope for increasing unity. It remains, however, that there are deep differences. To me it appears that one of the greatest – at least in the dialogue between Churches that accepted the Reformation and the Roman Catholic Church which did not – is over the question whether visible unity is only a goal to be aimed at, or whether it is a divinely guaranteed endowment of the koinonia. The Roman Catholic Church is irrevocably committed to the latter conviction. I think the time has come when this fact should be brought out into the open; and perhaps it may be more usefully done by one who is committed to ecumenism than by a 'traditionalist' who has never given more than lip-service to what the Second Vatican Council had to say about this great movement.

In the second place, I fear that to discard from the Christian tradition this faith in visible unity as a permanent endowment of the Church is, in principle and in the long run, to open the door to an undogmatic liberalism which, if pushed to its ultimate consequences, would mean a disintegration and eventual collapse of what God has given us in Christ and preserved for us by his Holy Spirit.

Thirdly, I ask myself what promise of stability could there be in a Great Church of the future which held, on principle, that its unity was a product of human striving, blessed no doubt by God but in no way guaranteed by him? If a Christianity which, through fifteen centuries, held firmly to the conviction that visible unity is of the essence of the Church, was nevertheless unable to escape the recurrent disaster of schism, what hope could there be for a Christianity which had deliberately surrendered that conviction as the price of escape from our present difficulties?

But finally, I believe that Christian faith is ultimately a matter of personal decision. I see assent to the gospel as something not less particular than falling in love:

> In every man's career are certain points
> Whereon he dares not be indifferent;
> The world detects him clearly, if he dare,
> As baffled at the game, and losing life. ...
> But certain points, *left wholly to himself*,
> When once a man has arbitrated on,
> We say he must succeed there or go hang.
> Thus, he should wed the woman he loves most
> Or needs most, whatsoe'er the love or need –
> For he can't wed twice. Then, he must avouch,
> Or follow, at the least, sufficiently,
> The form of faith his conscience holds the best,
> Whate'er the process of conviction was:
> For nothing can compensate his mistake
> On such a point, the man himself being judge:
> He cannot wed twice, nor twice lose his soul.[3]

I have the uncomfortable feeling that there is, at the present time, many a Christian who is postponing a personal decision on the greatest issue of all: How do I personally incorporate myself into historical Christianity?; in the hope that somehow the Church leaders and the theologians will patch up a union which will allow him to slip in, along with the mass of his fellows, to a Church more 'universal' than the one to which at present he belongs. This can be a form of escaping from one's personal responsibility. It is true that the call of Christ is universal and the response to it involves us with others in a collectivity, a koinonia. But the response of each is incommunicably and inescapably his own. Now it may be true that there are Christian bodies, other than the Roman Catholic one, whose basic stance is open to the possibility of growing into Catholicism, and where, concurrently, the principle of the magisterial authority of the Church leaders is such that those leaders could take virtually the whole population of their Church into communion with the Roman Catholic Church through an act of assent to its constitutive beliefs. But at least where the principle of private judgement is deeply embedded in the ecclesiastical tradition, and where the authority of the leadership is real as regards discipline but little more than nominal as regards belief, the individual has to recognize that he cannot in principle wait till he has been given a lead by persons whose teaching authority in any case he does not accept.

IV

So, then, it will be said, you are advocating an immediate surrender to the old, pre-Vatican II, intolerant claims of an unreformed Roman Catholic Church?

My reply may be of little comfort to my ecumenical friends in the other Churches. It is, however, something that I suggest my fellow Catholics should ponder.

Someone has said that the road to Christian unity, like the road to resurrection, is a way of the Cross; that unless a Church is prepared to die to itself it cannot hope to be raised again into the Great Church of the future. There is truth in this saying, a truth that has to be worked out in different ways in the different Christian bodies. Catholics so far have perhaps been slow to apply this truth to themselves. Is it possible to say that the Catholic Church must 'die' in order to live? This essay has been devoted to arguing that there is a limit to such a suggestion: the Catholic Church, in loyalty to itself, its mission and commission, and to Christianity itself and the world to which Christianity is sent, cannot barter away the principle that God's Church 'subsists' in the Roman Catholic Communion, and that in that Communion are to be found the 'universal aids to salvation'. But granted that basic limitation, I think that there is much room for movement, a movement that has begun already in our own generation.

Apart from a closing paragraph or two, Newman wrote his *Essay on the Development of Christian Doctrine* before he became a Roman Catholic. The essay presents itself as offering a hypothesis to explain how it is that every extant form of Christianity seems markedly different from Christianity as it is disclosed in historical records of the past. The hypothesis is that Christianity is capable of development, particularly in its doctrine, that such development is in fact inevitable, and that a Christian is bound to conclude that it is willed by God and that God will have seen to it that the development is a change within abiding and necessary identity. Newman affirms that, granted the truth of the hypothesis, he is not responsible for the fact that the outcome of the resultant understanding of Christianity is that Roman Catholicism is shown to be the one authentic and divinely sanctioned development of the original gospel.

Although, however, the essay closely anticipates Newman's reception into the Church, the decisive intellectual shift in his mind had occurred some years earlier. Already well before he began to write the book he had reached the point where he could see no answer to his difficulties except the acknowledgement of the truth of the Catholic claim. He waited only because he feared that he was under some, perhaps diabolical, illusion.

It is possible to accept Newman's argument and its conclusion, and yet to hold that the argument can be pushed too far; and that, whereas Newman's aim was to justify Catholic dogmatic affirmations, the idea of development has been used to sanction other aspects of actual Catholicism, in his time or in ours, which are not in fact guaranteed by the essential argument – and would, in some cases, no doubt have been rejected or deplored by Newman himself (for instance, while he seeks to understand certain aspects of popular Marian devotion, it is clear enough that he feels bound only by the authentic teaching of the Church on the subject of the Mother of God). Moreover, it is to be borne in mind that, while the argument can validate developments that have actually occurred, it cannot demonstrate that development *must* occur in precisely the way it does. The argument cannot prove that Christianity *had* to domesticate itself first and foremost, in the early centuries, in the Graeco-Roman culture, and therefore to express itself, dogmatically, in language and thought-forms borrowed (with modifications) from that culture. The argument only assures us that, granted that Christianity *did* so ensconce itself particularly in that culture, its dogmatic decisions, even though expressed in Graeco-Roman concepts and terms, were true. It remains, so far as we can see, that the decision to establish the new religion in the cities of the Mediterranean and especially in Rome, was a human decision – that the Church could, instead, have moved eastwards and established itself in India and in the Indian culture and thought-world. Established there, its developments might have been very different from what they actually have been, though the argument shows that such developments would have been true; but their contingent conditioning, and conceptual and verbal expression, would have been different from what in fact they have been. Such considerations may warn us to distinguish carefully between the universal truth of the gospel (and of dogma) and the cultural vesture in which that truth comes to expression.

Leaving aside speculations about a Christian history that did not occur – for in fact the Church went not to India but to Rome – it seems to me to be of the utmost importance to remember that a great many developments in Catholicism are not dogmatic at all, but practical or theological. Such developments, as already indicated, cannot shelter behind Newman's brilliant argument. But often it is such non-dogmatic developments that make it difficult for our Christian friends to contemplate an acceptance of the claims of the Catholic Church. In particular, they may have very serious difficulties about the concentration of power at Rome and the assumptions that seem to underlie that concentration. It may be helpful to examine this matter, and to take it as an illustration of the flexibility that is still latent in the Church within the limits of what cannot be altered because it is true.

In an earlier chapter it has been observed that a Council of Aquileia, about the year 381, affirmed that 'the rights of communion derive from Rome'. The metaphor is of streams of water flowing from a single source. It aptly describes a state of things in which the local church of Rome, represented by its bishop, can grant to or withhold from an individual or a group that communion which symbolizes and effects its living participation in the reality of the universal koinonia. The same symbolism seems to me to underlie the important fourth chapter of Cyprian's *De Unitate Catholicae Ecclesiae.*[4] And it may well be that this is the thought underlying his remark that *unitas sacerdotum*, the unity of the bishops of the world in a single communion, had its origin (or had and maintains its origin, *exorta est*) in the See of Peter.

But while Cyprian may have seen the 'source of communion' as being the See of Peter, he never, I think, suggests that that See is the source of the gospel, that is, of Catholic orthodoxy. The source of Christian truth, for him, is Christ – or perhaps rather the Scriptures as recording the teaching of Christ.

And while he may affirm that the *unity* of the episcopate finds its source in Rome, he is careful to point out that the other apostles 'were what Peter was' and never, to my recollection, hints that they derived their episcopal powers from any other source than Christ.

If we now turn to Rome itself, in the first half of the fifth century, we find Pope Innocent I using the same 'source' metaphor, but with significant applications:

> ... you decided [he writes to a council of bishops which had met at Carthage] that it was proper to refer to our judgement, knowing what is due to the Apostolic See [sc. the See of Rome] since all we who are set in this place desire to follow the Apostle *from whom the very episcopate and whole authority of this name is derived.*

And he speaks of the 'customs of the Fathers' and of 'that which they decreed by a divine and not human sentence', so that from [this See of Rome] 'all other Churches (*like waters flowing from their natal source* and flowing through the different regions of the [whole] world, *the pure streams of one incorrupt head*) should receive what they ought to enjoin'.[5] Cyprian had said that the See of Peter was the source of the unity of the episcopate. Innocent appears to say that Peter was the source of the episcopate itself. Cyprian had, in my view, seen Rome as the centre of communion. Innocent appears to see it as the source of correct doctrine.

We have to recognize that neither of these positions adopted by Innocent has been sanctioned by an infallible definition. The Second Vatican Council is clear that the authority of bishops is given to them not by a Roman delegation but by Christ in the sacrament of Orders. And according to the First Vatican Council, when the Pope defines a dogma he is exercising an infallibility which belongs to the Church; moreover, it is clear that he is bound to discover the truth which he defines, not by a private communication from heaven but by examining the tradition of the Church at large. The whole Church, in her sacred tradition, is the 'source' on which he draws and which he articulates.

Nevertheless, it is hardly disputable that Popes have frequently behaved as though bishops were merely their delegates, enjoying only such authority as Rome chose to dispense to them; and as though their doctrine were due to some private relationship with the Holy Spirit rather than to what they could learn from the Church as a whole.

The question of the relation of the authority of the Pope to that of the other bishops brings up the question of what Vatican I called the 'universal, immediate, ordinary jurisdiction' of the Pope. That the Pope's authority is universal is clear from the fact that, by withholding the right of communion, he can ultimately bend all who remain within the koinonia to his will: if they rebel, he can exclude them. That this authority is 'ordinary' means, in the language of the Council, that it is not derived from some other human source. But the word 'ordinary' is very dangerously equivocal. It can be taken to mean (and has often, even recently, been so taken) that the Pope's universal jurisdiction is something of daily and normal exercise: that, day by day, the Pope rules the Church in somewhat the way that the Roman Emperor's rule was both co-extensive with the Empire and in continuous exercise. The result of this practical misunderstanding has been, down the centuries, a monopoly of power in the Church which the Popes have claimed and the Church, including the other bishops, has been too willing to concede and indeed to encourage: it is so much easier to leave the burden of decision upon the shoulders of a distant monarch than to take responsibility oneself. But there has been another disastrous result. The grievances of the Eastern patriarchates against Rome stemmed in no small measure from papal interference in their own affairs and their legitimate customs. We have seen that the East could, in the centuries before the eleventh, put up with and indeed appeal to a papal primacy (cf. the second Council of Nicaea). When, however, the Pope treated the East as a mere extension of his own patriarchate, the East was justly indignant. After all, Northern Africa, well within the sphere of the Pope's special powers in the West, had, not only in the days of Cyprian but in the time of Augustine, acknowledged, indeed, the legitimate Roman prerogatives – 'causa finita est', said Augustine, when Rome condemned Pelagianism – and yet had stoutly protested against Rome's attempts to take local affairs out of the hands of the local hierarchy. Unfortunately the Vandals were at the gates as Augustine lay dying and the sturdy independence of the North African Church was lost to our common patrimony. Rome's over-calling of her hand went practically unchallenged thereafter in the West. In the East it contributed to that estrangement which we deplore today.

This misconceived idea that Rome is the fount not only of communion (which it is) but of everything in the Church finds expression in the notion that all canon law stems from the Pope, a notion which may need now to be vigorously contested. It can be argued that law is the crystallization of good custom, and that its roots are therefore not in the authority of the administrators but in the *sensus fidelium*, the Christian good sense of the collectivity. It is true that laws have to be 'promulgated', and that this is the responsibility of official authorities. But they are 'confirmed when they are accepted by those who use them'.[6]

The First Vatican Council, to which we owe the formulation of the universal ordinary jurisdiction of the Pope, was well aware that there were *some* limitations upon this primacy. But it felt itself unable to specify these limitations in its formulation.[7] Perhaps one fruit of the reconciliation of the Eastern Orthodox Communion and the Roman Catholic Church might be a renewed attention to this area.

In short, the special position of the local church of Rome and its bishop in the universal Church can be described as either a primacy or a centre of communion. There is truth in both descriptions; indeed either can be derived from the other: if the Pope has a primacy of teaching and discipline he can exclude from communion; and if he is the centre of communion he can require compliance with his leadership as the price of communion. Both descriptions can appeal to one or other of the so-called Petrine texts of the New Testament. The shepherd of the flock could be called its primate. The rock on which the Church is built so as to be superior to the slings and arrows of outrageous fortune would be the God-given centre of the Church's communion. We have lived long with the notion of primacy, and it has been pushed to lengths which, it can be argued, have provoked schism and hindered reunion. Should we not change our emphasis now, and propose the papacy as the centre of a reunited Christianity? Should we not admit that Peter too needed 'conversion', so that he might fulfil his task of – not reducing to uniformity, but – strengthening the brethren?

From such a discussion of one instance of a flexibility that is inherent in the Church one could pass on to many other examples and indeed to the characteristic new orientations, over a wide field, opened up by the Second Vatican Council. I have taken other opportunities to declare my profound conviction that that Council was an epoch-making event in the history of Christianity. Here I would only repeat, what I have said elsewhere, that its spirit is more important than its letter, together with my conviction that this spirit has by no means yet permeated the Roman Catholic body. The ecumenical movement is a good school of patience, and I think also that Christians, both within and without the visible communion of the Catholic Church, must practise patience with regard to this slow but continuing influence of the Council on the Church as a whole. It has been pointed out very truly that individuals and collectivities alike can suffer from cultural shock, and particularly the shock of rapid change within their own cultural environment. Catholics have had to put up with a lot of changes since the Second Vatican Council began its discussions in 1962. Perhaps it would be not only imprudent but uncharitable to push them too far too fast. But the direction of change remains important, whatever its speed or gradualness. The Council was a solemn act of the Catholic Church and it stands as a norm, in the letter but above all in the spirit of its Acts, for future progress.

V

The upshot of these reflections is that the Catholic Church in its existential actuality is an imperfect representation of what it is called and chosen by God to be. This imperfection is chronic. It is not something that began to be only after some heroic age of a hardly discernible past. It is an ineluctable consequence of the fact that the Church is a communion of human beings in various stages of development from lesser to greater maturity, and of human beings who are fallible and, despite their baptism, liable to sin. The Church's imperfection may take different shapes at different epochs and in reaction to different circumstances. But we have no grounds for supposing that the Church on earth will ever be a perfect expression of its own ideal. The Second Vatican Council's words can be applied here:

> While Christ, 'holy, innocent, undefiled' (Hebr. 7:26), knew nothing of sin (2 Cor. 5:21), but came to expiate only the sins of the people (Hebr. 2:17), the Church, embracing sinners in her bosom, is at the same time holy and always in need of being purified, and incessantly pursues the path of penance and renewal.[8]

To admit as much is, it might be thought, dangerous. Is it not to invite those who are not yet within the koinonia, whether as individuals or as Christian churches and groups, to postpone their reconciliation with the Church?

The contrary is the case. Had we any reason to hope that the Church might at length, or even quickly, so put her house in order that there would be nothing scandalous about her, then a case, insufficient but plausible, might be constructed for remaining outside until the interior reformation should be accomplished. But if the Church never will be what she ought to be, then an inescapable question arises: Is it not our duty to join her without more ado and to lend our aid to her continual 'purification' from within her ranks? For, imperfect though she is and will always be, she is the divinely given and guaranteed, new and supernatural, historical reality within which and by means of which God's eternal purpose for the salvation of all men and the supernatural elevation of his creation is being accomplished.

The Church, in fact, is the 'sacramental' re-presentation of the appeal of God in Christ, an appeal directed to every man everywhere and at all times. It is an appeal of love and calls for an answer of not theoretical but actual, existential, love which gives itself as fully and immediately as God has given himself in Christ. On the one hand, the appeal is: 'Come to me, all who labour and are heavy laden, and I will give you rest ... My yoke is easy, and my burden is light'. On the other hand, it is inexorable with all the inexorability of perfect love. And because it is inexorable it is 'judgemental'. 'The Father judges no one, but has given all judgement to the Son ... He who hears my word and believes him who sent me, has eternal life; he does not come into judgement, but has passed from death to life'. The message of Christian history is that the way to come to Christ is to belong to the koinonia; and that hearing Christ and believing him who sent him entails, not as a distant aspiration but as a here-and-now urgency, seeking membership of that koinonia.

References

Introductory

1 Bernard J. F. Lonergan, S. J., *Insight: A Study of Human Understanding* (London 1957), p. 573; cf. pp. 573–7, in which Lonergan's profound wisdom is characteristically lighted up by a radiance of humour approaching satire.

2 The classical case is Oedipus' (legendary) incestuous marriage with his own mother. Such incest was and is believed to be an objective moral evil of a very grave and repulsive kind. But Oedipus was, through the accidents of his life, entirely unaware that his wife Jocasta was also his mother. Subjectively, then, his marriage to her was not morally evil. Nevertheless, Sophocles exhibits him as totally appalled by the eventual discovery of the truth about the marriage, and it appears that everyone in the play agrees that Oedipus is henceforth to be an exile from civilized society. His future is to be determined not by his moral innocence but by the objective fact of his incest.

3 *The Documents of Vatican II*, ed. Walter M. Abbott, S. J. (London 1966): Decree on Ecumenism, n. 3; pp. 345–6.

4 ibid., Decree on Ecumenism, n. 14.

5 *Foundations of Christian Faith* (London 1978), p. 353.

Chapter I

1 We have to take the 'new creaturehood' realistically. But we must not assert a sheer and total discontinuity between the old and the new. It has been observed that, to make a baby a Christian, we do not kill him; we baptize him. And the resurrection Christ disclosed himself to the disciples as recognizably identical with the crucified Jesus.

2 A. E. Harvey, *The New English Bible: Companion to the New Testament* (Oxford/Cambridge 1970), ii, 618.

3   In R. E. Brown, J. A. Fitzmyer, R. E. Murphy (eds), *The Jerome Biblical Commentary* (London 1970), p. 342.

4   I think it is clear enough, from the Epistle as a whole, that the divine plan is already *(a)* accomplished in the resurrection of Christ, *(b)* being accomplished here and now in the believers and the Church, though *(c)* still awaiting its full accomplishment, in believers, in Church, and in the whole universe – till at last, as Paul says elsewhere, Christ will hand over his kingdom to the Father.

5   We have also to hold fast to Paul's affirmation that the divine purpose will be realized in a transformation of the whole created order. It is insufficient to say that it is only a question of producing harmony among men. I therefore have my reservations about the following comment of J. A. Grassi (*Jerome Biblical Commentary*, ii, 344): 'In present-day terms we would say that God's purpose was to give new hope to a world divided by barriers of race, colour, culture, or political divisions and make possible a unity of men through Christ'. Apart from the fact that Paul focuses on sin as the root cause of human evils, one may surely observe *(a)* that the hope given to Christians is rooted not simply in a consoling prospect in the future but in an act, the redemptive death of Christ, already historically accomplished; and *(b)* that Paul does not restrict his vision to the creation of a happier human race; he holds that the whole created order to its roots is in process of transformation in Christ. For Christianity to retreat from this view of the total, creation-wide, relevance of the redemption into a man-centred concern for political, ethnic and cultural harmony is to sell out to agnostic humanism.

6   Instead of 'the foundation of the apostles and prophets' the New English Bible offers in its text: 'the foundation laid by the apostles and prophets' – which would mean that the apostles are not themselves the foundations. The alternative understanding of the passage is, however, offered in a footnote in N.E.B.; cf. also Revelation 21:10–14: '... the holy city of Jerusalem ... had twelve foundation-stones, and on them were the names of the twelve apostles of the Lamb'.

7   One may add: it is not a system of theological truths or of

'things to be believed'. Theologians are the servants, not the masters, of the Church.

8   (London 1908), pp. 5, 8–9. A comment seems obvious. If Paul could not admit of a broken Christianity, one Jewish and the other Gentile, would he have admitted of the possibility of a Church broken up into several churches, e.g. the Anglican Communion, the Protestant bodies, the Eastern Orthodox Communion and the Roman Catholic Church?

9   J. Armitage Robinson, *St Paul's Epistle to the Ephesians* (London 1903), pp. 130f.

10 ibid., p. 26.

11 C. Gore, H. L. Goudge, A. Guillaume (eds), *A New Commentary on Holy Scripture, including the Apocrypha* (London 1928), pp. 539–40.

Chapter II

1   (Dublin 1976), pp. 7–8.

2   (London/Baltimore, Md 1962).

3   (London 1975).

4   In what follows I shall use the word 'communion' for general purposes, but shall tend to use *koinonia* when referring more particularly to the Church.

5   cf. H. A. Williams, in *The Times*, 21 July 1977, p. 15.

6   *The Times*, 3 August 1977, p. 14.

7   ibid.

8   In Roman Catholic theology it produced a monstrously one-sided ecclesiology (in treatises *De Ecclesia*; correctives have lain scattered about in treatises on other departments of theology, and the life of the Church has usually been better, if sometimes worse, than the theory).

9   6 August 1977.

10 J. H. Newman, Sermon entitled 'The Prophetical Office of the Church', quoted in *An Essay on the Development of Christian Doctrine* (London 1845), pp. 115–16. It will be observed that Newman distinguishes 'episcopal' from 'prophetical' tradition. My use of the word 'tradition' covers both of these, and includes the Creeds.

11 With a touch of humour, Ronald Knox once observed to me:

'I know that one is too easily the victim of prejudice; but the older I get the more persistent is my conviction that Eton is better than Harrow, and Oxford than Cambridge.'

12 *Documents of Vatican II*: Constitution On the Church, n. 26; p. 50.

Chapter III

1 We must bear in mind that, in New Testament parlance, a 'word' is not, for example, a noun or a preposition, but a whole statement.

2 *The Ascent of Mount Carmel*, ii, 22; in *The Collected Works of St. John of the Cross*, tr. K. Kavanaugh & O. Rodriguez (London 1966), pp. 179, 181.

3 In this passage, 'the Lord' is presumably Christ; cf. verse 9: 'If on your lips is the confession, "Jesus is Lord", and in your heart the faith that God raised him from the dead, then you will find salvation'. Notice also Paul's question: '... how could anyone spread the news without a commission to do so?' Obviously, news can be spread by anyone, with or without a commission. It looks as if Paul is concerned that the 'news' should be purely and integrally communicated, for which purpose commissioned communicators are necessary.

4 E. L. Mascall, *Theology and the Gospel of Christ: An Essay in Reorientation* (London 1977), p. 149. Dr Mascall refers us to Karl Rahner, Louis Bouyer, Bernard Lonergan, Thomas F. Torrance and Jean Galot.

5 Mascall, op. cit., pp. 136–7.

6 ibid., p. 135. After all, one's pet dog can hardly know what it 'feels like' to be a human being. And if the objection to that comparison is made, that a dog is of a different species from his master, whereas Jesus was in his humanity consubstantial with us, one can add that it is impossible for me to know what it feels like to be Einstein or St John of the Cross.

7 *Collected Works*, pp. 553–4.

8 ibid., p. 554.

9 By what stages did this awareness provide the occasion for an 'insight' and the need for conceptualization? Of course we do not know. We can, however, make conjectures; remembering

that significant knowledge is something that grows not merely by the accumulation of items but by interior development. (a) Judging by the experience of wise adoptive parents, Mary would have found an opportunity of explaining to the Child Jesus, at a suitable age, that Joseph was not his 'father' in the ordinary sense of that word. This information would have left a 'vacuum' in the Child's psychology, to be filled, I suggest, immediately by the 'insight' that, after all, he had a 'Father in heaven'. (b) St Luke – and I still think he was probably dependent here on information ultimately derived from Mary herself – recounts that strange occurrence when the boy Jesus stayed behind in Jerusalem and, when found by Mary and Joseph, seems to have expressed surprise at their anxiety about him. Many readers must have been left vaguely uneasy by this story: how did it happen that a boy of twelve years old – by no means a mere baby – was so neglectful as to create a situation of such anxiety for his parents? And what is the meaning of his surprise? I suggest that, at this turning-point of a Jewish boy's life, when he was assuming the religious responsibilities of adulthood, the festival visit to the Temple was for Jesus a tremendous spiritual experience. This, as his words suggest, was 'his Father's house'. Here, where the divine liturgy was accomplished by God's priests and the sacred tradition was expounded by the scribes and doctors, he was at the centre of God's dealings with his People. The experience was overwhelming and, like Copernicus when his heliocentric hypothesis crystallized, he was in a state of 'ecstasy' that left him oblivious of his circumstances. The arrival of Mary and Joseph restored him to ordinary consciousness. I repeat that all this is sheer speculation. I suggest, however, that such speculation may help us to understand how the original revelation was both given and gradually received, while remaining throughout the same revelation and something entirely consonant with Jesus' primordial awareness: he had 'always known' it, and yet at each stage he knew it afresh and more profoundly. The Gospel of St Mark may encourage us to think that a further stage was reached at the baptism of Jesus by John the Baptist.

Chapter IV

1 In what follows I am deeply indebted to the cognitional theory of Bernard Lonergan, particularly as expounded in *Insight*.

2 B. Lonergan, *Method in Theology* (London 1972), p. 256.

3 Lonergan has pointed out how inadequate the pre-philosophic concepts and language of Greece were for the insights of the philosophers; and how the development of philosophy went hand in hand with an enormous development of language. The problem of inadequate linguistic resources recurred for Cicero when trying to present Greek philosophical ideas in the Latin tongue. He found himself reduced to inventing a Latin word *(essentia)*, for which he duly apologized. So too Lucretius regrets the 'poverty of our native tongue' when he sought to use it as a vehicle for Epicureanism.

4 *Insight*, p. 696: '... the solution [of the problem of evil] will be a harmonious continuation of the actual order of this universe.'

5 This principle can be illustrated in the education of children. Until a child has reached a certain stage of development, it is of no use offering it logical principles which it is quite incapable of digesting.

6 It may be suggested that the basic intention of the Fathers in their emphasis on Scripture as the sole norm was to exclude 'developments' which deviated from Christian origins. The Bible, for them, represented the appeal to antiquity. It is interesting to note that in the later patristic period appeal began to be made to past Councils and the earlier Fathers, not merely to Scripture.

Chapter V

1 My ideas on the Johannine literature are those of a mere interested amateur. Although each of the Synoptic Gospels has its own ethos, it is obvious that they are in a shared and sharp contrast with the Fourth Gospel. My mind turns to the contrast between the two pictures of Socrates, that of Xenophon in the *Memorabilia* and that of Plato. Xenophon

may be thought of as a retired army officer living on his country estate and foreshadowing Colonel Blimp. He could recognize a good and great man when he saw one, but was perhaps hardly competent to penetrate the depths of the thought of the Athenian private soldier whose name stands at the head of the Roll of Honour of the *philosophia perennis*. Plato, on the other hand, was a philosopher in his own right and of outstanding genius. He was also a poet and a master of the craft of prose literature. He had several axes of his own to grind; and it is easy to suppose that he has 'read into' the historical Socrates insights and lines of thought that would more than considerably have surprised his master. It is also possible to think that Plato gives us a deeper understanding of what Socrates was about than do the charming anecdotes of Xenophon. Obviously, the comparison with the evangelists limps in a number of ways. But it remains true that only a genius can deeply sympathize with a genius.

2   A. Feuillet, 'Le "Commencement" de l'économie Chrétienne d'après He 2:3–4; Mc 1:1 et Ac. 1:1–2', in *New Testament Studies*, January 1978, writes (my translation): 'Without ever using the word, the author of the Fourth Gospel is constantly thinking of the Church in which Jesus will prolong his illuminating and sanctifying action ... the long discourses after the Supper are a prophecy of the time of the Church, when Christ, absent from bodily sight, will be invisibly present to his own, continuing to instruct them and enlighten them by the Spirit the Comforter ... Thus that idea of the Church which the beginning and end of St Mark's Gospel only suggest ... has been expressed by John in his Gospel ... with singular force. But he is definitely not innovating; all he is doing is to give greater depth to an idea already present in his predecessors'.

3   John Macquarrie, *Martin Heidegger* (London 1968), p. 13. My other quotations from, and relating to, Heidegger are from this admirable and lucid little book.

4   ibid., p. 29.

5   ibid., p. 30.

6   ibid., p. 31.

7   'Look then busily that thy ghostly work be nowhere bodily; ... And although thy bodily wits can find there

nothing to feed them on, for they think it nought that thou dost, yea! do on then this nought, and do it for God's love. ... Reck thee never if thy wits cannot understand this nought; for surely I love it much the better. ... What is he that calleth it nought? Surely it is our outer man and not our inner. Our inner man calleth it All' (*The Cloud of Unknowing*, chap. 68; in *The Cloud of Unknowing And other Treatises by an English mystic of the fourteenth century; with a Commentary on the Cloud by Father Augustine Baker, O.S.B.*; ed. Dom Justin McCann, London 1924, pp. 159–60). Augustine Baker comments: 'The *nought* here mentioned is God'; and he speaks of the 'union of spirits, of the man's spirit with God's spirit' as being a '*union of nothing with nothing*' (ibid., p. 401; italics in the original). When St John of the Cross urges us to choose the 'nothing' of creatures he implies that in this choice of nothing we are choosing God.

8   On the work of Christ in his heavenly priesthood, see Thomas F. Torrance, *Space, Time and Resurrection* (Edinburgh 1976), pp. 115–18.

9   'I shall be with you' is the covenantal promise of God to the Old Testament People of God and their leaders. In St Matthew's Gospel the incarnation is associated with the name *Emmanuel* ('God with us'); and Christ's farewell promise to the disciples after the resurrection is: 'Lo, I am with you always, to the close of the age'.

10   The last part of this citation, from 'And this is eternal life', may be an editorial addition to the original text.

11   The word 'before' here is of course 'mythical'. The author means to refer to the eternal (i.e. time-transcending) glory of the second Person of the Holy Trinity. There is no 'before' and 'after' in God.

12   The word here translated 'sanctify' is the same as the word translated 'consecrate'.

13   *The Gospel according to John*. Introduction, Translation, and Notes by Raymond E. Brown (London 1971), pp. ci–cii.

Chapter VI

1 Little direct evidence, sc. in the New Testament itself. Modern scholarship is perhaps too sceptical, or even negligent, concerning possible extra-biblical sources. Dr John A. T. Robinson in *Redating the New Testament* (London 1976), p. 112, has drawn attention to George Edmundson's book, *The Church in Rome in the First Century* (London 1913), based on the author's Bampton Lectures in that year. Edmundson adds to the New Testament data a mass of traditional material, whose value he assesses with some critical power, and succeeds in offering a reconstruction of some aspects of primitive Christian history which is fascinating and not without persuasive force. Those who have never read the book or whose memory of it is dimmed by the passage of half a century or more may be recommended to consult it for themselves. They will, I hope, agree with me that it is attractive and impressive. Its documentation and thoroughness reflect rather severely on the light-hearted theorizing of some modern historians.

2 The Introduction to Harnack's *The Acts of the Apostles* (English translation, London 1909) is still worth reading, as an appraisal of Luke's second volume by a brilliant critic.

3 *The Epistle of Privy Counsel,* in *The Cloud of Unknowing,* p. 214.

4 ibid., p. 215.

5 Definition of the Immaculate Conception, 1854.

6 In Acts 'the apostles' are always, it would seem, with one exception, the Twelve. Exceptionally, in 14:14, Barnabas and Paul are called apostles. This may be because they were at the time in question engaged on a missionary journey upon which they had been sent, with the laying-on of hands, by the Christian community at Antioch in Syria; thus, the meaning may be that they were not 'apostles' *tout court,* but 'apostles of a local church', for which use of the word 'apostles' there is evidence elsewhere in the New Testament. In the Pauline Epistles, St Paul himself vigorously claims, and argues for, his right to be considered an apostle of Christ himself – like the Twelve, although obviously not an original member of

that group (to which he once refers as to a body which does not include himself). There is no evidence that Paul was ever admitted into the group of the Twelve (as Matthias was). If Acts is indeed from the pen of a companion, as it certainly is from that of a warm admirer, of Paul, it is remarkable that this author never (with the improbable exception of 14:14) concedes that he was an apostle in the sense that seems to be of great significance for the author's ecclesiology. The Twelve, for him, are a group of direct dominical institution – he even, in the Gospel, attributes the conferring of the title 'apostles' upon the Twelve to Jesus Christ. And it is clear that, in his understanding, the Twelve were not only commissioned eyewitnesses of the risen Christ and of his earthly ministry, but leaders (we could almost say rulers) of the Church. The point is important; for although the role of eyewitness was obviously not transmissible, the role of leadership and governance obviously was. And it looks as if Luke did not conceive of a universal Church lacking commissioned general governance.

7 *Method in Theology*, p. 88.
8 See note 1, opposite.
9 Obviously, we must not place too much weight on this silence of Acts. We gather that Paul (whom Luke does not reckon as an apostle, but who was a typical Christian evangelizer) was prepared from time to time to spend months if not years in a single Christian community, whether because of its size and importance or because of local difficulties and opportunities. We can readily suppose that an ageing apostle would tend to settle down permanently somewhere. And if he did so, what more probable than that he would assume the leadership of the local church? Peter, it would seem, ended his life at Rome; and if Edmundson's proposals (op. cit., pp. 47, 51–5, 118, 120, 248) are accepted, his visits there amounted in all to a number of years. I am prepared to think that Peter could have reached the conclusion that Jerusalem would not remain a suitable centre of the koinonia, and saw Rome as occupying that position in the future. Even so, it is rather interesting that early evidence is more inclined to present Peter as the founder than as the first occupant of the See of Rome. (It may be observed that I have not been making use of the

Didachè of the Twelve Apostles, which scholars, since Jean-Paul Audet's great edition of this little book, have been inclined to regard as an extremely primitive Christian document, perhaps anterior even to the year 70. But I am not satisfied that Audet has got the date of the *Didachè* right. Some years ago I attempted to show – in 'The Literary Relations of Didachè, Ch. XVI', *Journal of Theological Studies*, 1960, pp. 265–83 – that the *Didachè* utilizes the Gospel of St Luke, and must therefore be subsequent in date to that Gospel. It would also have had to be written in a place where that Gospel was already known, and it may be doubted whether St Luke's very 'Hellenistic' writings were popular in the centres of primitive Palestinian Christianity.)

10   The only one we know of is Paul, and his claim to apostolic authority happens not to be confirmed, according to available evidence, by the Twelve themselves or by Peter, unless we discern such an implication in the narrative in the Epistle to the Galatians, 2:9, where a critical reading might suggest that, far from recognizing Paul's immediate authority as an apostle, Peter and his two companions removed the ambiguity of his position by themselves giving him a commission similar to their own – as they had earlier given such a commission to Matthias.

11   *The Heythrop Journal*, July 1977, p. 295.

12   *Foundations of Christian Faith*, pp. 331f.

13   The Pauline Epistles speak once or twice as though the fully 'catholic', that is to say Jewish-and-Gentile, mission of the Church was the very point of the divine revelation in Christ.

14   Edmundson argues that the local church of Rome, to which Paul addressed his Epistle to the Romans at a time when he had not yet visited the capital city, was composed mainly of Gentiles, but also of Jewish Christians. Among the latter, he thinks, was 'an extremely influential and energetic section of Judaeo-Christians, Jews rather than Christians, who ... were bitterly opposed to St Paul, disputed his Apostolic authority, traduced and misrepresented his teaching, and denounced him as a renegade from the faith of his fathers' (op. cit., p. 17). The Roman Catholic Church today is troubled by a similar, diversely organized, 'wing' of strong traditionalists; and our own experience thus helps us to understand

something of the state of affairs consequent upon the decision of the 'Council of Jerusalem' – and also to sympathize with the Judaeo-Christians. Deep issues of continuity and change underlie both crises. The guidance of the Holy Spirit is not a superfluous item in Christian belief; nor is the 'authority' of the koinonia over against the private judgement of its members.

15 *Jerome Biblical Commentary*, ii, 350.

16 Another name for these functionaries in New Testament circles was 'bishops' *(episkopoi)*. The word 'presbyter' evokes the organization of Jewish religious communities, while 'bishop' sounds more Hellenistic, but has an interesting parallel in the Qumran documents. Only by degrees, and perhaps earlier in the East than in the West, did the Church settle down to using 'bishop' as the title of the single leader of a local church, while 'presbyters' continued to be the name given to the group of functionaries who co-operated with him. Thus, with the addition of 'deacons' (also mentioned in the New Testament, but there apparently as assistants of apostles), was evolved the nomenclature of the 'threefold ordained ministry' of bishops, priests (presbyters) and deacons.

17 The word 'jurisdiction' here is rather anachronistic; but one understands what the author means.

18 *Jerome Biblical Commentary*, ii, 404.

19 ibid., ii, 405.

20 J.A.T. Robinson says that advocates and opponents of the traditional authorship of the several 'Johannine' books (Apocalypse, the Epistles and the Gospel) 'find common ground in dating both the Revelation and the gospel and epistles in the years ±90–100' (*Redating the New Testament*, p. 254).

21 ibid., p. 329.

22 Clearly, by 'bishops' Clement means those who are elsewhere named presbyters. Terminology is still fluid at this date.

23 (Oxford 1912), ii, 132–3. Hamilton was an Anglican scholar, at one time professor of pastoral theology in the University of Bishop's College, Lennoxville, Canada. His book, *The People of God: An Inquiry into Christian Origins* (Volume I: Israel; Volume II: The Church) was published by the Oxford

University Press, but it may be that, like Edmundson's Bampton Lectures, it has suffered undeserved neglect because its appearance was soon followed by the Great War of 1914–18 – after which the world of biblical scholarship became obsessed with new ideas from Germany.

24   ibid., ii, 133–4.

25   ibid., ii, 129. It is unfortunate that the Anglican/Rome Catholic International Commission, in its important Agreed Statement on Ministry and Ordination (1973), made no allusion to this cardinal text from the Epistle of Clement, which surely ought not to be neglected in a discussion of early evidence for the doctrine of the apostolic succession of the ordained ministry.

Chapter VII

1   *Documents of Vatican II*: Constitution On the Church, n. 48; pp. 78–9.

2   *The People of God*, p. 146.

3   *Ep. Smyrn.*, 1; M.P.G., v, 708.

4   ibid., 8; M.P.G., v, 713.

5   M.P.G., v, 684, 705, 717.

6   Since I have been dealing with the Letters of Ignatius, I may be permitted to draw attention to another intriguing phrase in the exordium of his letter to the Roman Christians. He there describes the local church of Rome as that which 'presides in the place of the region of the Romans'. Duchesne asks: 'Over what does the church [not the bishop] of the Romans preside? ... The most natural sense is that it presides over the generality of the churches' (*Églises Séparées*, Paris 1905, p. 128). For this reference, and for much else in this chapter, I acknowledge my deep debt to Pierre Batiffol, *L'Église Naissante* (of which there is an English translation with the title, *Primitive Catholicism*).

7   Whereas Judaeo-Christianity was apt to underplay the divine component in Jesus Christ, Greek Christianity was long plagued with the threat of something like docetism. Centuries after Ignatius, it was necessary to affirm that Jesus Christ has not only a human nature but a real human will. In our

own age a strong reaction against docetic tendencies is threatening the doctrine of Christ's divinity.

8   *Contra Haereses*, I, x, 1; M.P.G., vii, 549.

9   ibid., III, iv, 1; M.P.G., vii, 855.

10   One infers that an individual bishop might be in error; but in that case appeal can be made from him to bishops who have an even greater right than he to claim that their teaching is truly apostolic. Irenaeus does not ask the question, Suppose there is disagreement between the occupants of the 'apostolic' sees themselves? This question is what keeps Eastern Orthodoxy and the Roman Catholic Church separated today.

11   *Contra Haereses*, IV, xxxiii, 7; M.P.G., vii, 1076.

12   *Contra Haereses*, IV, xxxi, 3; M.P.G., vii, 1070.

13   *Downside Review*, lxxi (1953), 1–13, 119–34, 258–72.

14   The universal Church is apparently a threat to the Roman Empire itself. The emperor Decius 'would rather have heard of a pretender to the Empire than of the election of a new bishop to the church in Rome'. Cyprian was living in a time of persecution.

15   I shall be using a slightly revised Italian version published by the author in 1960.

16   cf. Ludwig Hertling, S. J., *Communio: Church and Papacy in Early Christianity*, translated with an Introduction by Jared Wicks, S. J., (Chicago 1972), p. 16: '*Communio* is the bond that united the bishops and the faithful, the bishops among themselves, and the faithful among themselves, a bond that was both effected and at the same time made manifest by eucharistic communion.' I find this description less illuminating than the one I have offered, in which emphasis is laid upon the common 'possession' on which communion is based, and this common possession is taken to be the incarnate Word of God. But one must agree with Hertling that the actual point at which communion 'comes into act' in a deeply religious sense is the Eucharist, the 'bread from heaven' which is Christ giving himself to his koinonia and thereby uniting its members into the one koinonia.

17   Catholic priests today, in similar circumstances, can carry a document from their bishop which serves as a certificate that they are in good standing as priests in their own diocese and may therefore be allowed to celebrate Mass elsewhere. But in

ancient times letters of communion could be issued not only to clerics but to lay people; and they authorized *per se* not the saying of Mass but the reception of Holy Communion.

18 *Liber de praescriptionibus*, cap. xx; M.P.L., ii, 37.

19 cf. *Ep.* xxxvi; M.P.L., iv, 335–40.

20 In H. B. Swete (ed.), *Essays on the Early History of the Church and the Ministry* (London 1918), p. 195; quoted by B. C. Butler, *The Idea of the Church*, pp. 59, 110.

21 cf. S. L. Greenslade, *Schism in the Early Church*, p. 175; quoted by B. C. Butler, *The Idea of the Church*, p. 110.

22 Geoffrey Grimshaw Willis, *Saint Augustine and the Donatist Controversy* (London 1950), p. 116.

23 *Ep.* xliii, cap. viii, 21; M.P.L., xxxiii, 170.

24 p. 124, above.

25 p. 125, above.

26 *In Joannis Evangelium Tractatus* VI, cc. 11, 26; M.P.L., xxxv, 1430, 1437.

27 References in *The Idea of the Church*, ch. 7.

28 *De Baptismo contra Donatistas*, V, cap. xxvii, 38; M.P.L., xliii, 196.

29 ibid.; M.P.L., xliii, 195.

30 ibid.; M.P.L., xliii, 196: 'aut etiam in haeresibus vel in Gentilium superstitionibus jaceant'.

31 ibid.; M.P.L., xliii, 195.

32 *Ep.* cxlix, cap. i, 3; M.P.L., xxxiii, 631.

33 *Ep.*, xliii, cap. viii, 21; M.P.L., xxxiii, 170.

34 *Contra Cresconium*, II, xxi, 39; M.P.L., xliii, 489.

Chapter VIII

1 (London 1964), p. 18.

2 ibid., p. 30.

3 (ed. 1964), p. xxi.

4 *Space, Time and Resurrection* (Edinburgh 1976), p. 19.

5 op. cit. (ed. 1964), pp. xviii–xix.

6 *Documents of Vatican II*: Decree on Ecumenism, n. 3; p. 345.

7 ibid., p. 346.

8 ibid. The concept of 'holy things', 'gifts' or endowments of

the Church was utilized by F. D. Maurice in his important book, *The Kingdom of Christ*, an outstanding Anglican contribution to ecclesiology in the nineteenth century. It is found much earlier in Optatus of Milevis (fourth century, Africa) in his writing against the Donatists. Among these *dotes* (endowments) Optatus reckons 'the see *(cathedra)* of Peter', occupied, he says, by the bishop of Rome.

9   *Documents of Vatican II*: Constitution On the Church, n. 8; p. 23.

10 A friend who has read the manuscript of this essay finds some obscurity in my distinction between 'Church' and 'churchness'. Perhaps the following may help to explain my thought. In considering a human being one may distinguish between him and his human qualities, properties and attributes. He has the human qualities of corporeality and spirituality. He is humanly rational, passionate and intelligent. He has a pedigree and a milieu. Without such attributes he would not be a human being. But the sum of his attributes is not identical with the man himself. He *has* the attributes, and in particular he *has* his human nature. But he *is* himself; we do not say that he *is* his nature. We could call his nature 'humanness' (as I have spoken about 'churchness'). But the man is not his humanness; and the Church is not its churchness. A man, we say, *has* personality but *is* the particular person that he is: John Smith, or Mary Brown. To be a person is, in philosophic parlance, to 'subsist'. To subsist, on the other hand, is not necessarily to be human: the angels subsist – they are persons – but they are not human. (On person and nature, cf. John Cowburn, *Love and the Person*, London 1967, Chapter I, ' "What?" and "Which?" or "Who?" '.) Now, the attributes of John Smith cannot exist apart from John Smith himself; nobody else can have John Smith's (individual) nature and attributes. But the attributes of the Church, its churchness, can exist as attributes of entities which are not themselves the Church, though in those entities they can never exist in their full totality. John Smith's attributes are inalienably his own. The essential properties of the Church are separable gifts of God, and to the extent that some other body possesses some of these attributes it can be described as possessing churchness. As,

according to my argument and the central Christian tradition, complete communion (koinonia) is an attribute of the Church, it is obvious that the churchness of bodies which exist in separation from that complete communion is itself, though real, incomplete: one of the Church's attributes is lacking to them.

It will be noticed that I have here spoken of a person as 'subsisting', and it will be remembered that the Second Vatican Council says that the Church which we confess in the Creed 'subsists' in the Catholic Church, which is governed by the successor of Peter and by the bishops in union with that successor, although many elements of sanctification and of truth can be found outside of her visible structure (*Documents of Vatican II*: Constitution On the Church, n. 8; p. 23). I would not go so far as to affirm that the Council is here using the verb 'subsist' in the full sense which it has in philosophy, but I suggest that the choice of this word may mean that, while attributes and properties which, taken together with the gift of unity, constitute the 'nature' of the Church may be found elsewhere, nevertheless the answer to the question, Which (of the Christian bodies) *is* the Church, remains: The Church is uniquely the Catholic Church, though as regards its attributes it may be said to exist also elsewhere. Finally, it is to be observed that only in the godhead can an identical nature belong to more than one 'subsistence': the three 'persons' of the Holy Trinity are *subsistent* relations within the divine 'nature'. But the Church cannot have more than one subsistence. And the Second Vatican Council never says that the Church *subsists* except in the Catholic Church.

11   cf. *Documents of Vatican II*: Constitution On the Church, n. 14; pp. 32–3: 'Whosoever, therefore, knowing that the Catholic Church was made necessary', sc. for salvation, 'by God through Jesus Christ, would refuse to enter her or to remain in her could not be saved.' The wording of this sentence is extremely interesting (in the original Latin) and is indicative of the spirit animating the Council. The state of things it speaks of is represented as a remote (almost theoretical) possibility: the possibility that someone might *know* that he ought to be a Roman Catholic, yet *refuse* to be

such. A modern moral theologian might say that there was something wrong with such a man's 'fundamental option'.

12 We are perhaps more selective today. But how many people there are who would say that they 'cannot forgive Hitler' – despite the truth that no one of us can judge his internal guilt; he may have been mad.

13 *Ep.*, xliii, cap. i, 3; M.P.L., xxxiii, 160.

14 *Documents of Vatican II*: Decree on Ecumenism, n. 3; p. 346.

15 *Schism in the Early Church* (ed. 1964), p. xxi.

16 I understand that the Highest Common Factor of three numbers is the highest number that can be divided into each of them without remainder. Thus, of the three numbers 6, 14, 28, the Highest Common Factor is 2. On the other hand, the Lowest Common Multiple of three numbers is the lowest number into which each of these numbers will divide without remainder. In the case of the three numbers of our example, this is 84. In simple arithmetic, no H.C.F. can be greater than the lowest of the numbers involved; no L.C.M. can be smaller than the largest of the numbers involved.

17 It is noteworthy that Greenslade eschewed the question, When is a group of believers not 'Church'?

18 Some readers may recall Ronald Knox's satire, *Reunion All Round*. The extravagant wit of that book springs from the author's exploration of the potentialities of the H.C.F. programme of Reunion.

19 J. H. Newman, *Fifteen Sermons preached before The University of Oxford*, 3rd edn (London 1900), p. 313.

20 In the Essay on Development (Chapter I), Newman treats the revealed realities of Christianity as constituting an 'object', and our reception of them as constituting the idea of that object. It is a 'real' idea, in his language, because it is an idea of a real object. He argues that an idea which is 'of a nature to arrest and possess the mind' can be said to 'have life'. Having life, it responds actively to ever-changing environments, ever new challenges from within and from without, and thus responding it develops. A great idea, he says, 'is elicited and expanded by trial, and battles into perfection and supremacy. ... It is indeed sometimes said that the stream is clearest near the spring. Whatever use may

254 THE CHURCH AND UNITY

fairly be made of this image, it does not apply to the history of a philosophy or belief ', i.e. to a great 'idea', 'which on the contrary is more equable, and purer, and stronger, when its bed has become deep, and broad, and full. It necessarily rises out of an existing state of things, and for a time savours of the soil. Its vital element needs disengaging from what is foreign and temporary, and is employed in efforts after freedom which become more vigorous and hopeful as its years increase. Its beginnings are no measure of its capabilities, nor of its scope. At first, no one knows what it is worth. It remains perhaps for a time quiescent; it tries, as it were, its limbs, and proves the ground under it, and feels its way. From time to time it makes essays which fail, and are in consequence abandoned. It seems in suspense which way to go; it wavers, and at length strikes out in one definite direction. In time it enters upon strange territory; points of controversy alter their bearing; parties rise and fall around it; dangers and hopes appear in new relations; and old principles reappear under new forms. It changes with them in order to remain the same. In a higher world it is otherwise, but here below to live is to change, and to be perfect is to have changed often.' We have to ask ourselves whether the principle of the indivisible visible unity of the Church is an 'essay' which has failed and must in consequence be abandoned; or whether perhaps it is a principle which has not to die but to 'reappear under new forms'.

Chapter IX

1   *Space, Time and Resurrection*, pp. 21–2.
2   In modern jargon, just as metaphysics is a level of understanding above Aristotelian physics, yet presupposing physics, and gives a new and higher dimension to our understanding, so each 'level' of mathematics or science finds a higher context in a 'meta-level' presupposing and 'sublating' it. Algebra is a meta-level to arithmetic. Chemistry is a meta-level to physical science (which is not quite the same as the Aristotelian 'physics' in reference to

which metaphysics is a meta-level). I have even seen a reference to 'meta-music'.

3 ibid., pp. 22–3; the italics are in the original.

4 It should be noted that 'plans' here is, owing to the poverty of the English language, in form, indeed, in the present tense; but has to be understood in a supra-temporal sense.

5 Origen was not afraid to apply this line of thought to the Christian dispensation itself. He pronounced that the physical body of Jesus was a 'type' of his body the Church. We might say: the former is the *sacramentum* of which the latter is the *res*.

6 Late, compared with the millions of years that preceded it. For all we know, this lapse of time that has so far occurred may be minimal compared with the prospective age of the universe.

7 He describes the Son as the image of the invisible God. But the Word, considered in abstraction from his incarnation, is just as invisible as his divine Father. It is surely Jesus, the incarnate Word, who images forth for us the invisible God: 'He that hath seen me hath seen the Father.'

8 *Infallibility: The Crossroads of Doctrine* (London 1977), pp. 167, 168–9.

9 *Self-Abandonment to Divine Providence* (London 1971), p. 50. The presence and action of the incarnate Word are not dependent on our faith; and I see no doctrinal reason to believe that de Caussade's doctrine on the subject of this universal presence has to be restricted to that portion of historical time that is subsequent to the historical life of Jesus. My argument would be that, wherever in human history there has been fundamental 'good will', there we must suppose the presence of the grace gift of faith. The doctrine that Christ is present throughout the whole of creation and in the whole of history in all its elements may serve to reassure those who rightly hold that the object of faith, while it is formally God self-disclosed *(Deus revelans)*, requires also a 'material object' to serve as a *medium in quo* for the act of faith. The humanity of Christ in his historical life was of course such a material object: 'That ... which we have heard, which we have seen with our eyes, which we have looked upon and touched with our hands ... we proclaim also to

you' (1 John 1:1–3). This 'material object' is presented to us particularly in the Eucharistic sacrament and in the Church, the body of Christ. It is presented to the unevangelized in every element and event of the created order, since the whole of that order is orientated to the incarnate Word, and in it he is 'immanent' or implied.

10 In *A Second Collection* (London 1974), pp. 117–33: 'Natural Knowledge of God', reproducing a lecture given in 1968.

11 ibid., p. 121.

12 ibid., p. 122.

13 ibid., p. 123.

14 Pierre Charles, S. J., *La Prière de toutes les Heures* (Paris 1955), pp. 142–4; the translation is mine.

15 Francis Thompson, 'The Kingdom of God', in *Works: Poems* (London 1913), ii, 226.

16 We used to speak of 'uncovenanted mercies'. I doubt whether this was a correct use of language. The Christ who is present in every atom of the created universe and in every event of human history is precisely the Covenant Christ. It is because he has honoured his Covenant by becoming incarnate that he is present everywhere – present as the covenantal Word incarnate.

17 It is well known that Karl Rahner has coined the term 'anonymous Christianity'. His use of the term has been criticized. I am entirely at one with Rahner in what he seeks to convey by the term. But I wonder whether the term itself is not misleading. It is at least convenient to keep the word 'Christian' for what belongs to or derives from the historical proclamation of the gospel. Similarly, while I gladly recognize 'churchness' in the wide extension that Greenslade gives to that neologism, I think that to talk about separate 'churches' can be misleading, and that it has misled some Catholic theologians. The Second Vatican Council does use the word with reference to communions separated from the Catholic Church (it speaks of 'churches or ecclesial bodies'). But when you go from its language to its general doctrine, you discover *(a)* that it fully preserves the uniqueness of the indivisible visible communion which is the Roman Catholic Church, *(b)* that it uses the word 'churches' of separated communions to the extent that they share some of the 'gifts'

of God to his Church; it never justifies the inference: 'Since we call these separated bodies "churches" it follows that each and all of them have, though perhaps in imperfect forms, *all* the gifts that go to constitute the Church established by Christ'. One gift which they plainly do not possess and which is basic is the gift of visible unity.

18 · For similar reasons, we can say of a man who is not sacramentally baptized but is of good will that he has the 'baptism of desire': did he know that baptism is the divinely appointed 'door of salvation', he would, in virtue of his good will, undoubtedly will to be baptized and would take occasion to receive the sacrament. Such was the condition of the catechumens of whose salvation the ancient Church had such good hope.

19 Invincible ignorance is an unawareness of some obligation, an unawareness which is free from guilt. If you are innocently unaware of a duty you are not, in God's eyes, guilty if you do not perform that duty. The word 'invincible' sounds strange: it means that your ignorance is not something that you would have overcome if you had used reasonable care to discover what your duty was. Oedipus was invincibly ignorant that Jocasta was his mother.

Chapter X

1 Athenagoras, Archbishop of Thyateira and Great Britain, *Ecclesiological Problems* (London 1976), p. 3.

2 ibid., p. 19.

3 ibid., p. 20.

4 ibid., p. 23.

5 *One Baptism, One Eucharist and a mutually recognized Ministry: Three agreed statements.* Faith and Order Paper No. 73 (World Council of Churches, Geneva, Switzerland 1975), p. 6.

6 ibid., pp. 9, 10, 11, 16.

7 The Catholic answer to each of these questions is Yes.

8 It must steadily be borne in mind that the Arians would have claimed that their christology was that of Scripture. Their dispute with the Church illuminates the unavoidable

necessity of exegesis, and the need of some authority to decide between inconsistent exegeses. The authority which saved the faith in 325, the Council of Nicaea, is the authority which bequeaths to us the principle of indivisible unity.

9   My use of the terms 'scribes' and 'Pharisees' is not intended as any reflection upon the groups designated by those names in antiquity. Rather is it a reminder that Jesus refused to accept the religious horizons and limits laid down by representatives of those groups. 'Scribal' religion would thus be religion as determined by theologians; 'Pharisaic' religion would be a religion of the 'unco guid' – or perhaps of those committed to the 'religious life' (monks and nuns, for instance). Christianity is a religion of grace seeking out profound religious need, not of intellectual competence or moral achievement.

10   *Schism in the Early Church* (ed. 1964), p. xvii.

11   John Hick (ed.), *The Myth of God Incarnate* (London 1977), p. 178.

12   ibid., p. 183.

13   'Changing Views on the uniqueness of Christ', in *The Times*, 11 October 1975, p. 14.

14   *The Myth of God Incarnate*, p. 188.

15   ibid., pp. 202–3.

16   *The Rubaiyát of Omar Kháyyám: from the Fourth Version of Edward FitzGerald's Translation* (London 1908), stanzas 65, 98, 99; pp. 141, 171.

17   Karl R. Popper, *Conjectures and Refutations: The Growth of Scientific Knowledge*, 3rd edn (London 1969), pp. 120–1.

18   ibid., p. 122.

19   ibid., pp. 126–7.

20   ibid., p. 129.

21   ibid., pp. 130–1.

22   ibid., pp. 131–2, 134. I cannot decide whether Sir Karl Popper would welcome my use of his arguments in the context of the Christian religion. The fact that he was addressing the Rationalist Press Association certainly does not prove that he is a 'rationalist' in quite the sense intended by that Association. On the other hand, he has said, *en passant*, of theology: 'Theology, I still think, is due to lack of

faith'! (*Unended Quest: An Intellectual Autobiography*, rev. edn, London 1976, p. 18).

23   *Method in Theology*, p. 332.

24   'Dimensions of Meaning', in F. E. Crowe, S. J. (ed.), *Collection*: Papers by Bernard Lonergan, S. J. (London 1967), pp. 266–7. The years that have passed since those words were written have gone far to confirm Lonergan's prognostications.

Chapter XI

1   *L'Église de Dieu*, p. 47. I am heavily indebted to this very important book in what follows.

2   cf. ibid., pp. 629–34. Bouyer writes: 'At first sight there are, today, two Churches, the Catholic Church ... and the Orthodox Church ... each claiming to be exclusively that "one, holy, catholic" Church which each confesses in the same Creed. Surely one or the other may be right, but not both at once. ... Only one answer seems possible: [these two Churches], though both terribly tempted by the spirit of division, nevertheless remain one Church, in fact as in right, despite appearances to the contrary'. He points out that instances of intercommunion are 'innumerable' up to about 1800. After that date, Latin missionaries started applying to the Easterns Tridentine or later rules which had been devised against Protestants; and were met with a 'tit for tat'. Similarly, theologians started treating the respective Churches as schismatic and even heretical. (There seems, however, to be a curious relative lack of such *official* acts on either side as would amount to a full endorsement of these theological affirmations. And it is interesting that the Roman Catholic Church maintained the practice of speaking of its sisters in the East as 'churches', even when it carefully avoided such language about the churches of the Reformation.)

3   I am here indebted to Vittorio Peri, *I Concili e le Chiese: Ricerca Storica sulla Tradizione d'Universalità dei Sinodi Ecumenici* (Roma 1965).

4   Mansi, *Conciliorum Collectio*, xiii, 208–9.

5   Francis Dvornik, with reference to the controversy involving Photius and the See of Rome a hundred years after the second council of Nicaea, states: 'The documentation of this controversy provides sufficient proof that the Roman primacy as such was not denied by the Eastern hierarchy, not even by Photius. The acts of the local synod held under Photius in 861 contain statements which indicate that the Eastern Church acknowledged the right of appeal to the Roman pontiff. And even the supporters of Photius appealed to the Pope against a decision of the Patriarch [of Constantinople] Ignatius' (Karl Rahner and others, eds, *Sacramentum Mundi*, vi, London 1970, 14: *s.v.* Schism: III, Eastern Schism).

6   Denzinger-Schönmetzer, *Enchiridion Symbolorum* (Freiburg 1967), p. 129. The Patriarch's signed acceptance of the Formula is dated 519. A similar version of the Formula was signed by the Patriarch Menas in 536.

7   Socrates, *Historia Ecclesiastica*, II, xvii, 96; M.P.G., lxvii, 220.

8   Sozomen, *Historia Ecclesiastica*, III, x, 105; M.P.G., lxvii, 1057.

9   Denzinger-Schönmetzer, op. cit., p. 55.

10   *Ep.* xv, 39; M.P.L., xxii, 355.

11   He had asked for guidance on the formula which had confronted him at Antioch to the effect that there are three hypostases in the Godhead.

12   *De Schismate Donatistarum*, II, ii; M.P.L., xi, 947, 948–9.

13   In at least an informal sense, the Archbishop of Canterbury is the centre of the Anglican Communion. He might claim that, apart from his position as bishop of his own diocese, archbishop of his own province, and primate of all England, he has only a 'primacy of honour' in that Communion as a whole. It is therefore most interesting that, in a recent dispute in the U.S.A., he has pronounced (in concurrence with the presiding bishop of the Protestant Episcopal Church of that country, but without overt consultation of any Anglican Synod or Lambeth Conference) that a group of dissidents there, who have proceeded to provide themselves with bishops not recognized by the P.E.C.U.S.A. as a whole,

are no longer in communion with himself. An informally primatial act?

14 (Paris 1920), pp. 192–209.

15 *Psalmus contra partem Donati*, line 228; M.P.L., xliii, 30: 'Numerate sacerdotes vel ab ipsa Petri sede'; the word is here probably substituted for 'cathedra' for rhythmical reasons.

16 *Ep. XLIII*, iii, 7; M.P.L., xxxiii, 163.

17 *De Unitate Ecclesiae*, IV; M.P.L., iv, 499–500.

18 *Ep.* lix; Rouët de Journel, *Enchiridion Patristicum* (Freiburg 1946), p. 207 (§580).

19 It should be noted that, for Cyprian, for whom bishop and (local) church are correlative, it is possible to move without explanation from 'church of Rome' or 'Romans' to 'bishop of Rome'.

20 In the 'thirties an attempt was made to argue that Eusebius has seriously misrepresented the whole affair. It was argued that the dispute about the date of Easter was a merely domestic affair of the local church of Rome and that Victor's proposed excommunication of the dissidents applied only to people resident in that city. I gave reasons for rejecting this hypothesis in an article, 'Eusebius and St Victor', in *The Downside Review*, lxix (1951), 393–410. But if the matter is regarded as still disputable, it must be borne in mind that Eusebius' account is good evidence for what he, a Greek historian in the early fourth century, thought was possible in the matter of relations between Rome and the rest of the Church.

21 *Hist. Eccl.*, V, xxiv, 192; M.P.G., xx, 497.

22 It seems sometimes to be assumed that the human Jesus could not have made arrangements for a long-continuing ›Church because he expected his own 'return' (the *parousia*), or rather the apocalyptic advent of the consummated Reign of God, to occur within at most a few years of his death. The assumption that he unreservedly accepted an apocalyptic eschatology of the sort supposed is questionable. But a Christian is bound to ask, Whatever the historical Jesus may be alleged to have thought about the future, since in fact the end of history has not yet occurred, what was the *divine* intention in the dispositions made by Jesus? If in the divine disposition of the economy of redemption a Petrine office was

necessary in the first generation, can one imagine that it would be less necessary in succeeding ages?

23   The Secretariat for Promoting Christian Unity, Information Service, No. 31. 1976/II, pp. 2–3.

Chapter XII

1   (London 1952).

2   *The Three Agreed Statements: Eucharist Doctrine 1971; Ministry and Ordination 1973; Authority in the Church 1976* (London 1978).

3   Robert Browning, 'Bishop Blougram's Apology'; the italics of course are mine.

4   In nature, so far as I am aware, a single source gives birth to a single stream – although estuaries are sometimes deltas. But one can imagine an artificial pleasure garden in which, from a single source, water is distributed along a number of diverse channels. As Canon Peter Hinchliff reminds us, in his charming book, *Cyprian of Carthage and the Unity of the Christian Church* (London 1974), Cyprian sold his garden when he became a Christian (but kind friends bought it back for him). In North Africa, 'even in spring continual watering is necessary to keep things alive' in one's garden (op. cit., p. 31), and an artificial water-system would be as useful as it could be gracious to the eye. I believe – though I have not checked the point – that Vitruvius gives guidance on the construction of such a system. The notion of a water-supply continuously maintained from a single source perhaps lies behind the neo-Platonic theory of divine emanations.

5   *Ep.* clxxxi; Denzinger-Schönmetzer, op. cit., pp. 80–1; trans. John Chapman, *Studies on the Early Papacy* (London 1928), pp. 146–7 (italics mine).

6   Canon law cited by Canon D. Shanahan, *The Tablet*, 18 March 1978.

7   cf. Garrett Sweeney, 'The Primacy: The Small Print of Vatican I', in *The Clergy Review*, lix, no. 2 (February 1974), pp. 96–121.

8   *Documents of Vatican II*: Constitution On the Church, n. 8; p. 24.

Index

Index